JAPANESE
FINANCIAL
INSTITUTIONS
IN EUROPE

ADVANCES IN FINANCE, INVESTMENT AND BANKING

SERIES EDITOR: ELROY DIMSON

VOLUME 1

Japanese Financial Institutions in Europe
D. Arora

JAPANESE
FINANCIAL
INSTITUTIONS
IN EUROPE

*International Competitiveness
of Japanese Banks and Securities Companies*

Dayanand Arora

1995
ELSEVIER
Amsterdam – Lausanne – New York – Oxford – Shannon – Tokyo

ELSEVIER SCIENCE B.V.
Sara Burgerhartstraat 25
P.O. Box 211, 1000 AE Amsterdam, The Netherlands

Library of Congress Cataloging-in-Publication Data

Arora, Dayanand, 1958-
   Japanese financial institutions in Europe : international
competitiveness of Japanese banks and securities companies /
Dayanand Arora.
      p.   cm. -- (Advances in finance, investment, and banking ; 1)
   Includes bibliographical references (p.).
   ISBN 0-444-82142-2
   1. Banks and banking, Japanese--Europe. 2. Financial
institutions--Europe.   I. Title. II. Series.
HG2974.A76   1995
332.1'5'0952--dc20   95-42984
                                                               CIP

From the same author:
Investment Banking in Japan

ISBN: 0 444 82142 2

This book is printed on acid-free paper.

Printed in The Netherlands.

Introduction to the Series

This series, presents a number of hitherto unpublished studies on a variety of financial themes.

The subjects covered by the *Advances in Finance Investment and Banking* (AFIB) book series include financial institutions and markets, corporate finance, portfolio investment, regulatory issues in banking and finance, comparative surveys, international taxation and accounting issues, and relevant macro-economics and asset pricing research studies. Books in this series include contributed volumes and edited conference proceedings, as well as single authored monographs such as this one. The attributes which bind these contributions together into a series are the focus on theoretical, empirical and applied issues within the field of finance.

Contributions stem from authors all over the world; their focus is consistently international. The editors of the AFIB series join me in hoping that the publication of these studies will help to stimulate international efforts in achieving advances within the fields covered by the series.

Elroy Dimson

To my mother
Subhadra Devi

Acknowledgements

The research work for this book was carried out under guidance and with personal support of Professor Dr. Wolfram Engels of the J.W. Goethe University, Frankfurt, Germany. While I was busy completing the revision of the manuscript, unfortunately he passed away on April 30, 1995. A proponent of the social market economy, he was a keen observer of the macroeconomic cobweb of society and published extensively on the subject. I gratefully acknowledge his contributions throughout my research work.

Elroy Dimson, Professor of Finance at London Business School and the editor of this series, took a personal interest in the book. His cooperation and advice during the revision process went a long way in improving the manuscript. The revised manuscript also benefitted from the suggestions of Michel Habib, Assistant Professor of Finance at London Business School. I am indebted to both of them for their precious help.

I would like to express my sincere thanks to the Foundation for Advanced Information and Research (FAIR), Japan, which provided me with a short-term scholarship under their 'Visiting-Scholars' program. The constructive support from FAIR in establishing contacts with the Japanese Ministry of Finance and financial institutions was very useful for the understanding of the intricacies of Japanese finance. I also wish to place on record my indebtedness to various experts from Japanese banks and securities companies who took interest in my research work and helped me obtain the relevant material in Japanese. The translation of many difficult texts from Japanese into English by Atsushi Kono of Bochum University is gratefully acknowledged.

A major part of the manuscript was written in the quiet and cozy environment of the Vechta University Library. Located in the northern part of Germany, this small University offers excellent library facilities for the purpose of obtaining the required literature. The library staff of the University deserve special mention for all their assistance during the research work.

I owe the greatest debt to my wife, Elisabeth, for her moral support and "endurance" during the research work. Lastly, I wish to acknowledge the unspoken support of my children Manu and Karen. They tolerated several lapses in my responsibilities towards them during the entire study period.

August 1995   *Dayanand Arora*

CONTENTS

List of Tables

List of Figures

List of Abbreviations

BIS	Bank for International Settlements
BOE	Bank of England
BOJ	Bank of Japan
BOT	Bank of Tokyo
CD	Certificate of Deposit
CME	Chicago Mercantile Exchange
CP	Commercial Paper
DM	Deutsch mark
ECU	European Currency Unit
EU	European Union
FDI	Foreign Direct Investment
FRN	Floating Rate Notes
GDP	Gross Domestic Product
HLT	Highly Leveraged Transactions
IBF	International Banking Facility
IBJ	Industrial Bank of Japan
IET	Interest Equalization Tax
IMF	International Monetary Fund
JCIF	Japan Center for International Finance
JETRO	Japan External Trade Organization
JOM	Japan Offshore Market
LIFFE	London International Financial Futures Exchange
LTCB	Long Term Credit Bank of Japan
M&A	Mergers and Acquisitions
MITI	Ministry of International Trade and Industry
MNBs	Multinational Banks
MOF	Ministry of Finance, Japan
NCB	Nippon Credit Bank of Japan
NIF	Note Issuance Facility
OECD	Organization for Economic Cooperation and Development
ROA	Return on Assets
TIFFE	Tokyo International Financial Futures Exchange
TSE	Tokyo Stock Exchange
UNCTC	United Nations Center for Transnational Corporations

Chapter 1

Introduction

Japan's expanding role in international financial markets was a subject of considerable interest in the 1980s. Of particular interest was Japan's role as a creditor nation. Indeed, Japan's long-term capital outflows increased substantially during this period. This led to a sharp rise in Japan's external assets from $10.9 billion at the end of 1981 to $610 billion at the end of 1993. It is often suggested that Japan's role as a capital exporting country has given its financial institutions the advantage of recycling a huge current account surplus. This also gave rise to concern that Japanese financial institutions are playing a dominant role in international financial markets. The present study centers upon the competitive position of Japanese banks and securities companies in the broader framework of international financial markets. The focus of this research is on the Japanese financial presence in Europe.

The idea of conducting research into this topic emanates from the phenomenon of the Japanese financial institutions' increased presence on European financial markets in the 1980s. The emphasis on this European presence is reflected in the dramatic growth of their network of offices and volume of business in Europe. The present investigation seeks to examine their growth in Europe with reference to operational strategies, types of business conducted and the sources of competitive advantage. The main objective is to explain the emergence of Japanese banks and securities companies as financial multinationals and juxtapose this with the changes in their domestic and international environments.

When the research work on the subject was initiated in early 1989, the optimism in the Japanese domestic financial markets was at its peak, which was also fueling the global expansion of Japanese financial institutions. By early 1995, when the research work was completed, the whole scenario had changed completely. With the collapse of the domestic stock market and bursting of the asset price bubble, Japanese financial institutions encountered significant pressures from a sharp decline in the value of their equity holdings, higher cost of capital, and increase in banks' non-performing loans. Surprisingly, the gravity of the situation and its impact on the foreign involvement of Japanese financial institutions was not evident until the end of 1992. Coupled with the constraints on balance sheet expansion imposed by the BIS capital requirements since March 1993, Japanese banks were forced to reduce their overseas assets and liabilities. In the changed circumstances, the Japanese financial institutions' overseas expansion strategy has become more cautious and selective. The findings of the study, which attributes overseas expansion largely to favorable macroeconomic conditions in the domestic markets, are confirmed and endorsed by recent developments.

The subject matter of the study could be grouped with the research work in the field of international banking, international financial markets and service multinationals. The chapter on Japanese securities companies in Europe extends the analysis of investment banking firms as multinationals. A full chapter on the competitive position of Japanese financial institutions offers new dimensions for the research on international competitiveness of service multinationals.

In the following sections, the existing literature on the above subject is surveyed. This helps in identifying that the Japanese financial presence in Europe needs to be analyzed in a systematic framework in order to put the subject in a proper perspective.

1.1   Financial Institutions as Multinationals - A Survey of the Literature

1.1.1   Banks as Multinationals

While multinational banking is not identical to international banking, the literature on these two subjects has been mostly overlapping. Notwithstanding the interconnectedness between the two areas, an attempt has been made here to segregate those aspects in the literature, which pertain more to the ownership characteristics of foreign banking (i.e., *multinational banking*) than to the cross-currency and cross-border facets of banking (i.e., *international banking*). The obvious logic for this treatment is to signify that some different questions are posed by the existence of multinational banking.[1] One question involves the motives that make foreign banks want to enter a country. Another question concerns the factors that enable foreign banks to compete successfully with local institutions.[2]

---

[1]Lewis and Davis (1987) p. 219.

[2]Lewis (1987) p. 30.

The literature on international banking is varied. The areas included in this category relate to (i) tracing the origins, characteristics and implications for the rapid growth of international banking; (ii) credit creation in international banking; (iii) analysis of risks in international banking; and (iv) international asset and liability management. On the other hand, the research on multinational banking occupies itself with issues such as the pattern of growth in multinational banking, the economic reasons for the emergence of MNBs, their strategies in the international banking sphere, the nature and explanations of the activities undertaken and the other such ownership-related factors. Seen in this perspective, Aliber's survey of international banking (1984), though the first exhaustive one of its kind, should be treated as a survey of the literature on multinational banking. Since the present study focuses on multinational banking, the research in this area is described in detail in the following pages.

The research on multinational banking before 1970 is scant and unrelated. The systematic literature on the subject starts to emerge towards the second half of the 1970s, and the earliest question was: why do banks go abroad? The first attempt at finding an answer was made by Aliber (1976) followed by Grubel (1977). While Grubel (1977) emphasized the knowledge-specific capital of foreign banks, which can be utilized at low marginal cost in alien markets, Aliber's focus was on the cost of intermediation. In his words:

> "International banks based in countries with relatively low spreads between the interest rates they pay on deposits and the interest rates they receive on loans would be more likely to establish branches abroad because they had developed low cost methods of intermediation."[3]

The most cited and tested hypothesis in the literature is that banks go abroad to serve those domestic clients who have established branches or subsidiaries in foreign markets. [Métais (1979); Caves (1977); UNCTC (1981); Pecchioli (1983), etc.]. The explanation for this hypothesis ranges from the defensive strategy of not losing domestic customers abroad [Konzul (1970)] to the competitive superiority stemming from the private knowledge and information held by a bank in its records [Caves (1977); Niehans (1983)]. Of late, banks are said to be opting for a policy of a global network of offices for competitive reasons, i.e., aggressive policy of winning market share and reaping the benefits of global fund management [Glüder (1988)].

---

[3]Aliber (1976) quoted in Aliber (1984) p. 665.

The growth pattern of multinational banking has not been unidirectional. Cross-hauling, i.e., two-way internationalization, is a characteristic feature of multinational banking [Aliber (1984, 1989)]. The 'follow-your-client' strategy largely explains the two-way internationalization of banking; banks from either country entering the other along with their clients. Other than a few global surveys of multinational banking [Pecchioli (1983); UNCTC (1981, 1989)], the research on the growth and direction of multinational banking is predominantly American. It is partly because of the availability of comprehensive data in the U.S. that the most extensive studies have dealt either with foreign banks in the U.S. [Goldberg and Saunders (1981a and 1981b); Houpt (1980); Hultman and McGee (1989); Cooper et al. (1989); Grosse and Goldberg (1991) and Heinkel and Levi (1992)] or with U.S. banks abroad [Fielke (1977); Jain (1986); Goldberg and Johnson (1990)]. The studies about foreign banks from one country entering another country are limited; included in this category are U.S. banks in the UK [Goldberg and Saunders (1980)], German Banks in London [Gramlich (1990)], Japanese banks in the U.S. [Khoury (1980) Poulsen (1986)] and in the UK [Terrell et al. (1989)]. Most of these studies focus on the empirical testing of the determinants of multinational banks' growth. Coulbeck's work (1984) cannot be included in any of these groupings as he analyses the overseas operations and strategy of the largest MNBs from seven industrialized countries, i.e., the U.S., Japan, France, Germany, Canada and Switzerland.

Are there any systematic advantages to explain why the foreign presence of banks headquartered in particular countries grows more rapidly than in others? This question has been investigated by Aliber (1984, 1989) and Giddy (1983). Aliber used the Q ratio as a tool for explaining that banks headquartered in countries with higher Q ratios (which, in his opinion, is the same thing as low cost of capital) would be in a more favorable position to expand abroad. Though the idea of the cost of capital and Q ratio was fascinating, it had all the inherent weaknesses of Q ratio analysis. This led to a change in the tools used by Aliber for substantiating the same thesis. Later, he (Aliber, 1989) used the price-earning ratio and dividend yield ratio as proxies for the cost of capital. In his view, a higher price-earning ratio and lower dividend yield implies a comparative cost of capital advantage and hence banks from countries with this advantage will expand their foreign presence. Aliber's model has predictive value and argues the case for leveling the playing field for MNBs.

1.1.2 Japanese Banks as Multinationals

As mentioned above, the multinationalization of U.S. banks has been extensively investigated and documented. The academic interest in the overseas expansion of Japanese banking began in earnest in the 1980s. Among the earlier works that have explored the Japanese banking presence overseas, Terrell's (1979) work was probably the first. He compared the expansion of U.S. banks in Japan with that of Japanese banks in the U.S. to test empirically certain determinants of multinational banking. He found out that both U.S. and Japanese banks relied extensively on the interbank market, rather than on deposits, as funding sources. Khoury (1980) tested the relationship between foreign direct investment in the U.S. and loan booking by foreign banks in the U.S. In his sample, the foreign banks were Japanese banks. He confirmed the 'follow-your-client' thesis through his results.

The nature and extent of the internationalization of Japanese banking during the 1970s has been investigated by Fujita and Ishigaki (1986). Reporting the findings of a survey, the authors perceive the initial internationalization of Japanese banks as customer-led. The subsequent expansion has been viewed as moving more in tune with the internationalization of the financial markets. Their work, though it cannot be used to explain the dramatic expansion after 1985, provides useful clues and direction for research. Two recent works seek to trace the reasons accounting for the growth of Japanese banks abroad. Iwami (1989) suggests that, apart from the connections with the Japanese firms, it must have been an offensive strategy for acquiring market shares at the cost of profitability that explains the expansion of Japanese banks. He supports his contentions with estimates of the amounts of international assets and their profitability for the Japanese banks, where he notices a tendency of shifting assets to less profitable international business. Dufey (1990) sees that the Japanese bank expansion in the U.S. is closely correlated with the growth of that country's international trade.

The Japanese banking presence in the U.S. has been covered in many studies. Poulsen (1986) provides evidence concerning the impact of Japanese and U.S. financial conditions on the activities of Japanese banks in the U.S. During the period of tight credits in Japan (1972-80), Japanese banks used U.S. markets as an alternative source of funds and that during these periods their activities increased. The underlying aim of this work was to trace the influence of the domestic regulations on the activities of the Japanese banks abroad. Hultman and McGee (1989) found that the asset values of Japanese banks' offices in the U.S. were most closely associated with Japanese direct investment in the

U.S. The Japan Center for International Finance (1991) scrutinized Japanese banks' expansion in the U.S. during the 1980s and attributed the expansion to various macroeconomic factors within Japan and the U.S.

A survey of the literature reveals that research into Japanese banks' overseas expansion has focused more on their activities *in the U.S.* The gross neglect of their presence in Europe, where they are equally strong, is a serious gap in the literature. There are just a few works that assess the trends in the growth of Japanese banks in Western Europe [Burton & Saelens (1983 and 1986); Walton & Trimble (1987); Terrell et al. (1989); Düser (1990) and Kitamura (1991]. Burton and Saelens (1983) explain the internationalization of Japanese banking in much the same way as Fujita and Ishigaki (1986), relating it to Japanese foreign direct investment in Europe. They also pinpoint imperfections in the domestic sector as a reason for the foreign involvement by Japanese banks. In their second work, Burton and Saelens (1986) extend their analysis to include the European investment undertaken by Japanese banks and securities companies in establishing subsidiaries and affiliates. Behind this investment by Japanese financial institutions, they identify the desire to achieve higher rates of return in unregulated markets as the main goal. Remarkably, this study is the only one that covers not only the European investment of Japanese banks but also of securities companies and other non-bank financial institutions.

The research work by Terrell et al. (1989) focuses on the activities of Japanese banks in the U.K. and the U.S. They also emphasize the fact [like Poulsen (1986); Brimmer and Dahl (1975); Goldberg and Saunders (1980, 1981a, 1981b); and Tschoegl (1987)] that a large proportion of Japanese banks' activities in the U.S. and the U.K. appears to be related to avoiding financial restrictions at home. The latest work with a European focus is that of Düser (1990). He devotes his analysis primarily to the international strategies of Japanese banks during the 1970s and 1980s.

Research into the European expansion of Japanese banks is still limited. The knowledge already gathered is still based more on casual observation than on rigorous analysis. There are several issues for which no methodical answers are available. Do Japanese financial institutions possess any systematic advantage over their competitors in Europe? What are the organizational strategies of Japanese banks? Do macroeconomic conditions within the Japanese economy explain their global growth? These and several other questions need to be analyzed in a larger systematic framework so that better judgment can be made about the strengths, weaknesses and role of Japanese financial institutions. An analysis of this type should contribute to correct policy formulations, both by regulators and by competitors. It should also fill gaps in the academic literature on the subject.

1.1.3 Japanese Securities Companies as Multinationals

There is an acute gap in the literature as regards the industrial organization[4] of international investment bankers and securities firms. One notices here that the industrial organization of multinational banking has not been neglected to the same extent as that of multinational securities firms. There are running references in the literature to the industrial characteristics of international securities markets. To the knowledge of the author, there is just one work that explicitly treats securities firms as multinationals, i.e., by Scott-Quinn (1990a). He also recognizes the lack of academic interest in the subject and attributes this to (i) the secretive, private partnership form of organization of these institutions in the past, (ii) the small size of the industry in terms of capital employed, and (iii) the not so prominent role played by international securities markets before the 1980s.[5]

Concentrating on the activities of the U.S. investment banks in the City of London, Scott-Quinn (1990a) contends that, "Given the value of brand name in building a business and the problems and costs of sharing the use of it with partners overseas, it has been necessary to internalize its use and thus make direct investments overseas in both sales and production to service clients rather than continuing to use arm-length relationship."[6] His work evidently dwells on and draws nurture from the internalization theory of Dunning (1981).[7] Another work by Hakim (1986) reviews the strategies of

---

[4]Any study of industrial organization should seek to establish the relationship between structure (concentration), conduct (marketing policies) and performance (profitability).

[5]Scott-Quinn (1990a) p. 268.

[6]ibid. p. 292.

[7]In terms of the ownership-location-internalization (OLI) paradigm developed by Dunning (1981), any theory of multinational enterprise - including banking organizations - must identify some specific firm assets, such as patent technology, or special know-how or certain organizational skills, and explain why these special factors are exploited within the organization rather than by licensing, franchises, etc. Once this is done,
(continued...)

international investment bankers and makes recommendations to the would-be global investment banking firms. This work supports the idea of growth from within to become an integrated investment banking firm.

Nowhere in the literature have the strategies of Japanese investment bankers in their global operations been systematically investigated. Locating this gap in the academic coverage, the present work seeks to introduce methodical information from the experience of Japanese securities companies as multinationals. The idea is not to see them only as a separate and isolated group of multinationals but also in the overall framework of financial institutions as multinationals. In this attempt, the work should be the first of its kind in providing a more complete view of the subject.

1.2   Objectives of the Study

The main objective of the present study is to investigate and document the growth in the European presence of Japanese banks and securities companies. Within the main objective, the research work seeks to achieve the following aims:

(i)   to provide a detailed account of the Japanese financial system, its markets and institutions along with the measures, which led to the internationalization of Japanese finance in the 1980s;

(ii)   to describe the characteristics of Japan's capital flows in the 1980s for the purpose of identifying the extent of international financial intermediation performed by Japan and its financial institutions;

(iii)   to analyze the presence, activities, strategies and performance of Japanese banks and securities companies in Europe;

(iv)   to assess the competitive position and the sources of competitive advantage(s) available to Japanese banks and securities companies vis-à-vis internationally active financial institutions from other countries.

(v)   to examine empirically the variables that have induced or supported the growth of Japanese banks in the European Union; and

(vi)   to present detailed case studies on the Japanese financial presence in two European countries, viz., the United Kingdom and Germany.

---

[7](...continued)
location theory is left to determine the worldwide distribution of production and the form of local representation. See Lewis and Davis (1987) p. 254.

1.3   Research Methodology

The study draws extensively on the vast amount of research and data from English, German and Japanese language literature. A pilot survey of Japanese financial institutions in Germany was conducted in order to collect primary data for the case study of Japanese financial presence in German financial markets. During a three-month stay in Japan, a series of interviews were carried out with Japanese financial experts and academicians in order to bring the research work closer to real-life practice. Apart from several statistical tools that have been used to collect and compile information, the technique of multiple regression analysis (Ordinary Least Squares) has been applied for the purpose of estimating the statistical significance of various determinants that have influenced Japanese banks' expansion in Europe.

1.4   Plan of the Study

After the introduction in this chapter, Chapter 2 gives a detailed account of the Japanese financial markets and institutions. The information serves as a background for understanding the behavior of Japanese financial institutions outside their domestic financial markets. The impact of financial deregulation and liberalization, in so far as they influence the cross-border transactions and the behavior of borrowers and investors, has also been examined here. Chapter 3 examines Japan's long-term and short-term capital flows to test the validity of the statement that Japan performed the role of international financial intermediary in the 1980s. The stance of Japanese financial institutions in international financial intermediation has been scrutinized to find out whether banks or non-banks were the main vehicles in the recycling of Japanese surplus.

The case of the Japanese banking presence in Europe has been dealt with in Chapter 4 and that of Japanese securities companies in Chapter 5. Taken together, these two chapters constitute the core segment of the study. The focus of inquiry is on the nature of the Japanese financial presence in Europe with reference to the forms of organization, types of activities, operational strategies and performance in Europe. The integration of European financial markets after 1992 and the ensuing impact on the Japanese financial presence is also evaluated here. The competitive position of Japanese banks and securities companies is analyzed in Chapter 6 with the help of several yardsticks. A major part of this chapter is devoted to examining the sources of competitive advantage available to them. Chapter 7 presents the macroeconomic determinants of Japanese banks' expansion in the European Union. This chapter provides empirical testing of several hypotheses on the subject with the help of multiple regression analysis. Chapter 8 explores Japanese financial presence in two European countries, viz. the United Kingdom and Germany. These case studies bring to light the contrasts in the European strategy of Japanese financial institutions.

The concluding section reflects upon the major findings of the study and provides directions for future research on the subject. One of the major conclusions is that the competitive position of Japanese financial institutions during the 1980s was assessed more with reference to their increasing share in international financial markets than in terms of improvements in their international competitiveness. The competitive challenge posed by Japanese banks and securities companies needs to be re-assessed in the light of the evidence provided in this study.

Chapter 2

The Japanese Financial System - A Domestic and International Perspective

The financial system of a country refers to the institutional arrangement designed to transform savings into investment and to allocate funds among alternative uses.[1] The institutional aspect of any financial system refers to the legal framework for a given set of intermediary institutions. The related financial structure reflects upon the nature of financial contracts, such as dominance of capital market or banks. Thus, financial systems of free economies are usually classified into two groups: bank-oriented and market-oriented systems.[2]

The *bank-oriented systems* are normally characterized by less developed financial markets. Savings in such systems are primarily channeled through banks and other savings institutions in the form of short-term and long-term credits. Typically, the government supports bank lending and actively intervenes to influence the costs of various forms of finance. On the other hand, the *market-oriented systems* are identified by the existence of a wider range of financial instruments and markets. Households invest a larger share of their savings directly, through capital markets, and banks primarily meet the short-term needs of the corporate sector. Government regulates the banking sector but refrains from active intervention.[3][4] The corporate capital structure is also significantly influenced by the type of financial system with bank-oriented systems contributing more to highly-leveraged corporate sector and relatively low

---

[1]Tobin (1984).

[2]Berglöf (1990) p. 244.

[3]ibid.

[4]Zysman (1983) uses the terms credit-based and capital-based instead of bank-oriented and market-oriented to convey the same meaning, except that his emphasis is on fund allocation by prices which are established through relatively competitive markets in capital-based systems. As against this, in credit-based system, prices are administered.

dispersion of debt.[5] Based on the above description, the financial systems of Anglo-Saxon countries (Canada, the U.K., and the U.S.) are usually labelled as market-oriented and that of the other countries in the Group of Seven (France, Germany, Italy and Japan) as bank-oriented.

Before providing a detailed account of the changes which led to greater internationalization of Japanese finance and their impact, the main features of its postwar financial system, followed by the present position of its institutions and markets, are discussed in the next section. However, it needs to be noted that the changing nature of financial contracts in Japan (evidenced by flow of funds and financing behavior of corporations) have made the financial system "less-administered" and these could be construed as positive moves towards a market-oriented system.

2.1   Basic Characteristics of the Japanese Financial System

A characteristic feature of the postwar Japanese economy is that it achieved a high rate of growth in real GNP.[6] Being a 'late starter' in the industrial revolution, Japan's higher economic growth has come to be viewed as an industrial 'catch-up' process with borrowed technology.[7] The acute demand for long-term funds in Japan in the 'catch-up' process constitutes the background to the postwar high growth period which led to the emergence of a highly regulated institutional arrangement for financing this need.[8] The fundamental shape of the financial system created to meet domestic requirements has been maintained long after the high growth period because of its success in supporting and promoting industrialization. The extensive regulations in the system were targeted at achieving high economic growth. The system was characterized by:

---

[5]Borio (1990a).

[6]Between 1957-62 and 1963-69, annual average real GNP growth rate in Japan was 9.4% and 10.3% respectively. Germany, the U. K. and the U. S. reported growth rates between 3 to 5.5% during these two periods.

[7]Teranishi (1986) pp. 133-146.

[8]The conventional view of postwar Japanese financial system is that it was highly regulated. See Teranishi (1990); Suzuki (1987); Wallich and Wallich (1976).

(i)   functional segmentation of private financial institutions (between short and long-term finance; banking and trust business; and banking and securities business);

(ii)   interest rate regulation, both deposit and loan rates;

(iii)   regulation of international transactions (e.g., exchange controls); and

(iv)   collateral requirements for bond issues, bank lending and interbank transactions.[9]

Though a functional segmentation of financial institutions is also found in other industrial countries, the Japanese system is peculiar in the sense that it has so far enforced this triple segmentation by law. Similarly, the interest rate regulations were implemented by law to ensure allocation of funds in the desired sectors of the economy. The exchange controls were required to insulate the economy from external disturbances.

During the high growth period, despite the low or negative real returns available to savers[10] on bank deposits, most savings were channeled into industry through banks. The over-reliance by the private corporate sector on bank borrowing[11] led to the predominance of indirect finance and hindered, in some ways, the development of the capital market in Japan. Notwithstanding the competitiveness of the regulated bank-oriented financial system,[12] it could be argued that fund allocation by banks was carried out

---

[9]For details on this subject, refer to Suzuki (1987) pp. 35-44.

[10]In some years during the 1960s, the inflation rate was higher than the nominal interest rate on bank deposits.

[11]The Japanese banks extended more credit than they acquired through deposits and capital. They filled the gap of 'over-loan' by borrowing from the Bank of Japan.

[12]Two divergent views are widespread regarding the competitiveness of the Japanese banking sector during the high growth period. The first view [Sakakibara et al. (1982); Sakakibara (1984); and Teranishi, (1990)] argues that the banking sector was more competitive during the high growth period than is commonly believed. The second view [Cargill (1985)], providing a U.S. perspective of the Japanese financial system, suggests

(continued...)

efficiently; the high growth rate of GNP attained by the Japanese economy justifies that.

Another important feature of the high growth financial system was that the Japanese government acted more as a financial intermediary than as borrower or regulator.[13] While the postal savings system, as a public financial intermediary, collected one-fifth of the nation's total deposits, other public institutions, such as the Japan Development Bank extended financial support to industries, like mining, marine transport and agriculture, which were facing difficulties in obtaining finance. The support extended by public institutions to the industry was seen as an implicit guarantee and encouraged participation by the private financial institutions.

However, the success of the regulated Japanese financial system must be seen from another point of view. The system succeeded also because it provided the borrowers with huge implicit subsidies in the form of differential between the regulated rate of interest, which they paid, and the competitive market rate, which they would have paid otherwise.[14] Even the financial intermediaries received implicit subsidies in the regulated system arising from the deposit rate regulations and cheaper loans from the Bank of Japan (henceforth BOJ). A recent attempts[15] at estimating these subsidies suggests that the annual average of implicit subsidies to the city banks during 1966-70 was ¥85 billion from regulation of deposit rates and ¥202 billion from low interest loans from the BOJ[16], the latter accounting for over 10 percent of the current earnings of the city banks

---

[12](...continued)

that both systems (Japanese and U.S.) operated under constraints that limit competition. Acknowledging the presence of interest rate regulation in Japan during the high growth period, it could be argued that the competition must have taken the form of non-price competition. Tsutsui (1990) provides details on this point.

[13]Sakakibara and Feldman (1983) p. 20.

[14]Aliber suggests that the implicit objective of regulation frequently is to subsidize certain groups. For details, refer to Aliber (1987) pp. 80-81.

[15]Teranishi (1990) p. 338.

[16]The annual average of implicit subsidies to Japanese industry has been estimated to be ¥451 billion between 1966-70 and ¥1006 billion between 1971-75. See Teranishi (1990).

during the 1960s.[17] This subsidy was over and above the tacit guarantee given by the BOJ for rescuing the financial institutions in distress.

The institutional arrangement of finance that was created during the Occupation Period (1945-52) was in force, with minor modifications, until the mid-1980s. After that, a multitude of new financial markets were set up in which the financial institutions operate with greater degrees of freedom. In addition to that, the recently completed process of interest rate deregulation (in June 1993) and the lowering of the functional segmentation amongst financial institutions (in April 1993) has further altered the basic nature of Japanese financial system. In the following section, a brief account of the existing financial institutions and markets along with their current position is presented.

2.1.1 Types of Financial Institution

In Japan, the various types of financial institutions cannot be precisely classified because of their historical development. The functional distinction among different types of institutions has been further blurred by a series of financial liberalizations during the 1980s. These measures have intensified the competition among the financial institutions for entering each other's domain. However, the postwar taxonomy of financial institutions, which is based on the main type of their business, still provides the best way of grouping them. Figure 2.1 provides a list of Japanese financial institutions according to this criterion.

The ordinary commercial banks, long-term credit banks, trust banks and regional banks are the main types of depository institutions in Japan. The securities companies and insurance companies are the two major groups of institutions in the category of non-depository institutions. Taken together, the above-mentioned institutions dominate in the institutional structure of Japanese finance as private financial institutions. The post office system in Japan, as a state-owned entity, competes directly with the depository institutions for mobilizing savings. The Japan Development Bank and the Export-Import Bank of Japan are the two major state-owned institutions entrusted with the job of allocating funds. Apart from these major institutions, there is a plethora of local or regional credit cooperatives and credit associations which cater to the needs of specific groups or communities.

---

[17]Tsutsui (1990) pp. 72-73.

Figure 2.1: Principal Financial Institutions in Japan (As of end-March 1994)

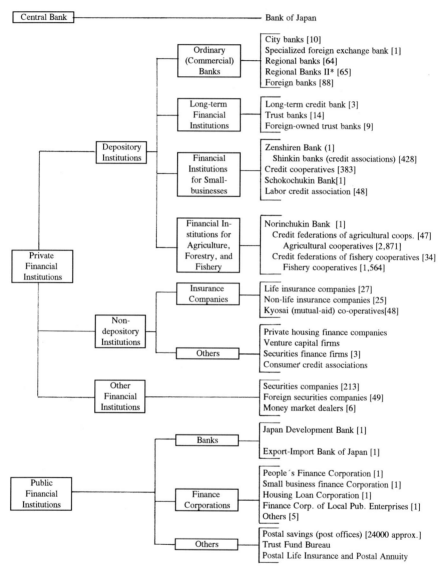

*Members Banks of the Second Association of Regional Banks
Figures in parenthesis show the number of institutions

Source: BOJ; Federation of Bankers Associations of Japan [Zenginkyo]etc.

Private depository intermediaries. This section confines the discussion about the domestic position of private depository institutions only to those institutions which are active in the overseas markets. Table 2.1 provides a summary view of the market position of each type of depository institution in Japan.

Table 2.1: Market Share of Depository Financial Institutions in Japan

Type of banks	Branches°		Market Share (%)*		Securities business (%)	
	Total	Over-seas	Funds raised	Funds lent	Under-writing²	Deal-ing²
City Banks (11)	3277	219	19.7	29.1	21.3	14.1
Regional Banks (64)	7140	54	15.3	16.7	5.6	3.5
Regional Banks II (65)	4524	7	5.8	6.7	1.3	0.9
Foreign Banks (88)			0.2	1.0		
Long-term credit Banks (3)	108	32	5.6	6.2	4.9	5.1
Trust Banks (8)	434	41	12.7	7.6	2.1	1.1
Total (151)³	15,483	353	59.1	66.3	35.2	24.7

° As of the end of September 1993
* As of the end of 1993
² For the fiscal year ending March 1992
³ Total represents member banks of the Federation of Bankers Associations of Japan and excludes foreign banks

Source: Federation of Bankers Associations of Japan [Zenginkyo] (1994a)

The 11 *city banks*,[18] including the Bank of Tokyo (BOT), constitute the single most important category of private depository institutions in Japan, accounting for about 22 percent of the total branches of all banks.[19] The city banks dominate institutional finance and account for 20 percent of the total funds raised and 30 percent of the total loans

---

[18] The merger of Mitsui Bank and Taiyo Kobe Bank on April 1, 1990 and that of Kyowa Bank and Saitama Bank on April 1, 1991 reduced the number of city banks from 13 to 11. The proposed merger between Mitsubishi Bank and Bank of Tokyo in 1996 will reduce the number of city banks to 10.

[19] All banks include city banks, regional banks, member banks of the second association of regional banks, long-term credit banks and trust banks.

made in Japan at the end of 1993.[20] However, the degree of concentration in the Japanese banking industry is not high when compared with the countries of Western Europe. Thus, the concentration ratio in Japan, based on the top five banks' deposits as a percentage of total banking systems' deposits, is 16 percent as against 57 percent in France, 45 percent in Switzerland, 36 percent in Italy, 32 percent in the U.K., and 31 percent in Germany.[21]

Traditionally, city banks have placed great emphasis on serving the needs of large corporations. As of March 1988, corporations capitalized at ¥1 billion or above account-ed for approximately 30 percent of the total lending of city banks. Large corporations also account for 50 percent of total deposits of city banks. Most large Japanese corpora-tions in the 1950s developed some affiliations with an industrial group or *keiretsu* in Japan. Constituted around a financial institution, these industrial groups were remarkably stable throughout the 1960s and 1970s. The influential role of the 'main bank system' in Japan, which owes its existence to the industrial groupings, is declining. As many as a quarter of the companies listed on the Tokyo Stock Exchange (henceforth TSE) switched their main bank (number one lender for the firm) between 1985 and 1990.[22] With decreased corporate dependency on bank loans and an increase of funding through securities,[23] in the 1980s all city banks sought to diversify their activities by extending loans to small and medium sized firms (45 percent of total lending of city banks as of March 1988) and expanding international activities. In the latter half of the 1980s, lending by city banks to the parties who wish to purchase real estate or invest in finan-cial assets and lending secured by real estate or securities increased rapidly.[24]

The regional banks constitute the second largest group of private depository institu-tions. Since the conversion of all *sogo* (mutual) banks into regional banks after February

---

[20]Federation of Bankers Association of Japan [*Zenginkyo*] (1994a).

[21]Moody's Inc. (1989) p. 17.

[22]For details, see Bank of Japan (1992a) p. 16.

[23]The ratio of funds raised through loans to securities declined from 6:1 in 1980 to 2:1 in 1988. for details, refer to Usuki (1991) pp. 32-41.

[24]Bank of Japan (1991a) p.12; In the boom years of 1987 and 1988, loans collateral-ized by property accounted for more than half of city banks' incremental loan growth. See Economist (1990a) p. 5.

1989, there were 129 regional banks as of the end of March 1994.[25] Most of the regional banks are based in the principal city of a prefecture and conduct the majority of their operations within that prefecture. In terms of the number of branches, all regional banks account for three-quarters of all banking branches as of the end of September 1993. Taken together, all the regional banks accounted for 21 percent of the total deposits and 23 percent of the total lending in Japan at the end of 1993 (see Table 2.1). Over half of their deposits are from individuals and over three-quarters of these deposits are time deposits. This aspect of regional banks' fund supply explains their behavior as net suppliers of funds in the interbank money markets and their high ratio of securities holdings. Many regional banks are sizable by international standards, with six of them figuring in the world's 100 largest commercial banks in terms of asset size. The largest regional bank, the Bank of Yokohama, is larger than the smallest city bank.

The long-term credit banks emerged in Japan in the postwar era to fulfill the continued demand for long-term funds which could not be satisfied by the commercial banks. The Industrial Bank of Japan (IBJ), Long-Term Credit Bank of Japan (LTCB) and Nippon Credit Bank (NCB) are the three banks under this category. They are authorized to issue debentures[26] but are restrained in their deposit taking activity, thereby making debentures their main source of funding. With a limited number of domestic branches, the three accounted for 5.6 percent of funds raised and 6.2 percent of lending by all financial institutions in Japan at the end of 1993. Though seen as wholesale banks in Japan, these banks have been striving to expand into the securities business to become full-fledged investment banks. Under the Financial System Reform Law, which came into force in April 1993, the long-term credit banks were the first to receive license for establishing securities subsidiaries. Outside Japan, the IBJ and the LTCB have already established themselves in this field.

There are seven specialized *trust banks* in Japan, which are involved both in trust and banking business. Other than these, nine foreign banks have been operating trust banking subsidiaries since 1985. In addition to this, one city bank (Daiwa Bank) and two regional banks (Bank of Okinawa and Bank of Ryukyu) are also engaged in trust business. Trust banks are long-term financial institutions in that they obtain most of their funds from

---

[25]The new 68 regional banks are distinguished by their membership of the Second Association of Regional Banks.

[26]The Bank of Tokyo is the only other bank authorized to issue debentures.

trusts, particularly loan trusts, and supply funds to major corporations for capital investment. Thus, trust banks differ from those in the U.S., which focus their activities in the area of asset management. At the end of 1993, the trust banks accounted for 13 percent of the total funds raised by the financial institutions and 8 percent of the total funds lent.

Private non-depository institutions. *The Japanese securities companies* constitute the most dominant group of non-depository institutions performing investment banking functions in Japan. Their dominant position in securities business resulted, to a considerable extent, from the Article 65 of the Securities and Exchange Law of 1948 which prohibited securities business by banks, trust corporations and other designated financial institutions. At the end of 1992, there were 265 securities companies in Japan, including 49 foreign securities firms. Under the Japanese Law, securities companies are required to obtain a separate license for each of the four kinds of securities businesses (viz. dealing on account, acting as broker, underwriting and retail distribution). Therefore, securities companies in Japan are usually classified on this basis. Table 2.2 provides details of all securities companies by the types of licenses and the size of capital.

Table 2.2 : Number of Securities Companies in Japan*
(by Types of Licences & Size of Capital)

(End of 1992)

Types of Licence[2]	Capital (yen in billion)					Total
	Under 0.2	0.2-0.99	1.0-2.99	3.0-4.99	5.0 & Over	
1, 2, 3, 4	...	50(24)	34(25)	28(21)	56(52)	168(122)
1, 2, 4	65(--)	22(1)	...	...	1(--)	88(1)
1, 2	...	1(--)	2(--)	...	...	3(--)
2	1(--)	1(1)	...	1(--)	...	3(1)
Total	66(--)	74(26)	36(25)	29(21)	57(52)	262[3](124)

*Includes foreign securities companies (Total 51; TSE members 25)
[2]There are four types of licenses: 1 for dealing; 2 for brokerage;
 3 for underwriting; and 4 for retail selling business.
[3]Total excludes 6 Saitori member companies
 Figures in parentheses indicate TSE membership

Source: Japan Securities Dealers Association

As the table shows, most of the securities companies are integrated securities companies having licenses for all four activities. Conversely, most of the integrated securities companies are also medium and large sized. As of the end of 1992, the 216 domestic securities companies conducted their business through 3072 business offices dispersed around the country with the largest of them having a dense network of offices.[27] Under the Financial System Reform Law of 1992 (enforced in April 1993), which allows financial institutions to compete in each other's sphere via subsidiaries, the Big Four securities companies (Nomura, Daiwa, Nikko, and Yamaichi) have established trust banking subsidiaries.

Functionally speaking, the relative strength of participants in any market is inversely related to the regulatory barriers to entry. The Article 65, as a regulatory barrier, seems to have reinforced the dominant position of a few securities companies in Japan. Thus, the Big Four securities companies predominate in all spheres of securities business. Taken together they accounted for 34 percent of all the stock transactions and 72 percent of all the bond transactions in the secondary markets in the business year ending March 1991.[28] Further, they acted as managing underwriter for 82 percent of all stock issues and 70 percent of all bonds issues in the domestic markets in 1990.[29] In new business areas too, such as M&A, investment advisory services, risk capital and derivative products, the Big Four play a significant role. Thus, the securities industry in Japan displays a high degree of market concentration and is oligopolistic in character. One implication of the oligopolistic character is that the behavior of the dominant Big Four in the domestic markets introduces an information bias in the securities prices and interferes with the free play of market forces.

The revenue mix of Japanese securities companies shows that the broker function is their main activity with over 50 percent of the revenue coming from brokerage commission. The fact that the Big Four also earned about 45 percent of their operating revenue in the business year ending 1990 from brokerage commission suggests that they still act

---

[27]Though the average number of offices per securities company turned out to be 13.4 at the end of 1989, the top four (Nomura, Daiwa, Nikko and Yamaichi) have the highest number of offices with an average of 128 offices. See Ministry of Finance, Japan (1991) p. 322.

[28]Tokyo Stock Exchange (1992a) pp. 270-273.

[29]Suto (1992) p. 85.

more as brokers than as full-fledged investment bankers. The Big Four obtain about 14 percent of their operating revenue from the underwriting business, which is higher than the industry average of 4.8 percent. This further hints at their prominent position in this area. Unlike the U.S. investment banks which report a quarter of their revenue from dealing on account, the Japanese securities companies earn only 12 percent of their revenue from this function.

In addition to securities companies, the *life and non-life insurance companies* are the other major group of non-bank financial intermediaries in Japan. As of the end of March 1994, there were 27 life and 25 non-life insurance companies in Japan. Taken together, they account for about 20 percent of the country's personal savings.[30] The large funds at the disposal of these institutions[31] and the diversification in their financial services has highlighted the similarities between insurance companies and other financial institutions.[32] Over the last ten years, they have grown at phenomenal rates and are active participants both in the loan market (as lenders) and capital markets (as institutional investors). Their portfolio investment in foreign securities was a significant factor of the capital outflows from Japan in the 1980s.

Public financial intermediaries. In the category of public financial intermediaries, two sets of institutions exist: those that collect savings and those that channel the collected funds into various investment opportunities. The funds collecting institution is the postal savings system. With over 24,000 offices throughout Japan, the postal savings system collected 17.2 percent of the funds raised by all financial institutions in Japan at the end of 1993.[33] The job of fund allocation is carried out by two public sector banks (Japan Development Bank and Export-Import Bank of Japan) and nine specific-purpose financial corporations. As a collective whole, the government financial sector accounted for 15.2 percent of the total loans at the end of 1993.[34]

---

[30]Bank of Japan, Economic Statistics Annual.

[31]As of the end of 1990, Japanese life insurance companies and non-life insurance companies had total assets of ¥130 trillion and ¥43 trillion respectively.

[32]Noguchi et al. (1991) p. 403.

[33]Federation of Bankers Associations of Japan [Zenginkyo] (1994a) p.8.

[34]ibid.

2.1.2 The Present Position of Financial Markets

Other than the traditional classification of the financial markets into short-term and long-term, the developments of the 1980s have given birth to a third group of financial markets, viz. derivative products markets. Lastly, there is a residual category of markets which, because of their peculiar character, cannot be covered by the above-mentioned categories. Two such markets are the foreign exchange market and the offshore market. A discussion of financial markets in Japan, under the above-mentioned grouping, is given here.

Short-term financial markets. The short-term markets in Japan are typically classified into the *interbank market* and the *open market*. An overview of the relative size of each segment of the market is provided in Table 2.3.

Table 2.3

Part I: Relative Position of Different Types of Short-Term Financial Markets in Japan

(Amount outstanding in percent)

Year	Interbank market (A)	Call market	Bill market	Open market (B)	CD market	CP market	FB market	TB market	Gensaki market	Total Yen in Trillion
1970	75.0	75.0		25.0					25.0	2.4
1975	78.8	27.1	51.8	21.2					21.2	8.5
1980	58.7	24.6	34.1	41.3	14.4				26.9	16.7
1985	50.3	17.3	32.6	49.7	33.7				16.0	28.8
1990	44.8	26.6	18.2	55.2	20.9	17.4	1.1	8.4	7.3	90.0
1992*	52.9	37.8	15.4	47.1	17.4	12.0	1.7	10.1	5.8	103.0

*Figures from Federation for Bankers Associations of Japan (1994)

Part II: International Comparison of the Size of Short-Term Financial Markets

(Total Size to GDP, in %)

Year	Japan	US	UK	Germany
1982	7.4	33.1	21.8	15.8
1991	21.3	30.6	29.8	26.0[2]

[2]Figure for year-end 1990

Source: Suzuki (1987); Sawayama (1991); BOJ etc.

The interbank market consists of the call and bill market, and the open market is composed of the CD (certificates of deposit) market, the CP (commercial paper) market, the FT/TB (financial bills/ treasury bills) market, the BA (bankers acceptance) market and the *gensaki* (securities repurchase) market. Though the interbank market is narrowly interpreted as a market in which only banks operate, securities companies have also been allowed access to this market since 1980.[35]

It is relevant to note that the absolute size of short-term financial markets in Japan has grown dramatically from ¥2.4 trillion in 1970 to ¥103 trillion at the end of 1992. This growth in absolute size has brought the Japanese money markets to a level comparable to that of other countries. [refer to Table 2.3 Part (II)]. The ratio of the total size of the Japanese short-term financial markets to GDP increased from 6.3 percent in 1975[36] to 21.3 percent of GDP at the end of 1991. The two countries with highly developed short-term financial markets are the U.K. and the U.S. where the size of the short-term money markets represents about 30 percent of GDP. The size of the short-term financial markets in Germany, which does not include the so-called open market, is only 26 percent of GDP and, in the case of France, which has made efforts to expand the open market since 1985, the proportion at the end of 1991 was 21.9 percent.

A closer look at the different market segments in Table 2.3 part (I) shows that, in comparison with the interbank markets, the open markets have gained in relative importance since 1980. The open markets now represent almost half the outstanding size of the short-term financial markets. This is largely due to the diversification of the open markets and the growth shown by the CD (authorized in May 1979) and CP (started in November 1987) markets. The Japanese financial institutions are the major debtors (about 70%) of the money markets. This phenomenon could be closely related to the fact that indirect financing has traditionally taken up a large share in the Japanese financial system. By way of comparison, in the U.S., where direct financing carries a greater weight, the treasury bills market (government debt) and the commercial paper (corporate debt) market account for a larger share of the total market.[37]

---

[35]In 1980, securities firms were allowed to re-enter the call money market and later in May 1985 they were allowed access to the bill market, too.

[36]Feldman (1986) p. 39.

[37]Watanabe and Muraoka (1991) p. 71.

Other than affording financial institutions greater ease in adjusting their liquidity positions, developments in short-term money markets should ensure greater efficacy of monetary policy. The recent developments in Japanese short-term money markets have brought mixed influence on the BOJ's monetary policy. On the one hand, there has been a diversification of the tools used by the BOJ for open market operations. Since March 1986, BOJ executes open market operation by using CDs and in May 1989, CPs were added to the list of instruments eligible for the purpose.[38] On the other hand, the treasury bill market, which plays a major role in the monetary policy of the Federal Reserve Board in the U.S., still does not have sufficient depth to become the core of BOJ's monetary policy.[39] The fast growth in the Euroyen market is another significant money market development which has negatively influenced the monetary policy. The expansion of the Euroyen market, which banks have increasingly used for their cross-border settlements, has often been viewed as reducing the importance of domestic interbank market as a powerful monetary policy tool.

Long-term financial markets. It is generally believed that the predominance of indirect financing, which was more popular during the high growth period, was one of the reasons for the slower evolution of the long-term financial markets in Japan. Further, the traditional methods of equity issues (par value issues to existing shareholders), coupled with excessively high underwriting fee made the use of stock exchange uneconomical.[40] The first impetus for the development of Japanese securities markets came around 1975 from large scale issue of public bonds necessitated by the huge government deficits. Thus, since 1975 the Japanese securities market (including the bond and equity markets) has grown rapidly both in terms of absolute size and in relation to GNP. The value of outstanding balances in the securities market increased (at the annual compound rate of over 18 percent) from 18 percent of GNP in 1953 to 52 percent of GNP in 1970 and 184 percent in 1987. In the overall capital market, the share of the equity market has decreased somewhat from 62% in 1953 to 55% in 1987, and that of the bond market has increased from 38% in 1953 to 46% in 1987.[41]

---

[38]For details, refer to Osugi (1990) pp. 38-40.

[39]Since January 1990, BOJ has started using treasury bill operations also.

[40]Suzuki (1987).

[41]Takagi (1989) p. 566.

The primary markets. The *primary market for bond issues* in Japan comprises two main categories of bonds: public bonds and corporate bonds. The first includes national government bonds, local government bonds and government guaranteed bonds. The second category includes bank debentures, corporate bonds, yen-denominated foreign (Samurai) bonds and foreign currency denominated foreign (Shogun) bonds. Though the prime mover in the growth of the bond market has been the public bond segment, the largest proportion of bond issues are bank debentures, accounting for 43 percent of all bonds issued in the fiscal year ending March 1993.[42] However, because of severe eligibility requirements, high issuing costs and procedural complexities, the new issue market in industrial bonds has been sluggish and has tended to develop more outside Japan. For some varieties of industrial bonds, such as straight and warrant bonds, the majority of the issues in the 1980s were made in overseas markets.[43] In the domestic market, only offerings of convertible bonds have started to pick up since 1984. Thus, taken together, the share of industrial bonds in total bonds issued declined from 11.7 percent in the fiscal year ending March 1989 to 4.5 percent in the fiscal year ending March 1993. Among the subscribers to the various types of bonds, financial institutions have been the main purchasers of the government bonds and individuals the main group of buyers for bank debentures.

In the *primary market for equity issues*, offerings to the public at market price is of recent origin. This method of equity issues was tried in 1969 and now accounts for three-quarters of all issues by listed companies in Japan. The popularity of this method has brought about a tendency for the market-value public offerings to occur more when stock prices are high. Between the fiscal years 1987 and 1989, the buoyancy of long-term financial markets enabled all types of listed companies, particularly financial institutions, to make large scale equity offering.[44] The downturn in the stock prices since late December 1989 and the consequent reduction in the volume of new issues shows

---

[42]The new issue volume of government bonds in the fiscal year ending March 1993 was 40% of the total.

[43]See Section 5.3.1 and Table 5.4 for details.

[44]In 1989 Japanese financial institutions raised a total of ¥3,551 billion in the form of equity capital in Japan which was more than 40 percent of the total new equity financing by listed companies in that year. See Tokyo Stock Exchange (1990) p. 129.

that the new issue market is still inhibitive in nature.[45] Although the decline in equity financing depressed overall fund raising via the capital market, it has not forced Japanese corporations to return to bank borrowing. Instead, with demand for funds declining along with the economic slowdown, corporations have rather increased their issuance of straight bonds in both domestic and overseas markets to partly offset the decline in equity financing.[46]

The secondary markets. In the *secondary market in bonds*, government bonds form the largest part of total trading, accounting for 94 percent of the total between April 1985 and March 93.[47] The trading volume of government bonds has expanded sharply because of the marked increase in the value of outstanding government securities. Because of the massive offering, 47% of all the outstanding bonds in Japan as of March 1993 were government bonds.[48] The growth of secondary market was further stimulated in April 1983, when banks were allowed to sell public bonds over-the-counter, and in June 1984, when banks were allowed to deal in public bonds. In addition to public bonds, bank debentures and corporate bonds are the other two kinds of bonds accounting for 2.2 percent and 1.1 percent respectively of the total trading volume in the fiscal year ending March 1993.

Though banks are vital participants in bond trading,[49] bond dealers accounted for about 58 percent of the total bond trading value in the fiscal year ending March 1993. Most of the bond trading (over 90 percent) takes place on over-the-counter markets. The

---

[45]The total value of equity issues by listed companies declined dramatically from its peak of ¥6,659 billion (excluding exercise of warrants) in 1989 to ¥217 billion in 1992 (Source: Tokyo Stock Exchange).

[46]See Bank of Japan (1993a) for the implications of stock market development for corporate financial activities.

[47]The Bond Underwriters Association of Japan (1993). For details on the subject, see Sakuma (1991) pp. 126-143.

[48]The long-term liabilities of the Japanese government accounted for 47% of GNP for the fiscal year ending March 1991 and were higher than those of the United Kingdom (31.6%, 1988), Germany (21.5%, 1988), France (13.0%, 1988) but lower than those of Italy (52.3%, 1988) and the United States (51.9%, 1988).

[49]Various types of Japanese banks and financial institutions accounted for about 20% of the total volume of trading in the fiscal year ending March 1992. See Japan Securities Dealer Association (1992).

growth of the secondary bond market, theoretically, should provide feedback for the new issue market and enforce the legitimacy of the market forces. The secondary market yield on government bonds in Japan now reflects market conditions and has become a representative for new issue market in bonds.

Unlike bond trading, *secondary market in equity* operates mainly through stock exchanges. Of the eight stock exchanges in Japan, the exchanges in Tokyo, Osaka and Nagoya are the prominent ones with TSE accounting for over 80 percent of total stock trading since 1975. Out of the 3,000 large companies (with a share capital of over ¥1 billion), roughly 2,000 are listed on the Japanese stock exchanges.[50] In contrast with the American or the British stock exchanges, where specialists act as market-makers on their own account, Japanese stock exchanges are pure order-driven markets which function without any help from responsible market-makers. The stock exchanges are a two-way continuous auction market where buy and sell orders interact directly with one another through specialists, called *saitori*. The *saitori* do not take positions on their own account and function solely as middlemen between members of the stock exchange. Membership of the stock exchange is limited by regulations and, as of April 1993, there are 124 members (including 25 foreign securities firms) on the TSE. Thus, in comparison with New York (516 members) and London (410 members), the TSE still continues to be a closed system. The brokerage commission rates, which have been successively reduced since April 1985,[51] are still regulated and contrast with other developed stock exchanges, such as New York, London where negotiable commission is the rule.

A conspicuous feature of the Japanese stock market is that the share ownership of financial institutions and industrial corporations has steadily increased from 15.5 percent at the end of 1949 to 70 percent at the end of March 1991 making them a dominant group of shareholders. The share ownership of banks and the corporate sector may be called the corporatization of share ownership and must be distinguished from the institutionalization of share ownership, which often implies shares held by institutional inves-

---

[50]In comparison with New York and London stock exchanges, where the number of listed companies at the end of 1990 was 1,678 (plus 125 foreign companies) and 1,946 (plus 613 foreign companies) respectively, the number of companies listed on the TSE was 1,627 (plus 125 foreign companies).

[51]Brokerage commission rates have been revised downwards four times since 1985: in April 1985 (1.5%), November 1986 (9.1%), October 1987 (9.8%), and June 1990 (7.05%). [Information obtained from the Tokyo Stock Exchange].

tors, such as pension funds whose primary motive in shareholding is portfolio returns and not corporate control. Conversely, the relative share of individual shareholding has been steadily declining, from 69.1 percent at the end of 1949 to 23 percent at the end of March 1991. Most of the corporate shareholding is in the form of stable crossholding of stocks[52] and acts as a barrier to hostile takeovers. Since financial institutions and corporations usually do not trade their stockholding,[53] the high turnover ratio of the shares actually traded hints at the speculative nature of stock trading in Japan.

Another feature of the Japanese stock market until the end of 1989 was the high price-earning ratio (P/E ratio) of Japanese stocks. The average P/E ratio of 71 for Japanese firms at the end of 1989 was well above the world average of 20 and considerably higher than those in other industrial countries.[54] Various reasons are given for the high P/E ratio of Japanese firms,[55] but the fall in the ratio to less than 38 in December 1991, after two years of monetary restraint in Japan, suggests that loose monetary policy had increased the amount of funds available in the 1980s and thus activated a speculative bubble in stock prices. The average P/E ratio of Japanese stocks surpassed its level of 1989 in June 1994 and stood at 74. This is despite the low volume of trading on the TSE.

Though the Japanese authorities have pumped in ¥12,000 billion between 1991 and 1994 to prop up the stock market through purchases of equities by public sector institutions, there is a general lack of activity in the market after 1990. Evidently the downturn in the stock market is not simply cyclical. The structural shift within Japan's financial markets seems to have created an imbalance between demand and supply of equities.[56]

---

[52]Banks hold a dominant position among financial institutions holding about 22 percent of the total stocks. The importance of bank holdings must be seen in the broader perspective of intercorporate stockholding involving nonfinancial corporations as well.

[53]Takagi (1989) p. 559 and Okumura (1989) p. 1066.

[54]The P/E ratio for other industrial countries at the end of 1990: USA (12.17), UK (10.29), Germany (16.0), France (11.4).

[55]While many authors emphasize the distortions created by the earning measurement problems as an important reason [Ando and Auerbach (1985, 1988), Bildersee et al. (1990), French and Poterba (1989)], others attribute high P/E ratio to the speculative bubble theory and cross-shareholding between corporations. See Ueda (1990).

[56]Baker (1995a) p. 19.

Derivative product markets. In the 1980s the derivative financial product markets, such as futures and options, gained in prominence in the financial markets of industrialized countries. The basic significance of these markets is that they provide investors with a means of hedging the risk inherent in price fluctuations of financial assets. In addition to that, these markets also provide new investment opportunities and help in the expansion and stabilization of spot markets through arbitrage.

In Japan, derivative product markets are of recent origin. The first such market in bond futures was created in October 1985 when the TSE launched long-term government bond future trading.[57] After that the stock index based-futures market (September 1988) and the options market (October 1989), the U.S. treasury bond futures market (December 1989) and the market for options in government bond futures (May 1990) were introduced for providing investors with additional hedging opportunities. In April 1989, the Tokyo International Financial Futures Exchange (TIFFE) was opened with three financial futures contracts - Euroyen and Eurodollar interest rate futures and Yen/ dollar currency futures. The derivative product markets have grown steadily since their creation and now rival the Chicago Mercantile Exchange (CME). In some markets the volume traded has stayed well ahead of cash markets.[58] However, by far the most popular derivative product is the 10-year Japanese government bond futures contract listed on the TSE, which trades an average of 2 million contracts a month.

The derivative product markets in Japan, very much like in other developed financial markets, are dominated by financial institutions and institutional investors, who understand the intricacies of such markets. In terms of investor groups, securities companies dominate in all types of derivative product markets (except for bond futures market where banks do 60 percent of the trading), accounting for more than three-quarters of the volume traded. The virtual absence of banks from most derivative product markets

---

[57]The product traded was 6% 10-year Japanese government bond. Later, in July, 1988, the TSE began trading in the 20-year Japanese government bond futures contract also.

[58]The daily average turnover (at the TSE and Osaka Stock Exchange taken together) for stock index based futures in 1991 was more than five times the amount of turnover in the cash market at the TSE. The value of trading in bond futures at the TSE was over 30 times the value of spot trading at the exchange, and amounted to about one-half of the total value of trading in the OTC market in 1990.

can be explained by the fact that banks, though having access to all markets as special participants, are restrained from doing stock brokerage business.

The influence of derivative markets on cash markets has been a controversial matter in Japan. The recent weakness of share prices has led to the suspicion that the speculative character of the futures markets is the source of violent price movements in the cash market. It is alleged that the growing volume of trading in the derivative product markets has confused the cash market. Various attempts have been made to tighten the control over stock index futures and options. For example, the margin deposit requirement for futures and options was increased three times in 1991.

Other financial markets. *Japan's foreign exchange market* is concentrated in Tokyo. The direct participants in the market include all the authorized foreign exchange banks (334 as of the end of 1992), 8 foreign exchange brokers and the BOJ as the central bank. The market in Tokyo is the third largest in the world, after London and New York, accounting for 14.5 percent of the net (daily average) global foreign exchange trading in April 1992.[59] The net average daily turnover in the Tokyo foreign exchange market has increased 140 percent from US$48 billion in 1986 to US$115 billion in 1989 and further to $128 billion in April 1992.[60] The growth of foreign exchange trading in Tokyo was supported not merely by the cross-border flow of trade in goods and services but also by capital flows.[61] The foreign currency transactions originating from financial transactions, arbitrage and speculative deals have become the mainstream of the foreign currency market in Tokyo.[62] A survey conducted by the Bank for International Settlements (henceforth BIS) suggests that the net foreign exchange market turnover exceeded foreign trade by a factor of 37 in the case of Japan and 25 in the case of the U.S. in April 1989.[63] The abolition of the 'real demand principle' by Japan in April 1984 was a dominant factor behind this growth. In terms of the currency composition, yen-dollar

---

[59]In a survey by the Bank for International Settlements, the size of the net global foreign exchange market (average daily turnover in April 1992) was estimated to be US$880 billion. For details see, Blitz (1993).

[60]Bank of Japan (1993b) p. 38.

[61]Nakaishi (1991) p. 249.

[62]ibid.

[63]BIS (1990) p. 7.

transactions account for 67 percent of the total daily trading in April 1992. This is because of the large share of cross-border transactions that are handled in US dollars. The analysis of counterparty in the foreign exchange market shows that interbank operations accounted for over 67 percent of the net exchange market turnover.[64] A review of the types of transactions indicates that the share of spot transactions is comparatively smaller in Tokyo (37%) than in London (50%) and New York (49%).[65] The high ratio of forward transactions in Tokyo could be explained by the growing tendency among customers to use more sophisticated financial management techniques.

The significance of the foreign exchange market must be seen in relation to international banking activity. A certain positive, albeit fairly loose, relationship seems to exist between the expansion of the foreign exchange market turnover and the growth of international banking activity.[66] Japan recorded the highest rate of increase in both international banking operations and foreign exchange market activity in the 1980s. In contrast, Canada, where the banks did not expand their international banking claims, registered the smallest rise in exchange market transactions during 1986-89.[67] Understandably, the ease of operations in the foreign exchange market gets translated into the growth of cross-border financial business because all foreign exchange transactions are inherently cross-border in nature. However, the reverse is also true where the expansion of international banking claims shows itself in increasing foreign exchange transactions.

The Japan offshore market (henceforth JOM). Conceptually, an offshore market is one in which financial institutions intermediate between non-residents. The International Finance Bureau of the Japanese Ministry of Finance (henceforth MOF) defines offshore markets as, "markets where operators are permitted to raise funds from non-residents and invest or lend that money to non-residents free from most regulations and taxes."[68] The JOM was established in December 1986 with the intent of fostering the international business of Japanese banking institutions and the activities of foreign banks in Japan. It

---

[64]Ministry of Finance, Japan, Annual Report of the International Finance Bureau (1991) p. 112.

[65]Bank of Japan (1993b) p. 41.

[66]BIS (1990) p. 6.

[67]ibid.

[68]Quoted in Hanzawa (1991) p. 284.

was further seen as a tool for aiding the internationalization of the yen and the liberalization of financial markets. The JOM has been modelled on the lines of New York's International Banking Facility (IBF). The operations of the JOM have been completely separated from other domestic financial transactions and made exempt from interest rate regulations, reserve requirements and deposit insurance. Furthermore, interest payments are excluded from withholding taxes. In the JOM, other than non-residents,[69] only banks with a JOM license are allowed to participate. At the end of 1989, a total of 192 banks (114 domestic and 78 foreign) were given licenses to participate in the market. In terms of the number of participants, the JOM is still smaller than that of the U.S. and the U.K. which have 534 (159 U.S. banks, 319 foreign banks and 59 Edge Act corporations)[70] and 594 (228 domestic and 366 foreign banks)[71] market participants respectively.

The JOM has grown rapidly since it was launched. Its business volume increased from US$89 billion in December 1986 to US$649 billion by the end of March 1993. In terms of business volume, the market size of the JOM is smaller than London but bigger than New York's IBF. Two important characteristics of the JOM need to be mentioned here: firstly, as regards types of currency, the share of yen in total assets increased from 22 percent in December 1986 to 59 percent by the end of 1991. Secondly, inter-office transactions and interbank transactions still account for more than 79 percent (97% in 1986) of total assets and liabilities. The main reason for the predominance of interbank transactions lies in the fact that the big Japanese banks use the market for arbitrage, which helps in exploiting the interest rate movements and differences between individual market segments.[72] The institutions that take part in the JOM are mainly city banks, long-term credit banks and trust banks, which together accounted for 85 percent of total offshore market financial assets at the end of 1989.

Although the JOM market prohibits the transfer of funds from offshore accounts to on-shore accounts, banks have been able to use the JOM as an indirect source of funds

---

[69]Non-residents for the purpose are foreign banks (including overseas branches of Japanese banks), foreign corporations (including overseas subsidiaries of Japanese firms), and the foreign government and international organizations. Individuals and overseas branches of Japanese firms are not allowed to participate in the JOM.

[70]As of June 1988.

[71]As of September 1989.

[72]Ungefehr (1990) p. 637.

for their short-term needs. The Japanese banks could do so by remitting funds obtained in the JOM to one of their overseas branches through offshore inter-office accounts and by subsequently borrowing these funds through the on-shore inter-office account. This kind of "round tripping" of funds had the effect of inflating the international banking assets and liabilities of Japanese banks. Since April 1989, when the limit of funds that could be transferred from the JOM to on-shore accounts was raised from 5 percent to 10 percent of the average balance of previous month's JOM assets, the urgency to engage in round tripping has somewhat declined and this is reflected in the declining volume of inter-office business of Japanese banks (See Figure 4.3).

2.2   Internationalization of the Japanese Financial System

The term internationalization of finance means that the financial systems of various countries have developed relationships that extend across national borders. As a result, the financial systems in those countries are subject to international influence which triggers financial innovation, liberalization and reform.[73] The internationalization of finance should be viewed as a continuous process which seeks to ease the prevailing set of conditions for the conduct of cross-border financial transactions. The deregulation of prohibited cross-border transactions or permission to engage in new ones reflects itself in the quantitative as well as qualitative changes in the cross-border flow of funds and finally gets translated into greater integration (indicated by the interest parity condition) across national financial markets.[74] The liberalization of international banking business, international securities issues and trading, and free access to foreign financial institutions in the domestic markets are some of the indicators of the internationalization process.

Historically, the internationalization of finance in Japan began when it became an IMF Article VIII status nation as a result of which exchange controls on current transactions were abolished. However, the first catalyst of the internationalization of Japanese

---

[73]Suzuki (1989) p. 157.

[74]Feldman (1986) discusses three approaches of internationalization of finance, viz. regulatory, quantitative and price in the same sequential order.

finance[75] is to be found in the structural changes in the balance of payments caused by the shift to the floating exchange system in February 1973.[76] It caused a major change in the risks associated with holding assets and liabilities denominated in foreign currencies.[77] The different means of hedging exchange risks became necessary for the effective functioning of floating rate system. The second catalyst of internationalization came from foreign pressure (particularly in the early 1980s) which sought greater access for foreign financial institutions and investors in Japan. In the present section, a detailed analysis of Japanese experience of internationalization of finance is made. After briefly reviewing the changes in the regulatory framework, first between 1973-83 and later from 1984 to the present, the section discusses the quantitative and qualitative implications of these changes. The ultimate aim is to present a background which assists in creating a better understanding of the international financial intermediation done by Japan (Chapter 3) and the overseas expansion of its financial institutions (Chapters 4 and 5).

2.2.1 Deregulation after Shifting to the Flexible Exchange Regime (1973-83)

As mentioned earlier, the move to the flexible exchange system was an important stimulus in the process of internationalization and it altered the risk complexion of cross-border financial transactions, inducing gradual liberalization of capital movements.[78] However, even after shifting to the flexible exchange system, Japan maintained strict

---

[75]There is general agreement in the literature regarding the catalysts of domestic financial reform in Japan [Cargill (1985); Suzuki (1987); Feldman (1986); Teranishi (1990); and Shimamura (1989)]. Thus, the origins of domestic financial reforms are to be traced to the slowed economic growth in the aftermath of first oil-crisis and its impact on the flow of funds in Japan. The public budget deficits led to sizable issues of government bonds after 1975 and the regulations under which government bonds were issued proved burdensome when the need for more public debt issue became imminent.

[76]Though Japanese yen began to float on 28th August, 1971, the Smithsonian Agreement of December 1971 caused a brief return to fixed exchange rates. In February 1973, Japan finally moved to flexible exchange rate regime.

[77]Fukao (1990) p. 27.

[78]An important move at removing exchange controls was initiated already in May 1972 when the foreign exchange concentration system was abolished. The system, which was introduced in June 1950, obliged all residents to sell their foreign exchange holdings to the Bank of Japan through authorized foreign exchange banks at official rates.

exchange controls until 1980. This implied that price formation in the foreign exchange market was guided by the monetary authorities. Thus, Japan followed a system of 'managed float' until 1980 with controls on capital movements.[79] All potential channels of capital movements, ranging from international payments, borrowing, direct and portfolio investment (both inward and outward) to the freedom of financial institutions to engage in international financial business, was kept under strict control.[80]

Generally speaking, the process of liberalization between 1973-80 revolves around Japan's current account position and conditions in the foreign exchange market. Exchange controls were frequently altered to encourage inflows when the yen was weak and outflows when the yen was strong. This defensive policy, though effective to some extent, did not seem to alter the value of the yen substantially.[81] Thus, the period 1973-80, as a whole, symbolizes minor and gradual easing of the regulations. The abolition of limits on the acquisition of Japanese equity by foreigners (November 1973), the relaxation of yen conversion controls on authorized foreign exchange banks (December 1973), the lifting of voluntary restraints on the purchase of foreign securities first for all types of financial institutions except banks (June 1975), and later for banks (March 1977), and the repeal of the prohibition of forward transactions for hedging external securities investment (April 1978) are some of the examples of the gradual approach. A comparison between the deregulation of cross-border borrowing and asset acquisition (direct and portfolio investments) shows an interesting contrast in timing. Whereas deregulation for asset acquisition began in the early 1960s, that for borrowing started in the 1970s.[82] The difference in timing is primarily attributable to the fact that deregulating borrowing transactions is not seen as a promising way of effecting quick changes in the flow of funds.[83]

One indicator of the internationalization of the financial system is the growth in external assets and liabilities. Figure 2.2 clearly shows that Japan's external assets and

---

[79]Fukao (1990) p. 27.

[80]For a detailed account of the regulatory framework of Japanese financial markets during the period 1973-83, see Feldman (1986).

[81]Fukao (1990) and Feldman (1986).

[82]Feldman (1986) p. 154.

[83]ibid.

liabilities grew very slowly between 1976 and 1983, suggesting that deregulation of cross-border transactions did not influence capital movements significantly. Thus, in the 1970s, the internationalization of financial markets did not progress substantially relative to the growth of the real economy. The reason for this could be traced to some of the strict controls, such as real demand principle, which made hedging through forward contracting impossible and discouraged financial transactions.

Figure 2.2: Growth in the External Assets and Liabilities of Japan

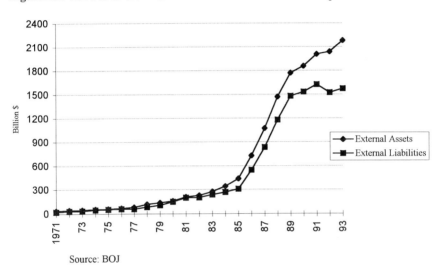

Source: BOJ

The revision of the Foreign Exchange Law in December 1980 was an important event in the process of liberalization. In contrast with the old law, under which all transactions were prohibited in principle, the new law permitted, in principle, all foreign exchange transactions unless specifically prohibited. Under the new law, cross-border portfolio investment, both inward and outward, did not require prior notification if carried out through designated securities companies. This implied the virtual abolition of all restrictions on the convertibility of the yen into foreign currencies. The freedom granted by the new law, coupled with the high interest rates in the U.S., led to a release of pent-up demand for portfolio diversification and long-term capital outflows increased substantially in the 1980s.

2.2.2 Deregulation after the 'U.S.-Japan Accord' in 1984

The process of the internationalization of finance in Japan gained momentum with the realization overseas that an economy as large as Japan's was continuing to maintain high barriers to foreign entry. The growing foreign pressure for greater access to Japanese financial markets found its first official expression in the U.S-Japan Accord of May 1984. Under the accord, Japan agreed to initiate action to open its financial markets and promote the internationalization of the yen. As a consequence, Japan's external assets and liabilities grew rapidly after 1984. Thus, external assets increased by a factor of 6 between 1984-93 from $341 billion at the end of 1984 to $2181 billion at the end of 1993 (see Figure 2.2). The faster pace of external asset growth implies increase in the net external asset position and shows Japan's role as a creditor nation. In the following pages, a brief account of the deregulation since 1984 is presented under five distinct categories:

In *the area of international banking*, the process has sought primarily to boost the Euroyen market. In June 1984 the ban on short-term Euroyen lending to residents (short-term yen lending by banks outside Japan to Japanese residents) was lifted.[84] Medium and long-term lending to non-residents was permitted in April 1985 and to residents in May 1989. The Euroyen loans have grown tremendously as a result of these deregulation and given new cross-border business opportunities to Japanese banks. The permission to issue Euroyen CDs to non-residents (including the foreign affiliates and branches of Japanese banks) was granted in December 1984. This provided Japanese banks with an additional source of funds. Later, in November, 1987, Euroyen CPs were allowed to non-residents (including the foreign affiliates of Japanese corporations). The above-mentioned liberalizations were coupled with a series of relaxations of foreign exchange controls discussed below, which further stimulated the international banking business conducted by the Japanese banks.

Foreign exchange controls were eased to adapt the Japanese market to changed conditions and to encourage the internationalization of the yen. Firstly, the real demand principle for forward contracts was abolished in April 1984.[85] The purpose of this deregulation was to provide room for active foreign exchange management by corpora-

---

[84]Short-term Euroyen lending to non-residents was liberalized in June 1983.

[85]Until April 1984, forward foreign exchange trading in Japan was confined to actual trade flows.

tions and financial institutions. Secondly, the abolition of spot position controls (yen conversion quotas) on authorized foreign exchange banks[86] and the liberalization of yen remittances abroad by Japanese offices of foreign exchange banks through inter-office accounts (June 1984) provided banks with greater scope for efficient asset and liability management. The fact that Japanese banks now assign more importance to treasury function is partly due to these deregulation. Raising the overall (spot plus forward) open foreign exchange position of banks and allowing direct interbank foreign exchange dealing for all currencies, except yen-dollar transactions in July 1984[87] further eased the liquidity adjustment process in the foreign exchange market.

In the field of *international securities issues,* the Euroyen bond market has been deregulated through a series of measures. The eligibility to issue Euroyen bonds was extended to private foreign corporations in December 1984 and to residents (de facto) in April 1985. Whereas the liberalization of Euroyen bonds issued *by non-residents* has stimulated the deregulation of *Samurai* (publicly offered yen-denominated bonds issued in Japan by foreigners) bonds and *Shogun* bonds (publicly offered foreign currency-denominated bonds issued in Japan by foreigners), those issued by residents has led to the deregulation of non-collateralized bond issues in the domestic market.[88] Various liberalization moves that have been initiated by the MOF in the domestic bond market are intended to avoid the hollowing out of the domestic capital markets. In a recent move, overseas entities have been permitted to issue yen-denominated floating rate notes in Japan (June 1991).

The *purchase of foreign securities by Japanese investors* has been rapidly liberalized since March 1986. The upper limits imposed on the proportion of assets that could be invested in foreign securities by institutional investors have been raised since 1980 (refer to Table 2.4).[89] Though the raising of the upper limit has encouraged capital outflow, the actual foreign investment by the institutional investors has stayed well below the

---

[86]This gave Japanese banks freedom to borrow in foreign currencies and invest the funds locally in yen.

[87]The permission for direct dealing was extended to Yen-dollar transactions in February 1985.

[88]Osugi (1990) p. 14.

[89]From February 1994, the ceiling on domestic and foreign portfolio investment requiring notification to the MOF was raised from ¥30 million to ¥100 million.

Japanese Financial Institutions in Europe

upper limit. The average investment in foreign bonds and equities at the end of 1993 stood at 15% and 2.9% of total assets respectively.[90] Thus, the effectiveness of these measures was limited because these restrictions did not constitute a restraint on institutional investors.[91] Recently, the foreign exchange losses faced by the Japanese institutional investors on their international portfolios[92] have been more important determinants of their overseas portfolio investment.

Table 2.4 : Deregulation of Controls on Foreign Securities Purchases by Institutional Investors

(Upper limits as % of total assets*)

Month/Year of Change	Life Insurance	Non-life Insurance	Postal life Insurance	Trust banks (loan trusts)	Trust banks (Pension funds)	Trust fund bureau
Situation in 1980	10	10	0	0	0	0
Jan-81					10	
May 83			10			
Feb-86				1		
March 86	25	25				
April 86					25	
June 86				3		
August 86	30	30			30	
April 87						10
June 87			20			
Feb-89				5		

*Upper limits here imply the permitted ratio of foreign investment holdings to total assets. The limit set on increases in foreign investment were removed between March and August 1986

Source: Fukao (1990) and Osugi (1990)

The internationalization of Japanese financial markets has often been measured in terms of the *foreign financial institutions' limited access to various markets*. To alleviate

---

[90]Euromoney (1994) p. 50.

[91]Fukao (1990) p. 46.

[92]Japanese life insurance companies suffered a total loss of $15 billion for the fiscal year ending March 1992 because of the yen's appreciation from ¥140.95 at the end of March 1991 to ¥130 in March 1992 against the dollar. See Schale (1992) p. 49. The yen's sharp appreciation between January and May 1995 has further aggravated the situation. In this short period, Japanese institutions have seen the yen value of their foreign assets decline by almost 20 percent.

the problem, the authorities allowed foreign financial institutions in a number of new markets. Foreign banks were granted membership of the government bond underwriting syndicate (April 1984), were allowed to deal in government bonds (October, 1984) and were given approval to participate in the trust banking business (November 1985). They can now 'own' a membership seat on the TSE (since February 1986), lead-manage Euroyen bonds (December 1984) and even own up to 50 percent (compared with 5 percent for the domestic financial institutions) of securities firms (since December 1985).[93] Foreign securities firms were allowed to set up investment trust subsidiaries (October 1990) and were issued banking licenses (March 1991).[94] In January 1995, Japan signed an agreement with the United States to grant U.S. and other foreign firms unrestricted access to Japan's $200 billion public pension funds market and to make a substantial increase in their access to the Japanese private pension fund sector.[95]

2.2.3 The Impact of Deregulation

The repercussions of the financial deregulation in Japan on the cross-border financial flows can be analyzed with reference to the:

(i) changes in the financing behavior of Japanese corporations;

(ii) changes in the international business of Japanese financial institutions;

(iii) presence and performance of foreign financial institutions in Japan;

(iv) internationalization of the yen; and

(v) linkages between the Japanese and overseas financial markets.

The influence of deregulation on the international business of Japanese banks and securities companies forms part of the detailed discussion in Chapters 4 and 5. In this section, a brief discussion of other aspects has been undertaken.

Changes in the financing behavior of corporations. It goes without saying that increased activity in the international flow of funds is intimately related to, and is

---

[93]The permission to establish securities subsidiaries was granted first to European banks which operate under the universal banking system. In June 1987, this permission was also extended to US banks.

[94]Goldman Sachs, Morgan Stanley and Salomon Brothers were the first to get banking licenses.

[95]The Banker (1995) p. 6.

mutually dependent on, the globalization of business financing.[96] The international financial transactions by Japanese enterprises registered significant changes in the 1980s. The share of foreign sources in fund procurement began to rise at an accelerated pace after 1980, from 27 percent in 1980 to 64 percent in 1991.[97] The most important foreign source was the issue of foreign bonds which increased from 1 percent at the end of 1980 to 13 percent of the total funds procured by Japan's corporate sector in 1989.[98] In employing the funds, the use of funds in foreign currencies showed a more persistent and rapid increase, especially for investment in foreign securities.[99] Starting from 0 in 1970, the share of investment in foreign securities increased to 19.5 percent of total financial assets in the fiscal year 1980 and to 37.5 percent in the fiscal year 1985[100] before falling to 21 percent in the fiscal year 1989. The essence of the above information is that the Japanese corporate sector pursued an aggressive policy of financial profits in the late 1980s.

It is evident that Japanese corporations used various forms of financial deregulation in Japan to diversify their fund procurement channels and to make attractive investments. The combined effect of the liberalization of foreign exchange controls and relaxation of securities issues was that overseas financial markets became attractive; they not only provided opportunities for raising cheaper funds but also offered a better return than that available on domestic financial assets. It should be noted that the changes in corporate financing behavior were not guided solely by deregulation but also by other factors, such as the reduction in the fund shortages experienced by Japanese enterprises, the improvement in the ratio of paid-up capital, and the emphasis on financial income in revenue strategies.[101]

Presence and performance of the foreign financial institutions in Japan. The problem of foreign participation in Japanese financial markets is not limited to econom-

---

[96]Inoue (1989) pp. 85-86.

[97]See Table 5.4 on direct financing activities of Japanese companies.

[98]When expressed in other terms, foreign bonds accounted for 45 percent of total financing through securities in 1989.

[99]Inoue (1989) p. 52.

[100]ibid. p. 61.

[101]Inoue (1989) p. 83.

ics, but is complicated by politics.[102] It is often seen with reference to the Japanese financial presence overseas. If measured in terms of the increase in the number of the foreign financial institutions in Japan and the markets in which they are eligible to participate, the response to the internationalization measures has been positive. Thus, the number of foreign banks in Japan increased from 5 (with 28 offices) in 1986 to 88 banks by the end of March 1994 (See Table 2.5 for an overview).[103]

Table 2.5: Presence of Foreign Financial Institutions in Japan

	(number of institutions)	
	1986	1994*
Foreign Banks		
Number of banks	5	88
Total number of offices[2]	28	262
Trust banking subsidiaries	9	9
Tokyo branch of 50%-owned securities subsidiaries of banks	...	25
Government bond dealing license		16
Syndicate member for government bond underwriting		26
Foreign Securities Firms		
Number of firms	14	58
Total number of offices[2]	45	166
Regular member of the Tokyo Stock Exchange	6	24
Government bond dealing license		48
Syndicate member for government bond underwriting		31
Banking license to securities firms	...	4

*As of the end of March 1994

[2]Includes branches, subsidiaries and representative offices

Source: MOF; Federation of Bankers Associations of Japan [Zenginkyo] (199

---

[102]Funabashi (1991) p. 418.

[103]Of the 86 foreign banks, there are 22 from North America, 31 from the European Community (9 German, 7 French, 6 British, 4 Italian, 3 Spanish and 2 Dutch) and the rest from Asia. See Takeda (1992) p. 84.

The number of foreign securities firms increased at a much faster pace from 2 firms at the end of 1984 to 14 in 1986 and further to 50 firms at the end of March 1994. The number of foreign securities firms with membership of the TSE also increased from 6 in 1986 to 25 in November 1990. A total of 9 foreign banks established trust banking subsidiaries in 1985/86 and 3 securities firms have set up subsidiaries for managing investment trust since November 1990. In the underwriting syndicate for government bonds, as at the end of March 1994, there are 57 foreign financial institutions (with 31 securities firms and 26 banks). A total of 64 foreign financial institutions (48 securities firms and 16 banks) have so far been granted government bond dealing licenses. Between 1985-90, the increasing presence and participation of foreign financial institutions in Japanese financial markets was seen as a necessity because Tokyo formed an essential link in the global 24-hour trading of securities. However, the low volume of activity in the Japanese stock market since early 1991 has reduced the attractiveness of the market for foreign financial institutions to some extent.

Despite the growing presence of foreign financial institutions in Japan, their overall performance has been grossly poor because of the domestic environment which is biased in favor of local financial institutions.[104] In a survey of opinions and strategies of foreign financial institutions in Japan conducted by the Japan Center for International Finance, 40 percent of those surveyed approved of the direction in which deregulation and internationalization was going but felt that much remained to be accomplished before Tokyo could be favorably compared to New York or London.[105] In addition, another 30 percent felt that true deregulation and internationalization remained distant goals. Thus, a total of 70 percent of foreign financial institutions expressed dissatisfaction with the actual state of the market.[106]

The experience of foreign financial institutions shows that foreign securities firms have been able to perform better than foreign banks. The foreign securities firms were able to increase their share of equity trading on the TSE from less than 2 percent of daily trading in 1987 to 9 percent in 1990.[107] In the derivative product markets, they are

---

[104]Osugi (1990) p. 25.

[105]Japan Center for International Finance (1990), p. 2.

[106]ibid.

[107]Feldman et al. (1991) p. 438.

widely perceived as the leaders. On the other hand, at the end of 1991, the foreign banks accounted for only 1 percent and 0.2 percent respectively of the loan and deposit market in Japan.[108] Even in trust banking, the 9 subsidiaries of foreign banks had only a small share of 1.8 percent of the entire trust banking industry at the end of March 1989.[109] The foreign banks owe their existence in Japan to the foreign exchange trading and dealing in government bonds from which they derive most of their profits.[110] Taken together, all foreign financial institutions account for about 8 percent of the government bond underwriting syndicate. On the whole, the entry of foreign financial institutions into Japan, as a consequence of deregulation, has boosted competition in Japanese financial markets.

The internationalization of the Yen. A currency is said to be international when it is employed in a 'significant' number of cross-border transactions (both for invoicing as well as for private investment) and one that is widely held around the world. An internationalized currency could also be used as a vehicle currency, i.e. to denominate and execute international trade and capital transactions that do not involve direct transactions with the issuing country.[111] The internationalization of the yen has been sought more vigorously in the recent past for two reasons: first, because of the increasing strength of the Japanese and German economies, as shown in their surging net external assets, demand for a multiple key currencies system based on the dollar, the German mark and the yen are increasing. Second, the internationalized yen is seen as a help in diminishing various nations' exposure to foreign exchange risks. For the domestic economy, the benefits are that the internationalization of the yen leads to the deregulation of domestic financial markets and serves as a hedge against foreign exchange risks. It would be interesting to survey the extent to which the recent deregulation have contributed to the internationalization of the yen. Table 2.6 provides a summary account of this point from various perspectives.

---

[108]Federation of Bankers Associations of Japan [Zenginkyo] (1994a) p. 8.

[109]Funabashi (1991) p. 421.

[110]Khoury (1990) p. 119.

[111]A currency is used as a vehicle currency when the transaction costs involved in using it are lower than transactions costs involved in using other currencies. For the theory of international currency use, see Tavlas and Ozeki (1992).

Table 2.6: Various Indicators of the Internationalization of Yen

Indicators	Period/Unit	1980	1982	1984	1986	1988	1989	1990	1991	1992
(I) International trade										
Ratio of yen-denominated exports to total exports	CY/%	29.4	32.2	33.7	35.3	34.3	34.7	37.5	39.4	40.1
Ratio of yen-denominated imports to total imports	CY/%	2.4	...	...	9.7	13.6	14.1	14.5	15.6	17.0
(II) Euroyen Market										
Share of Euroyen in Eurobonds issued	CY/%	1.2	1.6	1.8	4.5	5.3	7.3	12.6	13.9	12.2
Euroyen CDs outstanding	CYE/billion yen	...	...	155	44	341	348	231	207	78
Short-term Euroyen loans outstanding (non-resident)	CYE/billion yen	...	...	468	1,567	1,426	1,819	1,533	1,392	...
Long-term Euroyen loans outstanding (non-resident)	CYE/billion yen	...	...	...	818	1,896	2,126	1,588	1,443	...
(III) Fund raising by non-resident in Japan										
Yen-denominated foreign bond issues (Samurai)	CY/billion yen	261	856	1,115	785	797	999	575	504	1175
Equity offerings by foreign companies	CY/billion yen	...	...	72	152	137	269	67	...	...
(IV) Foreign investment in Japanese securities										
In Japanese bonds (share of outstanding issues)	CYE/%	2.7	3.2	3.2	3.0	2.1	2.1	2.7	...	...
In Japanese stocks (share of aggregate value of listed stock)	FYE/%	5.8	7.6	7.4	5.3	4.3	4.2	...	...	...
(V) Yen's share in foreign exchange reserves	CYE/%	4.4	4.7	5.8	7.9	7.7	7.8	9.1	9.9	...

FY = fiscal year; FYE = Fiscal year-end; CY = Calendar year; CYE = Calendar year-end

Source: MOF; Bank of Tokyo; OECD etc.

The *use of the yen as an invoicing currency for international trade* increased from 29.4 percent of the total exports at the end of 1980 to 40 percent by the end of 1992. By 1994, the figure has risen to just 40.7 percent.[112] The ratio of imports denominated in yen to total imports, despite increasing from 2.4 percent in 1980 to 17 percent in 1992, is conspicuously low. It has more to do with composition of the Japanese imports, most of which comprise raw materials where dollar invoicing is common. When compared with the own currency-denominated trade of other industrial countries, the ratio of yen-denominated exports and imports is much lower. Thus, the own currency export and import ratio for the U.S. was 96 and 85 percent respectively at the end of 1988. The two figures for other countries were: Germany (81% and 52.6%), U.K. (57% and 40%), France (58.5% and 48.9%).[113] The geographical distribution of yen-denominated trade brings the striking fact to light that, in 1990, 43 percent of Japanese exports to and 27 percent of Japanese imports from the European Union (henceforth EU) were yen-denominated.[114]

The use of the yen in cross-border capital transactions is indicated through fund raising and investment by non-residents in the Japanese capital markets and yen-denominated transactions in the Euromarket (i.e. Euroyen transactions). From amongst the methods of fund raising available to non-residents, both yen-denominated syndicated loan and bond issues have declined in importance. This is mostly because of the popularity of the Euroyen market, where growth has been tremendous. Foreign investment in Japanese bonds and stocks has increased in absolute terms but, in relative terms, still accounts for a meager 2.1 percent and 4.2 percent respectively. The Euroyen markets have contributed most to the international use of the yen. Further, the share of yen-denominated bonds in the total value of bonds issued on international markets leaped from less than 1 percent in 1983 to 14 percent in 1991.[115] A much higher proportion of yen-denominated bonds is employed in currency swaps when compared with bonds

---

[112]Baker (1995b) p. 11.

[113]Whereas the high ratios of the United States are because of dollar as the main vehicle currency, the high ratio of European countries stems from the European Union as a trading block where intra-Union trade is dominant.

[114]Bank of Tokyo (1991) p. 4.

[115]OECD (1992a) p. 49.

denominated in other currencies.[116] In international banking, the share of the yen in cross-border banking assets (on stock basis) increased from 3 percent at the end of 1983 to 13.7 percent at the end of 1991.[117]

The *role of the yen as an international reserve currency* can also be understood by looking at its share in the official foreign exchange reserves of IMF member countries. Thus, yen's share in the total foreign exchange reserves increased from 0.1 percent in 1973 to 9.1 percent at the end of 1991.[118] By way comparison, German mark's share rose from 7.1 percent in 1973 to 19.3 percent in 1989. Thus, the yen is the third most important currency in terms of its position in total official reserves next to the US dollar and the German mark.

Yet another indicator of the international position of the yen is the proportion of Japan's external assets and liabilities which are denominated in yen. It is estimated that about 38.4 percent of Japan's external assets and 35.7 percent of its external liabilities were denominated in yen at the end of 1989. The greater proportion of external assets denominated in yen implies a lower need for managing exchange risks. As Japan's net external assets grow rapidly, foreign currency-denominated assets pose additional exchange risks and significantly alter the portfolio decisions of creditors and investors.

To sum up, the Japanese yen is used more widely in capital transactions than in current transactions. Even in capital transactions, more progress has been made in the fund raising area than in the fund investment area. The internationalization of the yen has occurred more in long-term rather than in short-term fund raising. Further, though the international use of the yen has progressed, most of yen transactions are often intermediated by the Japanese banks, used by the Japanese residents or made the basis of currency swaps.[119] However, it is believed that Japan's good performance with respect to inflation during the 1980s (and the associated gain in the credibility of Japa-

---

[116]This implies that yen procured in international markets are not employed immediately but first swapped into other currencies, mostly dollars.

[117]BIS.

[118]The portion of yen holdings by EU countries in their total foreign exchange reserves was 4.7 percent at the end of 1989.

[119]Fuji Bank (1990) p. 7.

nese monetary policy), the liberalization of financial markets and the increase in Japan's share of world exports imply a growing role for the yen as an international currency.[120]

Linkage between the domestic and the foreign financial markets. The ultimate impact of the international financial deregulation can be observed on the linkages between the domestic and the overseas financial markets, which manifests itself in the price of similar financial assets across borders. The main indicator of the strengthened linkage is the interest parity condition. The interest parity condition implies that the domestic interest rate must equal the sum of the foreign interest rate plus the expected appreciation of the foreign currency.[121] Thus, the arbitrage between the financial markets shows a convergence between Euroyen and Eurodollar rates. The differential between Euroyen rates and *adjusted* Eurodollar rates (Eurodollar rates plus dollar forward premium/discount annualized) became negligible after 1984.[122] The absolute value of the differential was 0.2915 between 1983-85 and declined to 0.0511 between 1984-88.[123] Further, the differential between the *gensaki* and Euroyen interest rates is now very small. So, in terms of interest parity condition, the internationalization has progressed successfully.

One could also assume that the elimination of capital controls has increased the substitutability between assets denominated in yen and those denominated in other currencies. Though some researchers[124] provide evidence for the hypothesis that short-term yen assets and dollar assets are still imperfect substitutes for one another,[125] it is

---

[120]Tavlas and Ozeki (1992) p. 15.

[121] In equational form, the interest parity condition used in exchange models could be expressed as:

$$r^* = r + x$$

where r^* is the domestic interest rate, r is the foreign interest rate and x is the expected appreciation of the foreign currency. It is always formulated in terms of the interest rates and exchange rate of two countries.

[122]Conversely speaking, deviations from covered interest parity between Euroyen and Eurodollar rates became smaller and more stable around zero after 1984.

[123]Osugi (1990) p. 61.

[124]McKenzie (1986).

[125]McKenzie (1992) p. 41.

still not clear whether the degree of substitutability between these assets has, in fact, increased since 1984.

2.3   The Emerging Shape of the Japanese Financial System

With all the piecemeal deregulation in Japanese finance in the 1980s, the future shape of the financial system has started emerging. Three forces will influence radically the evolution of the system: the fluctuations in asset prices, the ongoing process of interest rate deregulation and the attempts at removing the functional segmentation between the different types of financial institutions. A brief account of the repercussions of these forces is presented in this section.

Influence of shift in asset prices. The wealth effect generated by the increase in asset prices, especially those of shares and real estate, substantially influenced the functioning of the Japanese economy and finance in the 1980s. The decline in asset prices[126] caused by the tight monetary policy since the end of 1989 has reversed the trend. This decline in asset prices influenced the performance of the Japanese financial system in several ways. The plunge in the capital gains from securities investments hit a potential source of profit for the financial institutions. For the Japanese banks it implied a slowdown in their volume-oriented business policy. The decline of the stock market further reduced the capital ratios of the Japanese banks because they are allowed to count 45 percent of the unrealized capital gain on their stock holdings as Tier II capital for BIS capital adequacy standards. Not only this, the declining stock market made the raising of cheap equity still more difficult and robbed the Japanese institutions, both financial and non-financial, of the cost of capital advantage.

For the Japanese securities companies, a declining stock market means a reduction in brokerage commission income caused by falling market volumes. The mounting book losses on their own stock holdings is another cause for concern. The effect on smaller and medium sized securities companies will be more severe because, unlike the Big Four which have underwriting business to support their profits, they rely heavily on

---

[126]The Nikkei stock price index declined 57% from its record height in December 1989 and land prices in six largest cities of Japan fell by an average of 10% between 1990-92.

brokerage commissions. In such precarious circumstances, the possibilities of forced restructuring within the financial services industry become imminent.[127]

The Effects of interest rate deregulation. The process of interest rate deregulation in Japan, which began earnestly in 1985, was completed by the end of June 1993 when interest rates on all types of time deposits were liberalized. This has tightened the linkage between funds procurement costs and market rates[128] and has a direct impact on the funding costs of the financial institutions. Though the financial institutions, particularly banks, registered declining margins after 1985 because of the increased funding costs,[129] they did not pass all of the funding cost increase on to lending rates. Even then, the Japanese banks have been able to avert a decline in their overall profitability. This has been achieved primarily through increased lending to small and medium sized firms[130] as well as through capital gains from portfolio investments.

However, the real impact of interest rate deregulation has been noticed since 1989 when tight money policy initiated a correction process in the asset prices. Not only has extending credit to the real estate sector, a growth area for banks in 1980s,[131] become more risky, but the leaning on capital gains from securities disposal no longer provides a buffer. The Japanese financial institutions will have to develop alternative business strategies in the 1990s to cope with this acute situation of declining margins and profitability. It is very likely that the cost-profit structure will be an important determinant

---

[127]In a survey conducted by the Institute for Financial Affairs in December 1990, 50% of the respondents predicted that restructuring through mergers and tie-ups would increase in the financial arena. Many felt that mergers between small and medium-sized securities firms were likely to increase. See Institute for Financial Affairs (1991) for details.

[128]Bank of Japan (1991b).

[129]The differential between short-term lending rate and funding costs has declined from an average of 3 percent between 1970-85 to 1.6 percent between 1985-91. See Bank of Japan (1991b) p. 36.

[130]The loans to small and medium-sized firms by city banks increased from 26% in the fiscal year 1975 to 51% of the total loans outstanding at the end of 1990. Refer to Bank of Japan (1991a) p. 6.

[131]The ratio of loans to real estate industry, directly or indirectly (through non-bank financial intermediaries), to total loans outstanding increased from 9.9 percent in fiscal year 1980 to 25.7 percent at the end of 1990. See Bank of Japan (1991a) p. 9.

of their business policy. This would, in all likelihood, affect the competitive position of Japanese banks in the domestic market.

Removal of the functional segmentation between the financial institutions. The functional segmentation created after the War between the various types of financial institutions continued until end March 1993. However, the barrier between commercial banking and securities business, enforced through Article 65 of the Securities and Exchange Law, had been blurred by a series of newly authorized activities since 1982.[132] The debate on financial system reform, which began in 1985, for the effective removal of functional segmentation, sought to identify a viable model for allowing all types of financial institutions (except insurance companies) to enter each other's field. The Financial Systems Research Council, an advisory body to the MOF, submitted its final report in June 1991 recommending that the principal method for removing the barriers was to allow mutual entry through subsidiaries specializing in different business fields.[133] The subsidiary idea ended the debate about an appropriate model of reform, which ranged from gradual reform to allowing German-type universal banking. The report also suggested an immediate revaluation of any regulations that prevent unfettered competition.

The Japanese parliament passed a series of bills in June 1992 for reforming the financial system, and the Japanese financial system is set for a major change through legislative action which came into effect in April 1993. This means that the Article 65 stands repealed even before the Glass-Steagall Act in the U.S.. The key aspect of the latest reform package is that different types of financial institutions will be allowed to enter each other's field through special-purpose subsidiaries.[134] This evidently implies that the MOF has to provide certain exceptions to Article 11 of the Japanese Anti-

---

[132]For details on the subject, see Osugi (1990) pp. 41-45 and Arora (1991) pp. 136-139.

[133]Financial Systems Research Council (1991) Chapter 4.

[134]Since regional institutions, such as smaller regional banks and *shinkin* banks, would have difficulty establishing separate subsidiaries, the reforms allow these institutions to compete in trust banking business directly or to act as agents for trust banks. This step has resulted in a growing number of tie-ups between trust banks and regional banks. By the end of May 1994, 16 banks had started trust business by themselves and 105 banks had become agents for trust banks. See Federation of Bankers Associations of Japan (1994b) p. 1.

Monopoly Law which sets a 5 percent limit on equity participation by banks. Furthermore, as planned by the MOF, banks would not be allowed to engage in retail brokerage in the beginning. Similarly, securities companies may not be permitted to conduct foreign exchange business immediately. It is relevant to note that stock brokerage business for banks and foreign exchange business for securities companies have been the most contentious areas in the reform process.

2.4 Summary and Conclusions

The Japanese financial system still depicts several characteristics of a 'bank-oriented' rather than a 'market-oriented' system. The predominance of indirect finance and the underdeveloped character of the corporate bond market support this. In such a system, the commercial banks, particularly major city banks, play a pivotal role. Among non-depository institutions, securities companies constitute the dominant group of institutions performing investment banking functions. The diversification of Japanese financial markets and the opening of new ones has given Japanese banks new options for asset and liability management. Domestic deregulation have altered the financial behavior of corporations and this is transforming the role of banks from the main supplier of funds to a provider of comprehensive financial services. Consequently, the intensity of competition among different types of institutions has increased.

The internationalization of Japanese finance is a phenomenon of the 1980s, which gathered momentum after 1984. The liberalization of cross-border financial transactions and the related aspects has been piecemeal and gradual. The process of deregulation has sought to lift various exchange controls, ease international banking business, relax the issuing of capital and diversifying of portfolio through overseas markets and provide foreign financial institutions with greater access to Japanese markets. The impact of these regulations has been observed in (i) the financing behavior of Japanese corporations, which increased their overseas funding activity; (ii) increased presence of foreign financial institutions in Japan, (iii) increased outflow of long-term capital from Japan, particularly foreign securities investment by institutional investors; and (iv) the strengthened linkage between the domestic and foreign financial markets. Another area stimulated by the series of deregulation has been the international business of Japanese banks and securities companies.

The effect of surging asset prices influenced the Japanese economy and financial system in a big way. The return of asset prices to normality, the completion of interest rate deregulation and the recent removal of functional segmentation between financial institutions would radically influence the evolution of Japanese finance in the 1990s. The impact of domestic conditions on the position of Japanese financial institutions overseas should, as is always the case, be strong and noticeable.

Chapter 3

International Financial Intermediation by Japan and its Financial Institutions

Within a single economy, the flow of funds account describes how deficits are financed and surpluses are disposed of. It also shows how the funds of saving surplus units in an economy are channeled to the saving deficit units. In other words, this is the process of financial intermediation. The channels through which the process takes place may be direct (whereby saving surplus units lend directly to the saving deficit units) or indirect (whereby a financial intermediary operates between saving surplus and saving deficit units). In particular, the intermediary role of a financial institution usually implies maturity transformation (in as far as the intermediary offers the saving surplus units a relatively short-term claim and the saving deficit units a long-term liability), and risk transformation (in so far as saving surplus units face a lower risk than would occur if lending were made directly by them to saving deficit units). Broadly, the same is true of international financial intermediation (henceforth IFI). Generally speaking, IFI is nothing other than an extension of the single economy financial flows to a two economy model.

3.1 The Concept of International Financial Intermediation

3.1.1 Historical Background

The concept of calling a country a banker was first introduced by Lary.[1] However, he made very little out of it and was, in fact, skeptical of the analogy.[2] The concept was translated into a workable IFI hypothesis by Kindleberger's essay on international market for liquidity in 1965[3]. The hypothesis grew out of a combination of the general theory

---

[1]Lary (1963).

[2]ibid. p. 147.

[3]Kindleberger (1965).

of financial intermediation pioneered by Gurley and Shaw[4] and the observation that, beginning in 1950, the United States had persistent "liquidity deficits" reflecting a strong demand for dollar assets by both private foreigners as well as foreign monetary authorities. At the same time, outflows of American private capital, mainly long-term, increased. Thus, the United States was increasing its foreign assets and its liquid liabilities to foreigners at the same time. It appeared, therefore, that the United States was performing the role of a financial intermediary. The role of the United States as international financial intermediary was further expounded and developed by Despres, Kindleberger and Salant[5]. The D.K.S. thesis, as it popularly came to be known later, contended that the United States was playing the role of a banker for the world whereby it was borrowing short and lending long.

3.1.2 Meaning and Significance

The main implication of the D.K.S. thesis was that a country can export long-term capital in exchange for short-term debts without running a current account surplus or in excess of its current account surplus. The thesis was the first "minority view" of its kind to go against the common view of capital account deficits (or surpluses) being a definitional equivalent of current account surpluses (or deficits). A remarkable inference from the D.K.S. thesis is that the capital account can also be autonomous, rather than induced. In a subsequent elaboration of the D.K.S. thesis, Salant[6] explained IFI in the following way:

> "Financial intermediation in general consists of the acquisition of a financial asset, accompanied by a simultaneous creation of a financial liability. It is represented by the intermediary's increase in financial assets or its financial liabilities, whichever is smaller... Application of this definition to the international transactions of a country suggests that the measure of IFI should be the increase in a country's foreign financial assets or the increase in its liabilities to foreigners, whichever is smaller. The excess of increase in assets over increase in liabilities, then, would be foreign investment that is transferred in the form of a current account surplus, rather than by *(international financial)* intermediation. .. One should, therefore, regard IFI as *excluding* the excess of increase in the

---

[4]Gurley and Shaw (1960).

[5]Despres, Kindleberger, and Salant (1966).

[6]Salant (1972).

country's foreign financial assets over the increase in its liabilities to foreigners".[7]

Thus, IFI is performed when, and to the degree that, foreign financial assets and liabilities increase simultaneously. It appears from the D.K.S. thesis that only those parts of international movements of capital in and out of a country should be construed as IFI which involve maturity transformation. This is evidently a very restricted definition of IFI because it ignores all other forms of international financial transactions where financial institutions perform numerous other useful functions. Salant's view sets aside with a single stroke the utility of:

(i)   collecting information about the rates of return and the bringing together of the lenders and borrowers;

(ii)   pooling assets with somewhat independent risks and thereby reducing the risk of portfolios; and

(iii)   lengthening the investment planning period, thereby lowering the relative weight of the risk factor.

Notwithstanding these limitations, the D.K.S. thesis offers a deeper insight into the concept of IFI for the first time. In addition, the world of finance is today far different from the way it was twenty years ago. The more recent example of IFI is provided by the recycling of the OPEC surplus. In the period after 1973, international banks intermediated by offering surplus OPEC states short-term claims and enabling developing countries with a balance of payments deficit or capital shortage to finance their needs by incurring medium-term (roll-over) debts. Noticing the reluctance of the OPEC states to lend directly to deficit countries and their preference for short-term deposits, the role of the international banks was decisive in the recycling process. Logically, IFI is reflected in various segments of international banking.[8] It is interesting to note that the developments in international banking bring to light many mechanisms which, in effect, are nothing other than examples of IFI. One prime type of IFI is where domestic banks lend to deficit units outside the country, either with funds secured from the surplus sector internally or by borrowing from non-residents. Domestic capital markets may also be a channel of IFI when bond issues are made by non-residents - the funding may again

---

[7]ibid. pp. 608-609.

[8]Llewellyn (1979).

either be from domestic sources (with non-residents tapping domestic savings) or external sources (e.g. European borrowers and investors both approach the American capital market to fulfil their needs).[9] Thus, to sum up, IFI may be defined "loosely but sufficiently as any asset or liability of a financial intermediary or a participant in the securities markets that has a cross-border or cross-currency dimension or both."[10]

Until very recently, the concepts 'international financial intermediation' and 'world banker' were often used interchangeably. In a recent study, Tavlas and Ozeki (1992) draw a distinction between a nation that functions as an international financial intermediary and one that serves as a world banker. Their judgement adds a new dimension to the research and needs elaboration here. According to the authors:

> "the fact that a country is serving as an international financial intermediary (borrowing short, on a net basis, from the rest of the world and lending long, on a net basis, to the rest of the world) does not ensure that it is also functioning as a world banker.....A nation functions as a world banker when its borrowing short (on a net basis) from, and lending long (on a net basis) to, the rest of the world enhances the liquidity of the international financial system. In order to provide liquidity to the rest of the world, the nation must be supplying short-term deposits (i.e. import short-term capital) denominated in its own currency to the rest of the world. When a nation's banks collectively engage in international liquidity transformation by accepting deposits from non-residents that are denominated in the nation's own currency, the nation may be said to be acting as a world banker."[11]

The authors also draw attention to the fact that a nation serves as world banker when its *banks* - as opposed to its non-bank financial institutions - borrow short, on a net basis, from the rest of the world and lend long, on a net basis, to the rest of the world.[12] It was precisely this process that contributed to the international use of sterling in the late nineteenth and early twentieth centuries and to that of the US dollar from 1945 to 1980. *Banks* in these countries provided liquidity - denominated in sterling and US dollars

---

[9]It has long been known that the European investors after World War II bought a large proportion of the bonds issued by European borrowers in New York. Recently, this mechanism has become more common place.

[10]Bryant (1987).

[11]Tavlas and Ozeki (1992) p. 18.

[12]ibid.

respectively - to the rest of world and used the funds so acquired to make longer-term investments in the rest of world, which were also denominated in sterling or US dollar.[13]

Why does a country perform the role of an international financial intermediary? There are three basic phenomena[14] that explain this role:

(i) the lower liquidity preference of resident (including the financial institutions) in the country that performs IFI than in the foreign countries. When the foreign asset holders have a higher demand for short-term assets, in relation to the supply of such assets in their local markets, than the asset holders in the country that performs IFI, they are said to have a higher liquidity preference. The point to note is that the local financial intermediaries do not fully bridge the gap between demand and supply for short-term assets at the prevailing rate, if the capital does not move in and out of the country that is performing IFI;

(ii) the degree of competitiveness of the financial intermediary industry. The country that performs IFI usually has a greater degree of competitiveness in the provision of its financial services. If a country or its financial intermediary industry has an edge in developing and marketing financial products and techniques, it would naturally have greater competitiveness; or

(iii) the cost of financial intermediation. The fact that there is a higher cost of financial intermediation is indicated by the wider spreads between the rates that the banks pay on their deposits and the rates that the banks charge to their borrowers. The differences in spread provide an opportunity for the country with lower spreads to perform IFI in countries with higher spreads.

These three phenomena are distinct and independent in their own right. Thus, if the IFI is more oligopolistic and is conducted at higher costs in country A than in country B, financial institutions from country B will have incentives to operate in country A, even if the liquidity preference patterns of the asset holders and the borrowers in country A is identical with those in country B. This also suggests that a country can continue to play the role of international financial intermediary as it moves from one phenomenon to the other. There were periods in the 1950s and 1960s when the United States performed IFI primarily because of the differences in the liquidity preference between Europe and

---

[13]ibid.

[14]The discussion in this section is based on Salant (1972) p. 612.

America. Later, it continued to strengthen its role as international financial intermediary because of greater competitiveness and innovativeness in the financial intermediation process.

Significance of IFI for the international economy. It is not difficult to trace the advantages accruing to the provider and receiver of IFI. *First*, to the extent that any country A lends long and borrows short, and lends at higher rates than it pays for what it borrows, it earns an interest differential. If foreigners find it profitable to lend short to country A and borrow long from it, then country A is evidently performing a financial service to the foreigners. The real gain to the foreigners from 'importing' financial intermediary services may be in the form of a larger bundle of utilities (more liquidity, reduced risks and higher return) than they are able to obtain at home. *Second*, the availability of IFI may cause the lenders to increase their savings out of the given incomes, as compared with what they would have saved if the intermediaries were provided only domestically. This naturally makes higher levels of international investments possible. *Third*, the better access of borrowers to capital is likely to result in a better allocation of a given amount of investment outlays than would occur otherwise. *Fourth*, IFI makes financial intermediation more efficient because it brings intense competition in its wake. This reduces, on a global level, the amount of capital and labor absorbed in the process of transporting savings and investment and thereby makes more resources available for investment.

3.2   International Financial Intermediation by Japan

Japan's balance of payments, in general, and current account balance, in particular, attracted much attention the 1980s. Related to its soaring current account surplus was the subject of huge capital outflows from Japan in the later part of the 1980s. The behavior of different components of capital account, as autonomous from the current account, has aroused renewed interest in the subject. Thus, Japan accumulated a current account surplus of $462 billion between 1981-90 but net long-term capital outflows from Japan totalled $688 billion during the same period. (see Table 3.1) The excess of net long-term capital outflows over the current account surplus (i.e. $226 billion) was financed mostly by short-term capital inflows. Hence, Japan is said to have performed the role of an international financial intermediary. This chapter analyses different aspects of Japan's capital account (both long-term and short-term) in order to put Japan's role as an international financial intermediary in a proper perspective. The intensity and magnitude of IFI performed by Japan in the 1980s warrants that attention be focused on the subject.

Table 3.1: Comparison of Japan's Current Account and Capital Account

(US$ billion)

Calendar Year	Current Account	Long-term Capital Account	Short-term Capital Account	Changes in Official Reserves
1973	0.14	-9.75	2.41	-6.12
74	-4.69	-3.88	1.78	1.27
75	-0.68	-0.27	-1.14	-0.70
76	3.68	-0.98	0.11	3.79
77	10.92	-3.18	-0.65	6.24
78	16.53	-12.39	1.54	10.17
79	-8.75	-12.98	2.74	-12.69
80	-10.75	2.32	3.14	4.91
81	4.77	-9.67	2.27	3.17
82	6.85	-14.97	-1.58	-5.14
83	20.80	-17.70	0.02	1.23
84	35.00	-49.65	-4.30	1.82
85	49.17	-64.54	-0.94	0.20
86	85.85	-131.46	-1.61	15.73
87	87.02	-136.53	23.87	39.24
88	79.63	-130.93	19.52	16.18
89	57.16	-89.25	20.81	-12.77
90	35.76	-43.59	21.47	7.84
91	72.90	37.06	-25.76	-8.07
92	117.55	-28.46	-7.04	295.00
93	131.49	-78.34	-14.43	26.90

Minus sign (-) for current account column indicates deficit; for capital account columns, it indicates outflow of capital and for official reserves column decrease in reserves

Source: BOJ, Balance of Payments Monthly

3.2.1 The Maturity Structure of Japan's External Assets and Liabilities

At the end of 1981, the value of Japan's net overseas assets (a measure of accumulated net capital outflows) was $10.9 billion compared with the $140 billion of the United States. By 1985, the situation was reversed as the United States became a debtor nation and Japan's overseas assets soared to $130 billion, making Japan the world's leading creditor nation.[15] Thus, after going through the stage of an immature creditor between 1970-1983, Japan has now entered the stage of being a mature creditor. As of December 1993, Japan's net overseas assets were over $612 billion, which reflects the speed and size of Japan's long-term capital outflows. The last column of Table 3.2 provides the growth pattern of Japan's net external assets. Japan's net overseas assets, which were less than 1 per cent of GNP at the end of 1980, reached 12.2 percent of GNP by the end of 1991. These figures are also a pointer to the faster pace of the internationalization and liberalization of Japanese finance in the 1980s.

Table 3.2: The Maturity Structure of Japan's Net External Assets (1980-93)

(US$ billion)

Calendar Year	Long-term Assets	Long-term Liabilities	Net Long-term Assets	Short-term Assets	Short-term Liabilities	Net Short-term Assets	Net Assets [Total]
	[1]	[2]	[3]=[1]-[2]	[4]	[5]	[6]=[4]-[5]	[7]=[3]-[6]
1980	87.9	47.3	40.6	71.7	100.8	-29.1	11.5
81	117.1	70.3	46.8	92.2	128.0	-35.8	10.9
82	139.5	77.7	61.8	88.2	125.4	-37.1	24.7
83	170.9	102.8	68.1	101.1	131.9	-30.9	37.3
84	229.2	113.2	116.0	112.0	153.6	-41.6	74.3
85	301.3	122.3	179.0	136.4	185.6	-49.2	129.8
86	476.1	192.3	283.8	251.2	354.6	-103.5	180.4
87	646.2	236.2	410.0	425.5	594.7	-169.3	240.7
88	832.7	311.6	521.0	636.7	866.0	-229.3	291.7
89	1,019.2	447.5	571.8	751.8	1,030.3	-278.5	293.2
90	1,096.1	464.0	632.1	761.8	1,065.8	-304.0	328.1
91	1,247.8	647.4	600.4	758.7	976.1	-217.4	383.1
92	1,315.6	658.5	657.1	719.7	863.2	-143.5	513.6
93	1,412.9	711.8	701.1	768.0	858.3	-90.3	610.8

Source: BOJ, Balance of Payments Monthly

The maturity structure and changes in the external assets and liabilities constitute the main indicators of the IFI. The maturity structure of Japan's external assets (see Table 3.2) shows that Japan had a net creditor position in the long-term capital account of $632 billion, showing an increase of $592 billion between 1980-90. However, in the short-term

---

[15]The position was held by Britain (1837-1910) and the United States (1914-1981) in the past.

capital account, Japan was a net debtor to the tune of $304 billion, showing an increase of $275 billion within the same period.[16] This manifests the scale of the IFI function performed by Japan. In terms of the D.K.S. thesis, where the simultaneous increase of external assets and liabilities implies IFI, the extent of Japan's role in maturity transformation at the international level should amount to $275 billion (i.e., about 47% of the increase in the net long-term assets), the criterion being external assets and liabilities, whichever is lower. The rest should be interpreted as the channeling or recycling of Japan's current account surplus into foreign investments. Fukao (1990) endorses this view when he says:

> "the outflow of long-term capital corresponding to the net inflow of capital may be seen in macro-terms as Japan's playing the role of international financial intermediary. In contrast, the outflow of long-term capital corresponding to the current account surplus may be seen as a supply of savings to the rest of the world".[17]

3.2.2 Changes in Japan's External Assets and Liabilities

Table 3.3 provides computations about *the changes* in Japan's external assets and liabilities for three blocks of time making up the period between 1978-93. Three inferences are drawn from the table which further underscore the IFI function performed by Japan:

First, on the asset side, increase in the long-term external assets has been the main component throughout the period between 1978-91, accounting for over half of the total increases in external assets. However, on the liabilities side, short-term liabilities predominate and account for about three-quarters of the total increase in external liabilities for the period 1984-89.

Second, in the period between 1984-89, the increase in Japan's *net* long-term assets ($456 billion) and short-term liabilities ($237 billion) of Japan was most dramatic. This means that Japan financed a sizable portion of its external asset build-up during this period through short-term commitments abroad. This period exemplifies Japan's role as an international financial intermediary.

Third, the private sector was the main force behind the IFI function. Japanese institutional investors and corporate sector stimulated long-term capital outflow through their portfolio

---

[16]Bank of Japan, Balance of Payments Monthly (1992).

[17]Fukao (1990) p. 41.

Table 3.3: Changes in Japan's External Assets and Liabilities (1978-93)

(U.S. $ in Billion)

	1978-84		1984-89		1989-93	
	$ value	% share	$ value	% share	$ value	% share
Assets						
Long-term (A)	166	74.4	790	55.3	394	96.1
of which						
Private	146	[65.5]	710	[49.7]	294	[71.7]
Government	20	[9.0]	80	[5.6]	100	[24.4]
Short-term (B)	57	25.6	640	44.7	16	3.9
of which						
Private	63	[28.3]	582	[40.7]	2	[0.5]
Government	-6	[-2.7]	58	[4.0]	15	[3.6]
Total (A+B)	**223**	**100.0**	**1,430**	**100.0**	**410**	**100.0**
Liabilities						
Long-term (C)	84	45.4	334	27.6	264	286.5
of which						
Private	61	[33.0]	322	[26.6]	218	[237.0]
Government	24	[13.0]	13	[1.0]	46	[50.0]
Short-term (D)	101	54.6	877	72.4	-172	-186.5
of which						
Private	98	[53.0]	858	[70.9]	-213	[-231.5]
Government	3	[1.6]	18	[1.5]	41	[44.6]
Total (C+D)	**185**	**100.0**	**1211**	**100.0**	**92**	**100.0**
Net Assets						
Long-term	82	215.8	456	208.2	129	40.7
of which						
Private	85		388		76	
Government	-4		68		54	
Short-term	-44	-115.8	-237	-108.2	188	59.3
of which						
Private	-35		-276		214	
Government	-9		39		-26	
Total (A+B) - (C+D)	**38**	**100.0**	**219**	**100.0**	**318**	**100.0**

Figures in bracket represent the share of each component in the respective totals
Source: Computations from BOJ, Balance of Payments Monthly

decisions, and Japanese banks provided foreign currency funds through their short-term borrowing overseas.

It is interesting to note that the pattern of capital flows exhibited by Japan in the 1980s was sharply reversed in 1991. Japan experienced net long-term capital inflows in 1991 for the first time in 11 years. Not only this, the long-term capital inflow and current account surplus was offset by large private short-term capital outflows. Japanese banks reduced their liabilities by as much as $93 billion in 1991. The 1991 pattern of capital flow has continued ever since. In the period between 1990-93, Japan reduced its net external liabilities by $172 billion. Japan's capital flows between 1991-93 could be characterized as moving in the opposite direction of what would be expected from a country performing IFI.[18]

As elucidated in detail in Section 3.4 below, the main contention of this chapter is as follows: what appears to be IFI by Japan at an aggregate level is not a deliberate strategy adopted by any single type of economic agents within Japan. It is more a consequence of several economic agents' rational behavior and the pursuit of a set of motives. Thus, for example, the majority of long-term capital outflows occurred because of the institutional investors' motive of exploiting interest rate differentials between Japan and rest of the world. Similarly, most of the short-term capital inflows occurred partly because of the Japanese banks' role in providing foreign currency funds to domestic investors for the purpose of buying foreign securities and partly because of their attempts at circumventing various regulations in Japan.

At this juncture, it would be desirable to trace whether the IFI function performed by Japan also implies that Japan acted as a world banker. Given the present status of the internationalization of the yen,[19] one could formulate a provisional judgement that Japan only marginally provided international liquidity to the rest of the world in its own currency. However, to ascertain whether Japan performed the role of a world banker, one has to examine various components of the long-term and the short-term capital account as well as their currency composition.

3.3   Japan's Long-term Capital Account

3.3.1 Main Features

It has already been mentioned that, in the 1980s, the net long-term capital outflows from Japan were larger than the current account surplus; even more so during 1984-89. It has been argued that, in the early 1980s, there was an autonomous increase in capital outflows leading to a depreciation of the yen which, in turn, led to the increases in the current account surplus.

---

[18]Bank of Japan (1992b) explains the reasons for the sudden change of direction in the capital flows for 1991.

[19]Refer to Section 2.2.3.

There are four major components of the international capital account: foreign direct investment (FDI), trade credits, loans extended and securities investment. Table 3.4 shows the share of each component of long-term capital outflows from Japan. From the table, it becomes clear that portfolio investment has been the most important component since 1981, and accounted for more than half of the total long-term capital outflow after 1983. Most of the securities investment overseas has been undertaken by Japanese institutional investors[20] and is concentrated in fixed-income securities.[21] Recognizing that the average turnover period of investment in foreign securities by Japanese investors is estimated at about 2 years,[22] a logical inference is that a sizable portion of Japan's long-term investment is inherently short to medium-term in character.

Table 3.4: Components of Long-term Capital Outflows from Japan

(in Percent)

Component	1981	1983	1985	1986	1987	1988	1989	1990	1991	1993
Direct Investment	21.46	11.13	7.89	10.96	14.69	22.82	22.97	39.77	25.30	18.6
Trade Credits	11.97	7.98	3.44	1.39	0.40	4.63	2.08	-0.56	-3.23	-7.35
Loans Extended	22.29	25.96	12.74	7.03	12.19	10.15	11.71	18.37	10.78	11.10
Securities	38.48	49.37	73.06	77.20	66.07	58.01	58.91	32.86	61.18	70.20
Others	5.80	5.57	2.87	3.42	6.65	4.39	4.33	9.57	5.97	7.42
Total	100	100	100	100	100	100	100	100	100	100
Total annual outflow ($ in billion)	10.82	32.46	81.82	132.10	132.83	149.88	192.12	120.77	121.45	73.6

Source: BOJ, Balance of Payments Monthly

---

[20]The eight types of Japanese institutional investors (banking accounts of all banks, trust accounts of all banks, The Norinchukin Bank, Life insurance companies, non-life insurance companies, securities investment trusts, *Shinkin* banks and Postal life insurance) together accounted for about 75 percent of the total foreign securities holdings of Japan as of end of 1989. See Fukao (1990) p. 46.

[21]Except for 1989, in all other years since 1985, well over 90 percent of investment in foreign securities has been in bonds. See Bank of Japan, Balance of Payments Monthly.

[22]Bank of Japan (1984) p. 5. Taiyo-Kobe Bank (1989) also confirms the decline in the average holding period of foreign securities held by Japanese investors in the mid-1980s.

Japanese foreign direct investment is the second most important component of long-term capital outflows and its share fluctuated between 8 percent in 1985 to 40 percent in 1990. However, the share of Japanese FDI fluctuated widely in the 1980s, depending upon the proportion of long-term capital channeled into securities investment. Both long-term trade credits and loans have declined in importance, but the decline is more conspicuous in the case of trade credits.

The fact that most of Japan's long-term capital outflow is in the form of securities investment uncovers the prominent role played by Japanese securities companies and other non-bank financial intermediaries in recycling Japan's current account surplus. This implies that the banks' role in the process was confined more to providing foreign currency funds to investors interested in making portfolio investment overseas. Takeda and Turner (1992) point out that "perhaps the most paradoxical feature of Japanese banks' international role was that they did not directly contribute to reinvesting the country's current account surplus abroad".[23] Healey (1991) also hints at the same fact when he recognizes that 'Japanese banks are not a channel for net capital outflows'.[24] In contrast, when the U. K. and the U. S. were performing IFI, the banks from the respective countries played a pivotal role.

3.3.2 Determinants of Long-term Capital Outflows

Views concerning the causes of large capital outflows from Japan are divided. While some writers point out the importance of the increase in U.S. interest rates, others focus on the impact of the relaxation of capital controls within Japan, such as the revision of the foreign exchange law. In reality, there is a multiplicity of factors that influences the capital outflow from a country. A review of the literature suggests that there are three major reasons for capital outflows :

(i)   an increase in the wealth (which is the sum of high powered money, outstanding government bonds and the market value of stocks);

(ii)   an exchange rate appreciation; and

(iii)   an increase in the ratio of foreign assets to the stock of wealth. This increase in the proportion of foreign assets, in turn, may come from a number of sources such as:

---

[23]Takeda and Turner (1992) p. 84.

[24]Healey (1991) p. 137.

-        a change in the expected return differential in favor of foreign assets;
-        a change in the expected risk of foreign assets;
-        a change in the degree of risk aversion of the domestic investors; and
-        relaxation of capital controls, which brings new types of investors in foreign assets.[25]

A point of controversy arises from the above factors as to which of these factors have had a greater impact on capital outflows from Japan. Many of the arguments in this debate are based mostly on common wisdom. Almost all previous analyses on the subject place emphasis on the high rate of savings in Japan and the absence of profitable investment opportunities within the country. Feldstein, based on his intensive mathematical analysis, confirms that there is no statistically significant relationship between sustained differences in domestic saving rates and the various components of international capital outflows of a country.[26] He argues that international differences in saving rates are associated with almost equal differences in investment rates. Hence net foreign investment, which is equal to the difference between the domestic savings and the domestic investment, has a weaker association with domestic savings. However, theoretical considerations suggest that short-run response of the international flows to the changes in domestic savings may be much greater than the long-run response. The reason for this is that the short-run capital outflow is part of a once-for-all adjustment of the international portfolio. Once the adjustment is complete, the rate of capital flow returns to a lower level governed by the rate of the growth of the world capital stock and the share of international assets is the equilibrium portfolio.

In the case of Japan, it is often said that the investment in external assets is made at the expense of the accumulation of physical assets, such as housing stock and social capital. The composition of its wealth is disproportionately greater in the form of the foreign assets than in the form of the domestic assets and consumer durables. If one attempts at analyzing the determinants of such a composition of national wealth, one finds that the equilibrium stock of external assets depends not only on the savings rate (i.e., the time preference rate) but also upon the consumers' preference between durables and non-durables. A system that favors, in effect, financial savings relative to the holding of the durable, produces a larger accumulation of financial assets in general and external

---

[25]Ueda (1989) p. 7.

[26]Feldstein (1983).

financial assets in particular.[27] Taking the argument a little further, as long as the world rate of interest is larger than the domestic rate, there would be a tendency for the equilibrium composition of financial assets to drift more in the direction of external financial assets.

The growth of Japanese direct investment overseas seems to have been induced by the necessity of having production facilities in Japan's major export markets, mainly because of the appreciation of the yen after 1985. This is also being influenced by an enormous structural shift in the Japanese economy;[28] direct investment overseas will have the dual effect of reducing the current account surplus: the *export-replacing effect* whereby increased production by overseas subsidiaries will cut Japan's exports, and a *reverse-import effect* due to overseas subsidiaries' stepped-up exports to Japan.[29]

It is also believed that the trend towards increased foreign securities investment has been reinforced by a portfolio shift within Japan, from depository type savings institutions with a low securities orientation, such as postal savings, towards more securities-oriented contractual-type savings institutions, such as insurance companies and investment companies. However, it is interesting to note that individual savers' investment behavior has not changed much in the last decade and a half. The tax benefits on savings accounts and the exchange risks involved in the international investment have, on balance, kept individuals' interest in deposits reasonably high, despite the controlled rates.

3.4 Japan's Short-term Capital Account

Japan's short-term capital account includes all external assets and liabilities with an original maturity period of one year or less. Other than monetary movements (revealing changes in gold and foreign exchange reserves as well as in short-term external assets and liabilities of authorized foreign exchange banks), it includes trade credits, short-term loans and sale/purchase of securities under repurchase agreements (called *Gensaki* transactions). The monetary account explains how the balance of payments movements, expressed by the overall balance, have been financed. Though Japan's overall balance,

---

[27]An econometric analysis of the relationship between international capital movements and domestic assets was carried out by Kudoh (1989).

[28]Independent, (1990).

[29]Sumitomo Life Research Institute quoted in Independent (1990).

with the exception of 1983, has been in deficit since 1979 (caused by a huge increase in long-term capital outflows), official foreign exchange reserves increased from $26.5 billion at the end of 1985 to $85 billion at the end of 1989. This increase in official exchange reserves in the face of the increasing deficit in the overall balance reflected the large *inflows* of short-term capital through foreign exchange banks.

3.4.1 Role of Japanese Banks in Short-Term Capital Inflows

It has already been demonstrated in Table 3.2 that Japan has had a net debtor position in its external short-term assets since 1980, which gradually increased from $29 billion in 1980 to its peak of $304 billion at the end of 1990 before decreasing to $90 billion at the end of 1993. Even on a flow basis (see Table 3.3), short-term capital inflows dominate the liabilities side and contributed an increase of $237 billion to Japan's net short-term liabilities within the short span of 1984-89. A considerable part of changes in short-term liabilities represent the short-term external position of Japan's authorized foreign exchange banks. The overseas branches of these banks actively participated in the Eurocurrency markets for borrowing short-term foreign currency funds. Table 3.5 provides data on the short-term external position of authorized foreign exchange banks.

Table 3.5: Short-term External Assets and Liabilities of Japan's Authorized Foreign Exchange Banks

(U.S.$ billion)

Year	Assets Total	Assets Foreign Currency	Assets Yen	Liabilities Total	Liabilities Foreign Currency	Liabilities Yen	Net Assets Total	Net Assets Foreign Currency	Net Assets Yen
1970	6.6	6.6	0.0	5.5	5.0	0.5	1.1	1.6	-0.5
75	13.0	11.9	1.0	26.4	25.0	1.5	-13.5	-13.0	-0.5
80	45.2	40.5	4.6	78.0	67.8	10.1	-32.8	-27.3	-5.5
85	99.7	78.0	21.8	161.0	122.0	39.0	-61.3	-44.0	-17.2
86	194.7	131.1	63.6	322.2	243.4	78.7	-127.5	-112.3	-15.1
87	320.2	162.6	157.5	530.1	349.5	180.6	-209.9	-186.8	-23.1
88	502.3	259.9	242.4	765.2	500.5	264.7	-262.9	-240.6	-22.3
89	627.9	319.4	308.5	894.7	576.3	318.4	-266.8	-256.9	-9.9
90	644.5	360.6	283.9	898.9	620.6	278.3	-254.4	-260.0	5.6
91	640.8	301.8	339.0	803.5	555.0	248.5	-162.7	-253.2	90.5
92	599.9	263.1	336.8	684.7	499.6	185.1	-84.8	-236.5	151.7
93	607.8	230.7	377.1	659.6	467.5	192.1	-51.8	-236.8	185.0

Source: BOJ

The table shows that the authorized foreign exchange banks have continuously been debtors to the rest of the world, on a net basis since 1975. However, until 1985, their net short-term liabilities were no more than $61 billion.[30] At the end of 1989, their net liabilities reached a peak level of $267 billion before falling below the 1985 level at the end of 1991. It is interesting to note that the considerable increase between 1986-89 coincided with the period of yen appreciation. Evidently, expectations of a depreciation in the dollar's value during this period hedged the exchange risk and activated dollar borrowing by Japanese banks.

The currency composition of assets and liabilities shows that yen-denominated external assets have increased at a faster pace than yen-denominated liabilities. In other words, foreign currency-denominated liabilities still account for over two-thirds of external liabilities. Since the net debtor position of Japanese banks results primarily from net foreign currency liabilities, international liquidity provided by Japan to the rest of the world in its currency continues to be insignificant. Consequently, Japan's role as an international financial intermediary does not imply that it performed the function of world banker.

Another important inference from Table 3.5 is that the short-term external assets and liabilities of banks both increased simultaneously during the 1980s. Thus, instead of liquidating their external short-term assets, Japanese banks satisfied their acute foreign currency needs[31] by committing short-term liabilities overseas. Because of their high credit rating, the overseas offices of many Japanese banks were able to raise foreign currency funds in the Eurocurrency markets at relatively cheaper rates. Walton and Trimble found evidence for this in their survey of Japanese banks in London when they contend that 'The most important element of Japanese banks' international activity in London has always been their treasury function... The Japanese banks are net takers of funds both

---

[30]Bank of Japan, *Economic Statistics Annual*

[31]The strongest demand for foreign currency funds (mostly U.S. dollars) came from institutional investors who wished to increase their portfolio investment in foreign securities. The domestic offices of Japanese banks also needed funds for their own portfolio investment in foreign securities as well as for extending foreign currency impact loans. However, some authors believe that borrowing foreign currency funds overseas was a legal necessity for Japanese banks because of the existence of prudential regulations that limit their net foreign exchange exposure *on a daily basis*. See Fukao and Okina (1989) and Fukao (1990).

from banks located outside the United Kingdom and from the U.K. interbank market'.[32]
A considerable proportion of funds borrowed in London were onlent by the overseas
branches to their head office through inter-office accounts.[33]

3.4.2 Impact Loans as an Ingredient of Short-Term Capital Inflows

'Impact loans' is the general term used in Japan for foreign currency lending made
by an authorized foreign exchange bank to a resident without restrictions on the use of
the funds.[34] Under the new Foreign Exchange Law of 1980, almost all the foreign
currency lending to residents from foreign exchange banks is in the form of impact
loans.[35] Impact loans are [generally] made either to securities companies for use in
arbitrage with domestic call loans or to companies using foreign currency loans to acquire
yen funds while avoiding borrowing at the regulated prime rate for yen loans.[36] Since
June 1984, when short-term Euroyen lending to residents was liberalized, Euroyen impact
loans extended by overseas offices of the Japanese banks to Japanese residents have also
increased in prominence.[37] Table 3.6 shows the notable contribution of Euroyen impact
loans on Japan's short-term and long-term capital transactions. Such loans account for
almost all cross-border loans received by Japanese residents.

---

[32]Walton and Trimble (1987) p. 520.

[33]Section 4.4.1.1 elaborates the role of overseas offices of the Japanese banks as
funding vehicles for their head offices.

[34]It differs from tied loans on which there are restrictions on the use of funds. See
Suzuki (1987) p. 185.

[35]Until May 1979, only foreign banks in Japan were authorized to make short-term
impact loans in foreign currencies. Since then, the Japanese foreign exchange banks have
also been allowed to make such loans. Medium- and long-term foreign currency impact
loans were permitted in March 1980. Short-term foreign currency loans registered a
dramatic increase from $0.26 billion in 1980 to $269 billion at the end of 1990. Medium
and long-term loans, on the other hand, increased slowly from $0.82 billion in 1980 to
$112 billion at the end of 1990. See Ministry of Finance, Japan, Annual Reports of the
International Finance Bureau.

[36]Turner (1991) p. 79.

[37]Nearly all Euroyen impact loans are extended by overseas branches of Japanese
banks.

Table 3.6: Euroyen Impact Loans in Japan's Capital Flows

($ in billion)

Calendar Year	Short-term Capital Account			Long-term Capital Account		
	Balance	Loans	Euroyen Impact Loans	Balance	Loans	Euroyen Impact Loans*
1986	-1.6	3.9	4.0	-131.5	-0.03	NA
87	23.9	27.4	27.3	-136.5	-0.12	NA
88	19.5	16.9	17.3	-130.9	-0.08	NA
89	20.8	26.0	26.7	-89.2	17.8	17.6
90	21.5	29.6	28.8	-43.6	39.1	37.1
91	-25.8	-14.2	-15.2	36.6	38.1	36.8

Minus sign (-) for a figure indicates outflow of capital
*Long-term Euroyen impact loans to residents were liberalized in May 1989

Source: BOJ, Balance of Payments Monthly; MOF etc.

Figure 3.1 illustrates some rudimentary facts about impact loans and their effect on capital flows. The factor with the greatest influence on the changes in the capital transactions (both short and long-term) is Euroyen impact loans. Since the funds for such impact loans are sent from head offices of Japanese banks [item (3) in the figure] through inter-office transactions to overseas branches, Euroyen impact loans are, in effect, nothing more than

Figure 3.1: The Mechanism of Impact Loans and Japan's Capital Account

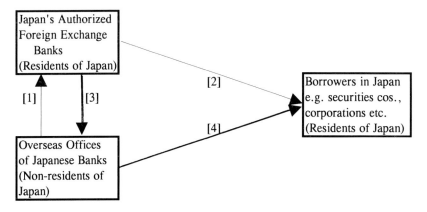

[1] Foreign currency funds lend by overseas offices of Japanese banks to their head offices
[2] Foreign currency impact loan by head offices of Japanese banks to borrowers in Japan
[3] Yen funds lend by Japan's authorized foreign exchange banks to their overseas branches
[4] Euroyen impact loan by overseas offices of Japanese banks to borrowers in Japan

a round-tripping of yen funds. For balance of payments statistics, item (3) is only a monetary movement but item (4) constitutes a cross-border transaction with residents of Japan and is a capital transaction, short or long-term depending upon its maturity. In sharp contrast with Euroyen impact loans, foreign currency impact loans [item (2) in the figure] do not appear in the balance of payments statistics because they do not have a cross-border character; only the inter-office transfer of foreign currency funds [item (1) in the figure] by overseas branches to their head office in Japan appears as a short-term external liability in monetary movements.

The net result of the above explanation is as follows: whereas short-term Euroyen impact loans have inflated the amount of short-term capital inflows, foreign currency impact loans have influenced only the short-term assets and liabilities of Japanese banks. The short-term Euroyen impact loans are, in effect, only recycling of yen funds and should be excluded in any computation of net short-term capital inflows for measuring the extent of the IFI performed by Japan.

To sum up the findings from Section 3.4, it could be said that:

(i)   Japanese banks have been the main vehicles for financing the short-term foreign currency needs of Japanese residents. Borrowing in the Eurocurrency markets, particularly of dollar funds, was the dominant method used for this purpose, which seems to have been automatically hedged by the expectations of a depreciation in the value of dollar.

(ii)   The Japanese banks' role in maturity transformation at the international level is overstated by the amount of short-term Euroyen impact loans, which inflate the short-term capital inflows into Japan.

(iii)   Since the majority of short-term external liabilities of Japanese banks are in foreign currencies, the provision of international liquidity to the rest of the world in yen, on a net basis, has been negligible.

3.5   International Financial Intermediation by Japan and Germany - A Comparative Analysis

Japan and Germany were the two major countries to have a current account surplus in the 1980s. It would be useful to compare the capital account of the two to see whether, and to what extent, Germany performed IFI. An analysis of the basic differences between the current account of these two countries will help in evaluating the impact of institutional factors on the IFI function. Table 3.7 presents different components of Germany's capital account.

3.5.1 The Basic Differences

The data in Table 3.7 reveals that, from 1982, Germany has recycled its current account surplus by exporting capital of all maturities, with the outflows of shorter maturities being the dominant ones. Except for the year 1981, the long-term capital account shows net capital outflows with large variations in the amount of net outflow over 1982-93. Similarly, the short-term capital account also exhibits net outflows throughout 1983-93. Thus, it emerges that Germany did not perform maturity transformation at the international level. Despite the fact that the Deutsche mark occupies second position as an international currency, Germany did not provide, on a net basis, international liquidity (short-term liabilities, such as deposits) to the rest of the world in its own currency. Very much like the case of Japan, because of the underdeveloped character of short-term financial markets in Germany, short-term Deutsche mark-denominated assets have remained less attractive for foreigners.

Table 3.7: Major Components of Gemany's Capital Flows* in the 1980s

(DM in Billion)

| Year | Long-term capital flows | | | | Short-term capital flows | | | | Net capital flows [1] + [2] |
	Direct Investment	Portfolio Investment	Others	Total [1]	Non-banks	Banks	Others	Total [2]	
1981	-8.0	-5.0	21.4	8.4	5.8	-10.3	1.8	-2.6	5.8
82	-4.0	-8.6	-1.5	-14.2	3.2	8.1	-0.3	11.0	-3.2
83	-3.6	3.2	-6.6	-7.0	-8.9	1.8	-4.3	-11.5	-18.4
84	-12.5	-15.7	-16.8	-45.0	-16.1	0.1	-1.6	-17.7	-62.7
85	-14.1	-31.5	-16.0	-61.7	-14.1	-27.7	0.1	-41.7	-103.4
86	-20.9	-21.3	-13.2	-55.4	-56.7	-59.0	-0.3	-116.0	-171.4
87	-16.4	-24.5	-21.3	-62.2	-11.5	-6.6	1.0	-17.0	-79.2
88	-20.1	-72.6	-5.3	-98.0	-21.4	-20.2	0.8	-40.8	-138.8
89	-27.4	-50.2	-17.5	-95.0	-51.6	-56.7	-4.6	-112.9	-207.9
90	-37.4	-22.9	-46.3	-106.6	-19.3	0.4	-5.0	-23.9	-130.5
91	-38.0	-27.3	-30.6	-95.9	11.1	39.7	-3.8	46.9	-48.9
92	-27.7	-70.4	-18.7	-116.8	3.6	63.8	-7.3	60.2	-56.6
93	-19.3	-40.3	-37.3	-97.0	-60.5	-102.6	-2.6	-165.7	-262.6

*From July 1990, data also includes the external transactions of the former GDR

Minus (-) against a figure implies outflow of capital

Source: Deutsche Bundesbank (1992a)

The magnitude of capital outflows of different maturities shows that the net long-term outflows from Germany have been smaller than those from Japan. Whereas the net long-term outflows from Japan between 1982-90 reached $678 billion (see Table 3.1), the figure for Germany amounted to about $152 billion (DM308 billion).[38] The explanation for this lies in the large net inflows of capital into Germany on account of portfolio investment made by foreigners in Deutsche mark securities which, in turn, reduced the overall figure of net long-term capital outflows. With regard to the short-term capital account, the contrast between Japan and Germany is not only one of magnitude but also of direction. While Japan shows a net short-term capital *inflow* of $78 billion between 1983-90, Germany records more than double of that as *net outflow* (i.e. $187 billion or DM383 billion). A considerable proportion of short-term capital outflows from Germany represents short-term borrowing by foreigners from German banks to finance their acquisition of Deutsche mark-denominated securities.[39] The active intervention of the Deutsche Bundesbank in the foreign currency markets to stabilize the markets at various stages after the Plaza Agreement of 1985 also explains some of the short-term capital outflows.

The dominance of short-term capital outflows from Germany and the pivotal role of the German banks in the process implies that they have been the main vehicles for the recycling of Germany's current account surplus. Table 3.7 clearly shows that between 1985-89, the German banks were the channels for net capital outflows. At the end of 1991, they had a net creditor position in their short-term external assets worth $73 million (DM114 million).[40]

3.5.2 Explanations for the Basic Differences[41]

The basic differences in the capital flows of Japan and Germany reflect the dissimilarities in the regulatory and institutional arrangements in the two countries. Characteristics of these arrangements include the relative sizes of financial intermediaries, the depth of

---

[38]Dollar values computed by converting DM values at the average exchange rate for each year.

[39]This is particularly true for the years 1986 and 1989.

[40]Deutsche Bundesbank (1992a).

[41] The line of argument in this section is based on a note published by the International Monetary Fund [IMF] (1989).

short-term financial markets, the degree of integration with offshore financial centers and the degree of segmentation of financial activities.[42]

The system of universal banking in Germany, which combines banking and securities business within the same institution, partly explains the predominant role of the German banks in the capital flows. On the contrary, the statutory segmentation of banking and securities business in Japan relegated a major part of foreign securities investment (capital outflows) to non-banks and institutional investors.

The relative size of different financial intermediaries in the economy also explains their role in cross-border financial transactions. Banks occupy a central role in the German economy and account for 85 percent of the assets of all private financial institutions, with insurance companies and investment companies accounting for about 12 percent and 3 percent respectively.[43] In Japan, the share of banks and other deposi-tory institutions in the assets of private financial institutions revolves around 75 percent, with insurance companies and trust banks[44] taking about 10 percent each.[45]

The factor which exerts maximum influence on the short-term bank flows is the prudential regulations on the foreign exchange exposure of banks. Though both Japan and Germany have such regulations, Germany's are stricter than Japan's[46] and subject to more extensive rules governing their permitted exposure in foreign exchange.[47] In Germany, the regulations prohibit net foreign currency positions from exceeding certain limits not only across maturities but also in instruments with maturities of one month and less and in instruments with maturities of six months and less.[48] In Japan, banks are only subject to overall limits on foreign currency exposure regardless of maturity. A consequence of these regulations is that the bulk of German bank outflows are denomi-

---

[42]IMF (1989) p. 84.

[43]These figures represent approximations based on the average share of different institutions during the 1980s. See Deutsche Bundesbank (1992b).

[44]The trust banks in Japan could be taken as the equivalent of investment companies (*Kapitalanlagegesellschaften*) in Germany.

[45]Bank of Japan, Economic Statistics Annual.

[46]IMF (1989) p. 86.

[47]Turner (1991) p. 74.

[48]IMF (1989) p. 86.

nated in local currency[49] and, hence, most of the currency-transformation activity as well as foreign currency maturity transformation activity is expatriated from Germany.[50]

The depth of the Euro-Deutsche mark market also makes it easier for German banks to lend Deutsche marks abroad and explains, to some extent, part of the net short-term capital outflows through the German banks. By way of comparison, the Euroyen market, though growing, was small in the 1980s. However, the reason why foreigners hold only negligible amounts of deposits in each country's national currency is common to both. The short-term money markets are less developed in both countries, thus constraining their role as providers of international liquidity to the rest of the world on a net basis.

The factor which globally increased long-term capital outflows in the 1980s was the shift of funds from amongst intermediaries. Generally known as disintermediation, the process has led to a shift of funds from banks towards non-bank intermediaries. In Japan, this trend was more conspicuous than in Germany because of the demographic reasons of a rapidly ageing population and also because of relatively attractive returns offered by them to savers under the regulated interest rate structure.[51]

To conclude, the above discussion brings to light the background reasons for the differences in the behavior of Japan's and Germany's capital account. This improves our understanding of IFI performed by Japan as well as reinforces the fact that surplus in the current account does not necessarily help a country perform IFI.

3.6   Implications of International Financial Intermediation by Japan

Large capital flows of all maturities in the 1980s led to the belief that international financial markets were integrated. In such a financially integrated world, fluctuations are readily transmitted across markets. The so-called 'financial internationalization' has its impact on the exchange rates (in a floating exchange regime), and on the speedy transmission of changes in overseas interest rates to domestic ones. This, in turn, is believed to exert pressure on the conduct of monetary policy. This section investigates the impact

---

[49]Turner (1991) p. 75.

[50]IMF (1989) p. 86.

[51]ibid. p. 89.

of the IFI performed by Japan on various macroeconomic variables in Japan as well as on Japanese financial institutions.

3.6.1 Impact on Macroeconomic Variables in Japan

Capital movements in and out of Japan affect the term structure of interest rates in the domestic markets and influence the exchange rate of the domestic currency.[52] At this juncture, one should separate the impact of long and short-term capital movements on these variables. Further, the impact of capital movements of different maturities depends on whether they are covered or uncovered. In covered capital movements, the value of the supply of (or demand for) spot U.S. dollars, by definition, equals the value of demand for (or supply of) forward U.S. dollars. Therefore, covered capital movements have the effect of making the spot-forward exchange spread equal to the interest rate differential, but cannot be considered to have a significant impact on the average level of the spot and forward exchange rates.[53] The uncovered capital movements, on the other hand, put direct upward or downward pressure on the spot market for U.S. dollars because the demand for (in the case of outflows) or supply of (in the case of inflows) spot U.S. dollars have no counterpart as in the case of covered capital movements.[54]

It is known that long-term capital outflows from Japan are generally not covered by a forward exchange contract.[55] This is particularly true of portfolio investment in foreign securities.[56] On the other hand, because of limits on banks' foreign exchange exposure,[57]

---

[52]Theoretically, when domestic short-term interest rates and overseas long and short-term interest rates are given, the three variables - domestic long-term interest rates, long-term capital movements and the exchange rate - are determined simultaneously.

[53]Bank of Japan (1984) p. 16.

[54]ibid.

[55]Bank of Japan (1984); Teranishi (1986) p. 145; Fukao (1990) p. 46; and Turner (1991).

[56]Though securities investment made by banking accounts of Japanese banks was covered because of the prudential regulations on the foreign exchange position of banks, a major part of the foreign securities holdings of Japanese insurance companies (the largest institutional investor in foreign securities) was not covered. See Fukao (1990) p. 46.

[57]Each bank's combined (spot and forward) net foreign currency exposure cannot exceed $1 million (positive or negative) at the close of each business day.

short-term capital movements are mostly covered. Thus, uncovered long-term capital outflows from Japan and covered short-term capital inflows into Japan should create a
situation of excess demand for the dollar in the process of intermediation and exert a
downward pressure on the real exchange rate of the yen.[58] Further, by virtue of their
being uncovered, long-term capital movements exert a larger influence on the exchange
rate than short-term flows.

The impact of capital movements on the term structure of interest rates in the domestic
economy also needs to be checked. The yield of long-term government bonds in Japan,
which is a leading indicator of the long-term interest rate, is affected by the capital
movements in so far as such movements influence the demand and supply conditions in
the domestic long-term bond market. Thus, to the extent that funds are invested in long-
term bonds, outflows and inflows of long-term capital exert a direct influence on long-
term interest rates.[59]

As far as the effects of short-term capital movements on the domestic short-term
interest rates are concerned, it is argued that these movements by themselves do not have
any significant influence on conditions prevailing in the short-term money market.[60] A
part of the explanation for this behavior lies in the fact that short-term capital movements,
particularly short-term bank flows, from a country are usually seen as residual and
accommodating items in balance of payments accounting.[61] In Section 3.4.2, Euroyen
impact loans have been recognized as an important ingredient of the capital movements
and IFI function performed by Japan. Except that the Euroyen impact loans inflate the
balance of long and short-term capital accounts, they do not directly affect the demand
and supply conditions of the foreign exchange market.

To conclude, one can discern a general impact of the IFI function which encompasses
the whole spectrum of financial markets in Japan: the IFI by Japan has created strong
linkages between domestic and overseas markets and in all policy matters, one needs to
be aware of this fact. Any attempt by monetary authorities to play down the influence
of international linkages may be ineffective and even counterproductive.

---

[58]Teranishi (1986) p. 145.

[59]Bank of Japan (1984) p. 9.

[60]ibid. p. 14.

[61]Turner (1991).

3.6.2 Impact on Japanese Financial Institutions

For Japanese financial institutions, and more so for authorized foreign exchange banks, IFI has meant a rapid diversification of international financial transactions. Not only did the assets of overseas offices of foreign exchange banks increase from ¥38 trillion at the end of 1980 to ¥190 trillion at the end of 1990,[62] but the share of external assets of Japanese deposit banks in their total assets also increased from 4.3 percent in 1980 to about 14 percent at the end of 1990.[63] The liberalization of cross-border financial transactions since 1980 also helped Japanese banks to increase their holdings of foreign securities, most of which were financed by short-term foreign currency borrowing on Eurocurrency markets.

The ease with which Japanese banks could raise cheaper foreign currency funds in the overseas markets for lending to domestic borrowers must have contributed to their overall profitability. Some operations, such as impact loans and bringing offshore funds to on-shore markets through round-tripping, helped them to circumvent various regulations in the domestic market.

For non-bank financial institutions, too, IFI by Japan eased the process by which they could diversify their portfolios and increase their share of foreign securities. Their short-term foreign currency borrowing in Japan helped them perform what one might characterize as 'currency transformations'; the Japanese institutional investors were able to hold foreign currency-denominated assets to back domestic yen-denominated liabilities.[64]

3.6.3 Some Policy Recommendations

It has been argued in this chapter that although Japan has served an important function as an international financial intermediary, it has not perform the role of a world banker. Implicit in this argument is that international liquidity supplied by Japan to the rest of the world in its own currency was very limited. In the case of the United Kingdom and the United States, the emergence of sterling and the dollar was a distinguishing feature of the IFI performed by them. If Japan is to continue to play the role of an international

---

[62]Bank of Japan, Economic Statistics Annual.

[63]The computation is based on IMF, International Financial Statistics. The figure of external assets does not include the foreign currency position of Japanese banks vis-a-vis residents of Japan.

[64]IMF (1989) p. 86.

financial intermediary, the first policy recommendation is that the yen's role in international transactions has to grow. In Section 2.2.3, it was pointed out that the Japanese yen is used more in international capital transactions than in current transactions. Even in capital transactions, the yen is used more in the fund raising area than in the fund investment area. Thus, increasing the use of the yen as an invoicing currency for international trade is the area where greater efforts are needed. It is generally believed that payment for the import bill is a very important motive for holding deposits denominated in the exporter's currency.

Until recently, there was an acute dearth of liquid short-term financial assets for attracting short-term funds denominated in yen. Some progress was made in this regard after 1984.[65] Japan would be able to provide international liquidity to the rest of the world in yen only if foreigners hold short-term yen-denominated claims. Thus, the second policy recommendation is that increasing efforts should be directed towards improving the depth and breadth of the short-term financial markets.

As shown in this chapter, Japanese IFI in the 1980s seems to have been spurred by the huge demand for foreign currency funds in Japan and the wave of deregulation. This implies that, as regards the IFI performed by Japan, the period 1985-89 was an exceptional one. There are signals that the intensity and magnitude of Japanese IFI has started slowing down since 1990. In 1991, Japan recorded a net inflow of long-term capital and outflow of short-term capital. Though a variety of domestic factors are also responsible for this slowing down, in the final analysis, the future of the IFI function performed by Japan depends upon the competitiveness of its financial institutions.

3.7   Summary and Conclusions

To understand clearly the global role of Japanese financial institutions, it needs to be known whether Japan has performed the role of a world banker, international financial intermediary or simply that of a capital exporter. The available evidence suggests that Japan's autonomous long-term capital outflows (exceeding current account surplus) were financed by short-term capital inflows. A large part of the long-term capital outflows were in the form of portfolio investment in foreign securities and the short-term capital inflows were in the form of Japanese banks' external borrowing. This suggests that Japan

---

[65]Refer to Section 2.1.2 for details.

performed international financial intermediation. However, since most of the short-term external liabilities of Japanese banks were in foreign currencies, they did not provide international liquidity to the rest of the world in their own currency. Thus, Japan's role as a world banker in the 1980s was not so significant.

A comparison of capital flows in Germany and Japan supports the hypothesis that a current account surplus is not a necessary condition for performing international financial intermediation. Further, the institutional and regulatory differences are important factors influencing the nature and the direction of capital flows. It has been argued here that performing international financial intermediation on a continuous and long-term basis depends upon the international competitive position of the financial institutions and playing the role of world banker depends upon a broad based short-term financial markets as well as the international position of the domestic currency.

In the performance of international financial intermediation, how far are the Japanese financial institutions competitive? What are their strengths and weaknesses? Chapter 6 seeks to provide some more insight into these questions.

Chapter 4

The Japanese Banking Presence in Europe

The internationalization of Japanese financial institutions is a privately-initiated phenomenon; practically all the financial institutions that have established offices overseas are in the private sector. At the same time, the phenomenon is officially controlled; the overseas expansion is strictly guarded and monitored by the MOF.[1] The fact that Japanese financial institutions' overseas expansion is strictly supervised by the authorities concerned implies the influence of state directives and national interests, all of which are not always responsive to economic reasoning.[2]

From amongst all the Japanese banks, only the so-called 'authorized foreign exchange banks' are eligible to seek permission from the MOF to establish overseas offices. Although the number of the authorized foreign exchange banks, excluding the foreign commercial and trust banks, stood at 236 at the end of 1992, only 76 of them have so far exercised their option of going overseas (Table 4.1). Of these 76 banks, 20 major banks [Specialized foreign exchange bank (1), City banks (10), Long-term credit bank (3) and Trust banks (6)] have an extensive network of overseas branches, subsidiaries and representative offices. They account for over 80 percent of all overseas branches and over 90 percent of all overseas subsidiaries of Japanese banks. They evidently also account for over 90 percent of the overseas business of Japanese banks. In this study, attention has been focused primarily on these major banks.

4.1   Evolution of Japanese Banks as Multinationals

The literature on the evolution of Japanese banks as multinationals has tended to revolve around a kind of 'flexible stage theory' [Hagura (1978); Oriental Economist (1976); Burton/Saelens (1983 and 1986); Fujita/Ishigaki (1986); Iwami (1989) etc.]. The common element in all the studies is that the Japanese banks have gone through three

---

[1] For example, from 1980, the MOF introduced the system of 'making a round' every two years for the approval of branches in a foreign country. This replaced the earlier system of 'making a round' every three years adopted in 1977. Bankers Research Unit (1981) provides more information on this point.

[2] Lewis and Davis (1987) p. 264.

Table 4.1: Japan's Authorized Foreign Exchange Banks and their
Internationalization

(As of end 1992)

Type of Bank	Number of Authorized Forex banks	Banks which have overseas-					
		Rep. Office(s)		Branch(es)		Subsi- diary(ies)	
		[A]	[B]	[A]	[B]	[A]	[B]
Specialized foreign exchange bank (1)	1	1	20	1	42	1	31
City banks (10)	10	10	189	10	173	10	198
Long-term credit banks (3)	3	3	40	3	30	3	47
Trust banks (16)	16	6	45	6	42	6	57
of which							
Foreign trust banks [9]	[9]	...		...		...	
Regional banks (64)	64	41	58	29	51	18	25
Second Regional banks group (66)	61	11	17	5	7	2	2
Shokin Banks (436)	87	1	2	1	1	1	1
Shoko Chukin bank Norinchukin bank (3) Zenshiren bank	3	3	20	2	3	1	2
Foreign banks (89)	89	...		...		...	
Total (688)	**334**	**76**	**391**	**57**	**349**	**42**	**363**

Figures in parenthesis indicate the total number of each type of bank

[A] = Number of banks; [B] = Number of offices

Source: MOF, International Finance Bureau, Annual Report No.17, 1993

stages of internationalization: starting from the pure domestic banking stage, with correspondent relationships in foreign countries (1950-61), through the expansion stage of opening new branches abroad (1962-70), to the stage of full-fledged international banking (1976-80). A modified and extended version of the different stages of Japanese banks' evolution as multinationals and its related aspects is presented in Table 4.2. An assessment of the Japanese banks' position in the period 1981-94 would suggest that they are in the fourth stage of 'experienced international banking', where they function as mature financial multinationals deriving advantages from an extensive network of overseas offices.

A noteworthy feature of the early stages of Japanese banks' internationalization was the dominance of the Bank of Tokyo (BOT); of the 70 subsidiaries and branches in 1971, about half belonged to the BOT. The reason for this could be traced back to the role of specialized foreign exchange bank that had been assigned to the BOT in the post-War period. Further, in their evolution as multinationals, Japanese banks had to work hard at improving their international credibility. Reflecting upon the credit standing of

Table 4.2 : Evolution of Japanese Banks as Multinationals

Period	Phase	International moves of domestic clients	Banks' focus in the International banking business	Client Base	Method of International banking	Nature of foreign expansion
1950-61	National Banking	Insignificant ; mostly based on import and export	1. Short-term trade financing 2. Foreign exchange needs of clients related with import export	Japanese	Transactions carried through correspondent relationship with banks in foreign countries	Mostly branches of Bank of Tokyo
1962-70	International Expansion	Foreign direct investment in manufacturing starts	1. Overseas funding needs of clients 2. Capital transactions start gaining in importance	Mostly Japanese	Emphasis on expansion of overseas network of branches begins for city banks [conspicuously lesser dependence on Subsidiaries]	1962-67: all city banks expand 1967-70: only Bank of Tokyo is allowed to expand
1971-76	Transitionary period	Japanese cos. make substantial FDI in the US and Europe	1. Overseas loans 2. Entry into investment banking 3. A limited sphere of retail banking overseas*	Search for non-Japanese clients begins	City banks do business through their own branches in all main financial centers of the world. Fully owned subsidiaries and joint ventures are made for non-commercial banking business	Focus on subsidiaries and consortium banking Geographically confined acquisition for retail banking*
1977-80	Full-fledged international banking	Large Japanese cos. turn into multinationals	1. Greater involvement in Investment banking activities 2. Balance of payment deficit financing for LDCs	Japanese as well as non-Japanese	Consortium form of international banking does not prove successful City banks try to complete the overseas network of offices.	Majority- and minority stakes in various forms of banking and non-banking institutions
1981-92	Experienced international banking	Medium and small size Japanese cos. go overseas to support local production of large Japanese cos.	1. Short-term borrowing for financing the foreign currency needs of resident 2. Foreign exchange business 3. Funds management 4. Revived interest in syndicated lending 5. Corporate financial services	Customers of all nationalities become target groups	Greater reliance on inter-office transactions for global fund management and arbitrage	Completion of overseas network of offices by city banks. Regional banks start positioning themselves in international financial markets . A period of most dramatic expansion of foreign branches and subsidiaries

* Japanese banks retail banking in foreign markets started in 1974 in California. However, the phenomenon remains geographically too limited to be a characteristic feature of their evolution

Japanese banks in 1974, Bachman pointed out that up to ten tiers of banks could be identified in 1974, ranking from U.S. banks as the best to Japanese banks as the worst.[3] This meant that Japanese banks had to pay very high premiums for interbank deposits, which virtually excluded them from participating in the market. However, the situation improved in June 1976 when there were 7 tiers of banks, with Japanese banks occupying fifth position.[4] Later, in the 1980s, Japanese banks commanded a very good standing in the market, with some of the city banks enjoying triple A rating from American rating agencies.

Commenting on the earlier stages of the internationalization of Japanese banking, Fujita and Ishigaki (1986) say that

> "...one of the features of the internationalization of Japanese banking is that it has been promoted by the internationalization of the Japanese economy but has not been accompanied by the internationalization of the yen or the Japanese capital market. It should be noted, however, that Japanese banks have themselves initiated internationalization of some aspects of their operations against the background of the development of international financial markets, such as the Eurodollar market".[5]

The aggressiveness with which Japanese banks have expanded and diversified their overseas operations and areas in which they have developed expertise is the subject of their global position in the 1980s. This is discussed in detail in chapter 6, which evaluates the competitive position of Japanese banks and securities companies. What follows here is a brief account of foreign banking presence in Europe. This serves as a background for assessing the position of Japanese banks in Europe.

4.2   The Foreign Banking Presence in Europe

The subject of foreign banking presence in Europe raises an immediate question as to who "foreign" banks are and what constitutes "Europe". One might say that a

---

[3]Bachman (1976) p. 10.

[4]Dufey and Giddy (1978) point out that the number of tiers and the difference between them have tended to increase whenever events focused attention on the risk of bank default.

[5]Fujita and Ishigaki (1986) pp. 198-99.

German bank in the City of London is as foreign as a Japanese bank. On the other hand, because of the linguistic and cultural affinity between the two Anglo-Saxon countries, one wonders if the American banks may be less foreign in London than a German bank.[6] However, in this study, the term foreign is used to imply the political demarcations and, thus, banks from within Europe, when entering each other's territories, would be termed as foreign. The logic of this argument might be weakening in the wake of the proposed unification of European markets, but it still holds true to a considerable extent. Furthermore, in spite of the fact that the crumbling boundaries between East and West are creating a bigger Europe, the emphasis in this work is on foreign banking presence in western Europe. This is largely because of the virtual absence of foreign banking in eastern European countries until recently.

4.2.1   A Brief History

Over the past three decades, the foreign banking presence in Europe has swelled steadily. Foreign banks have grown both in terms of numbers and in relative importance (see Table 4.3). This phenomenon could be interpreted simultaneously as a cause and effect of the greater integration of domestic and international financial markets. Table 4.3 illustrates foreign banking presence in Europe from the host countries' viewpoint. The growth of foreign banking presence in Europe has varied from country to country. These differences in the growth pattern reflect a number of factors, such as policies regarding the entry of foreign banks and the depth of the financial markets. Whereas countries like Belgium, France, Germany, Luxembourg, the Netherlands, Switzerland and United Kingdom applied a liberal policy towards foreign bank entry, other countries, such as Austria, Sweden and Norway, allowed entry to foreign banks only gradually.

The arrival of foreign banks in Europe was primarily concentrated in Belgium, France, Germany, the Netherlands and the United Kingdom. London was a natural choice throughout because of its liberal attitude, minimum regulatory barriers, historical position and the weightiness of its financial markets. Luxembourg established itself as a major financial center in Europe during the 1970s, with many of the foreign banks attracted by its favorable regulatory environment.

---

[6]Bresser (1982) p. 35.

Table 4.3: Foreign Banking Presence in Selected European Countries

(End of the year figures)

Host Country	Number of banks or offices				Foreign banks assets (%)[2]			
	1960	1970	1980	1986	1960	1970	1980	1985[2]
Austria	..	..	17	22	..	..	..	..
Belgium*	14°	26	51	57[2]	8.2°	22.5	41.5	51.0
Denmark	0	0	5	8	..	..	..	..
France	33	58	122	152	7.2	12.3	15.0	18.2**
Germany	24	77	213	283[3]	0.5	1.4	1.9	2.4
Italy*#	1	4	25	36	..	..	0.9	2.4
Luxembourg	3	23	99	110	8.0	57.8	85.4	85.4
Netherlands*	1	23	39	42	..	..	17.4~	23.6
Norway	..	..	..	7	..	..	..	..
Spain	4	4	25	49	..	..	..	..
Sweden	0	0	0	12	..	..	..	..
Switzerland*	8	97	99	125	..	10.3	11.1	12.2
United Kingdom*	51°°	95	214	293	6.7	37.5	55.6	62.6

*indicates the number of foreign banking institutions represented. For other
countries, figures refer to the number of banking offices
[2]percent of total assets of all banks operating in selected countries
[3]end-June 1985
°1958
°°end-1962
#branches only
~end-1983
**end-1984

Source : BIS (1986) pp. 151-52; Bröker (1989) p. 147

It would be of equal importance to see foreign banking presence in Europe from the
point of view of source countries. The largest banks from all over the world have at
least one branch in London. Banks from industrialized countries of the world, especially
G-10 countries, constitute the central force of the foreign presence. From amongst the
foreign banks of non-European origin, Canadian and Australian banks were the first to
establish branches in Europe, owing more to their traditional ties with England. In the
twentieth century, American banks constitute the second important group of non-
European banks in Europe. Since the American banking presence in Europe represents
a distinct era in foreign banking, a brief description of that is warranted here.

4.2.2 The Era of American Banking

"If you trace the development of foreign banks' presence in Europe, the year 1914 and the passage of the Federal Reserve Act are critical, because this legislation permitted U.S. banks for the first time to branch and establish subsidiaries abroad".[7] In 1920, U.S. banks had 20 branches in Europe,[8] but many overseas branches ceased operations between 1921-45 owing to the inexperience of the banks and the banking crisis of 1931. The U.S. banks operated at a very low profile until the early 1950s when the postwar reconstruction of Europe and the Marshall Plan provided new opportunities for expansion. The real increase in the U.S. banking presence in Europe occurred in the 1960s. The restrictive policies of the U.S. government regarding capital outflows which gave birth to the Eurodollar and Eurobond markets, the growth of U.S. FDI and trade, and the tight credit policies of the U.S. during 1966 and 1969-70 all reinforced U.S. banking in Europe. Table 4.4 provides country-by-country details of U.S. bank branches and the assets of these branches in Europe over the period 1965-85.

Table 4.4: U.S. Banking Presence in Europe (Member Banks of the Federal Reserve System)

Country	Number of foreign branches					Assets of foreign branches*			
	1965	1970	1975	1980	1985	1970[2]	1975	1980	1985
Belgium	2[3]	11[3]	10	8	9	2.8	4.3	4.0	4.8
France	4	11	19	12	12	6.7	8.0	7.1	6.7
W. Germany	3	17	31	27	18	6.5	6.8	3.5	4.0
Greece	1	8	18	16	21	0.6	1.1	1.3	1.5
Italy	1	3	10	14	22	2.8	2.2	2.5	2.9
Luxembourg	..	..	7	4	3	2.0	1.1	0.3	0.6
Netherlands	3	7	6	6	3	0.9	1.1	0.9	0.6
Spain	0	0	0	6	15	0.0	0.0	0.9	2.5
Switzerland	1	6	9	9	12	1.7	1.1	1.3	1.8
United Kingdom	17	37	55	57	68	75.5	73.5	76.0	72.7
others	..	..	9	10	10	0.6	0.8	2.2	1.7
European Total (A)	32	103	174	169	193	$53.9	$92.0	$170.3	$154.0
World Total (B)	180	460	762	787	916	$77.4	$162.7	$343.5	$329.2
Europe´s share (A/B)	17.8	22.4	22.8	21.5	21.1	69.6	56.5	54.4	46.8

*Percent share of each country in the European total
[2]figures are for end-1972
[3]also includes Luxembourg
Source: Federal Reserve System; Quoted in Goldberg and Johnson (1990) pp.128-31
     Number of branches for 1965 and 1970 from Khoury (1980) pp.42-43.

---

[7]McMillen (1982) p. 44.

[8]Khoury (1980) p. 40.

The data clearly shows that Europe has more or less maintained its share of the number of branches in the world total of U.S. banks. However, the volume of the business conducted by the U.S. banks in Europe has declined over time. Within Europe, the United Kingdom is the main base of the U.S. banking activity, both in terms of the number of branches and total assets. While, as per the number of branches, Italy, Greece, Germany, Spain and France in order of importance were the other countries of preference in 1985, France, Belgium and Germany boasted the maximum concentration of the U.S. banking business in terms of asset size.

U.S. banks and other financial institutions have been active not only on the wholesale side of cross-border banking but they have been equally dominant players in investment banking. Though some major U.S. banks have attempted the difficult job of entering the retail banking sphere of domestic markets in Europe, their experience in this particular area has been mixed. With little success, retail banking in European markets has proved a costly and disappointing form of foreign banking for banks from many countries.

Recently, the international position of the U.S. banks has dwindled a little. According to BIS estimates, their share of international banking assets declined from 28 percent at the end of 1983 to 11.6 percent at the end of March 1992. It partly reflects the aftermath of the LDC debt crisis in which the U.S. banks were deeply involved. The need to strengthen their loan loss reserves has squeezed their earnings and led to a rationalization of global network by many U.S. banks. The effects of difficult times in the U.S. banking industry are being felt in their European presence, too.

In retrospect, the contribution made by the U.S. banks to the development of multinational banking is indisputable. Their proactive stance towards selling banking services and innovative skills in developing streams of financial products constitute an ideal background for MNBs from other countries.

4.3   Organizational Aspects of the Japanese Banking Presence in Europe

The trailblazers for Japanese business in Europe, and elsewhere, were the Japanese trading companies. As soon as external trade resumed after the Second World War, Japanese trading companies started dealing through the European commodity markets of Europe for trade not just within Europe, but globally.[9] In order to handle the

---

[9]Takagaki (1986) p. 46.

concomitant financial transactions, the BOT reopened the branch office of its predecessor, Yokohama Specie Bank, in London (1952) and Hamburg (1954). This marks the beginning of the Japanese banks' arrival into Europe. Later, their expansion in Europe, with some basic differences, conforms to their global evolution as MNBs (see Table 4.2). These differences are discussed in Section 4.3.3.

Where does Europe stand in the Japanese banks' overseas strategy? A reasonably good indicator of Europe's position in the Japanese banks' global strategy is its share in the total branches and subsidiaries of Japanese banks. The continental spread of offices opened by Japanese banks is shown in Figure 4.1. The figure shows that Europe occupies second position after North America, accounting for 24 percent of all overseas branches and 33 percent of all overseas subsidiaries of Japanese banks at the end of June 1992. The fact that Europe has the largest share of Japanese banks' overseas subsidiaries provides evidence, firstly, for their desire to participate in the international securities markets in London and, secondly, their wish to be recognized as true EU banks in the wake of the 1992 banking regulation. North America, because of historical ties and trade relations, and Asia, because of the geographical proximity and the presence of offshore centers like Hong Kong and Singapore, relegate Europe to third place in terms of its share of Japanese banks' overseas branches.

Figure 4.1:Geographical Distribution of Japanese Banks' Overseas Offices (as of June 1992)

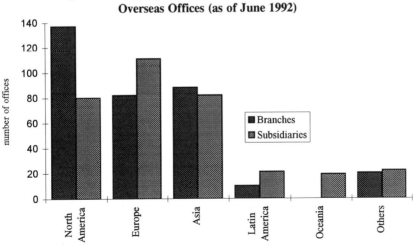

Source: Kinyu Zaisei Jijo (in Japanese)

4.3.1 Geographical Distribution of Offices within Europe

A better idea about Japanese banks' involvement in Europe can be obtained from the geographical spread of their offices within Europe and different forms of organizations in which it manifests itself. Table 4.5 shows the number of Japanese banks' branches, subsidiaries and representative offices in individual European countries. In terms of the degree of concentration of branch offices, Japanese banks have a heavy cluster in the United Kingdom, Germany, France and Spain; these four countries together accounted for about 80 percent of all branches in Europe at the end of June 1994. The itinerary of Japanese banks' subsidiaries in Europe is drawn around the United Kingdom, Switzerland, Germany, Luxembourg and Belgium, with 85 percent of all European subsidiaries at the end of June 1994. The increasing number of Japanese banks' representative offices in Europe, seen as an indicator of their future strategy, shows a continuation of the above-mentioned pattern. Thus, the prognosis about the future is more of the same, except that southern Europe, particularly Italy and Spain, appears to be gaining in prominence.

Table 4.5: Japanese Banks' Network of Offices within Europe
(In Individual Countries)

	1975			1985			1994*			
	B	S	R	B	S	R	B	S	R	Total
United Kingdom	19	5	4	23	16	16	28	32	21	81
Germany	12		1	13	3	15	15	19	20	54
France	1	1	3	3	1	11	10	2	5	17
Belgium	5	3		5	7	0	6	13	2	21
Spain				3	0	9	13	1	2	16
Italy				2	2	1	8	3	2	13
Netherlands				0	4	1	0	7	4	11
Luxembourg	0	2		0	5	0	0	9	0	9
Portugal						1	1	0	2	3
Subtotal (EU)	37	2	18	49	38	54	81	86	58	225
Austria		2				2	1	0	5	6
Switzerland	0	4	0	0	18	10	0	22	2	24
Others						3	0	4	4	8
Europe total	37	6	20	49	56	69	82	112	69	263

*Figures as of end-June 1994
B = Branches; S = Subsidiaries; R = Representative Offices

Source: MOF, Japan; Kinyu Zaisei Jijo etc.

The Japanese banking presence in Europe at present shows that they have:

- no or very little representation in the Scandinavian countries;
- very little or no presence in Austria, Ireland and the southern European countries of Greece, Portugal etc.

Therefore, despite the widely held belief that the establishment of the European network by Japanese banks is almost complete,[10] their heavy concentration in a couple of countries implies low geographical diversification within Europe. How far this can be regarded as an indicator of Japanese banks' 'herding behavior' is open to debate.[11] However, there are indications to the effect that Japanese banks have a tendency to watch each other and follow the leader. Japanese banks, in this context, may be characterized as *convoy banks*. A characteristic feature of this convoy behavior is that it inclines banks to serve the same set of customers and acquire similar portfolios. It is often said that international banks "herded" or demonstrated a "pack instinct" in extending loans to developing countries during the 1970s.[12] It might be useful to assess the riskiness of this type of behavior. However, the lack of concrete evidence makes it difficult to scrutinize this kind of behavior of Japanese banks.

The Japanese banks' network of offices in Europe should be seen, to a considerable extent, as strategic positioning where the aim is to take advantage of future developments, both at home and abroad. This is also borne out by the statement of a major Japanese bank:

> "..the establishing of subsidiaries for securities business in Germany has been undertaken probably a couple of years too early. At this point, I think of the present situation of the Japanese financial system. The financial liberalization and the reform of the financial system in Japan has begun already. But, it is likely to take a couple of years. Therefore, I want to emphasize here that the arrival of Japanese banks in Frankfurt has been motivated by medium and long-term strategies."[13]

---

[10]Naruse (1990) p. 4 and Hirota (1990) p. 18.

[11]Herding can be said to exist when some banks explicitly take only the portfolio allocation decisions of other banks into consideration while making their own portfolio decisions. For details, refer to Jain and Gupta (1987) p. 81.

[12]See Jain and Gupta (1987) for empirical evidence on the herding behavior of US banks.

[13]Tsuji (1990) p. 11.

4.3.2 Organizational Forms of Presence

The various forms of representation chosen by an MNB in foreign markets are an expression of its international strategies. The decision involves resolving the conflicting aims of retaining maximum parent bank control, on the one hand, and granting the necessary freedom to the overseas office for operational efficiency, on the other. Not only that, the decision about the form of organization is often constrained or favored by host country laws. The available choices of forms of organization to an MNB range from:

(i)   opening a representative office; and

(ii)   upgrading it to the level of a branch; or

(iii)   establishing a subsidiary under the local laws of the host country; and/or

(iv)   acquiring a non-controlling or controlling equity interest in a local bank; and/or

(v)   entering into a joint venture with a local bank; and/or

(vi)   establishing a consortium bank with other banks; and/or

(vii)   outright purchasing of a local bank in the host country.[14]

If one emphasizes the importance of brand name in business success, opening a branch or subsidiary is usually accorded preference over other forms of organizations.[15] Strategic alliances, of the (iv) and (v) type, with local banks, are quicker ways of entering a foreign market. However, they are difficult forms of overseas representation.[16] Consortium banking, a practice of the early 1970s, seems to have met with less success for various reasons.[17] Outright purchase of a local institution is mostly done for retail banking through a local network of branches.

---

[14]In the literature on international banking, the first three forms (i-iii) of organization are viewed as strong or autonomous forms, and the last three (iv-vi) as weak or cooperative forms of international banking. For details, see Gramlich (1990) pp. 6-8.

[15]The only distinction between a branch and a subsidiary is that a branch is treated as an integral part of its parent bank with unlimited liability, whereas a subsidiary is treated as a separate legal entity, with the liability of the parent bank, theoretically, limited to its capital investment in the subsidiary.

[16]Kohn (1990).

[17]In retrospect, many experts on the subject refer to them as an "episode of international banking". See, for example, Glüder, 1989, pp. 284 and 286. The diminished importance of consortium banks is a pointer to the fact that competition has taken over cooperation in international banking. See Germidis and Michalet (1984) p. 23.

The Japanese banks in Europe have used a combination of alternative forms of organization to achieve their goals. Because of the unique character of each host market, it is difficult to make any generalization of Japanese strategy for the whole of Europe in this regard. However, certain broad patterns can be identified:

(i) Opening overseas branches was the most popular form chosen by them until the late 1970s. Branches were established mostly for performing traditional commercial banking functions and for catering to the funding needs of the overseas operations of Japanese corporate clients in Europe.

(ii) Fully-owned subsidiaries in host countries became a popular form in the 1980s and the phenomenon is more striking in Europe (Figure 4.1). As mentioned earlier, Europe houses the largest number of Japanese banking subsidiaries. Most of them were established for the purpose of engaging in securities-related and other investment banking business.

(iii) Acquiring a controlling stake in an existing bank in Europe has rarely been used by Japanese banks. There are only two cases of this type: first, 55 percent equity investment in Swiss Banco del Gottardo made by the Sumitomo Bank in 1984 and the second, a majority stake in U.K. merchant bank Guinness Mahon by the Bank of Yokohama in 1989.[18] However, a number of non-controlling equity investments have been made by Japanese banks in Europe (see Table 4.6) for closer business relations and acquisition of management know-how. The table shows that out of 13 non-controlling alliances between Japanese banks and European financial institutions, 6 are in the United Kingdom.

(iv) Strategic alliances for establishing joint ventures have been used by Japanese banks as a rare option. There are two existing cases of joint ventures and both are in Germany: the first one has been between IBJ and Deutsche Bank since 1972 in which Deutsche Bank has a 16.7 percent stake and the second is between the Mitsubishi Trust and Banking Corporation and Westdeutsche Landesbank, established in 1988, in which both have an equal stake.[19]

---

[18]The Bank of Yokohama subsequently acquired full control of Guinness Mahon.

[19]In 1982, the Fuji bank acquired full control of its joint venture with U.K. merchant bank Kleinwort Benson (set up in 1973 with Fuji banks' share of 55 percent). Similarly, in 1983, Long Term Credit Bank acquired full control of the Nippon European Bank, a Brussels merchant bank, in which it held a 50 percent interest. See Burton and Saelens (1986) p. 30.

Table 4.6: Japanese Banks' Equity Investment Overseas: Geographical Classification of the Number of Cases

(As of June 1992)

Country/Continent	1-10%	11-25%	26-50%	51-75%	76-99%	100%	**Total**
United Kingdom	2	...	4	1	4	27	**38**
Germany	...	...	1	1	2	16	**20**
Switzerland	...	1	...	1	...	22	**24**
Luxembourg	...	...	...	...	1	8	**9**
Netherlands	...	...	...	...	1	6	**7**
Belgium	...	...	...	...	...	13	**13**
France	1	1	...	...	...	2	**4**
Italy	...	...	1	...	...	4	**5**
others	1	...	1	...	...	5	**7**
Europe Total	4	2	7	3	8	103	**127**
North America	4	1	2	5	7	75	**94**
Asia	10	24	27	7	12	63	**143**
Latin America	5	2	...	...	1	28	**36**
Australia	...	...	...	...	...	20	**20**
Africa/Middle East	...	1	...	...	...	1	**2**
World Total	**23**	**30**	**36**	**15**	**28**	**290**	**422**

Note: The financial institutions covered are: City banks (10), Specialized foreign exchange bank (1), Long-term credit banks(3), Trust banks (6) and Regional banks (21)

Source: Calculations from Kinyu Zaisei Jijo(in Japanese),

(v)   In early seventies, when establishing consortium banks was a popular form of international banking cooperation, Japanese banks also opted for participating in such consortia. Other than the two multinational consortia (ORION and SFE) in which one Japanese bank each had a minority stake, two purely Japanese consortia were set up in London in 1970: (i) the Associated Japanese Bank (International) by four city banks and one securities company; and (ii) the Japan International Bank by four city banks and three securities companies. The Japanese city banks and securities companies joined hands for consolidated loan-credit business in the Euromarket and for investment/merchant banking business. Recently, the Associated Japanese Bank (International) was taken over by the Sanwa Bank and the Japan International Bank was acquired by the Tokai Bank.

(vi)   To date, there has been no outright purchase of any European commercial bank by the Japanese banks. Consequently, no Japanese bank possesses a network of local branches for retail banking and wholesale banking continues to be the main business interest for them.

At this point, it would be relevant to analyze equity investment made by Japanese banks overseas according to the ownership ratio. This should manifest the nature of equity participation (controlling and non-controlling) in foreign countries. Table 4.6 reveals that out of 422 cases of equity investment by Japanese banks abroad (as of June 1992), 127 cases (30 percent of the total) are in Europe and more than 80 percent of these are wholly-owned or majority-owned affiliates. The fact that Japanese banks choose to carry out international operations in Europe through self-organized subsidiaries or through majority-owned affiliates hints at their strategy of maintaining maximum control over the operations. Conversely, this could also be traced to the varying degrees of freedom available to foreign financial institutions in the host countries. Ozawa suggests that countries whose financial markets are well developed and open to foreign participation provide incentives for such investment.[20]

The other explanation lies in the general behavior of Japanese multinationals which have adopted the path of overseas expansion through greenfield investments. The behavior of Japanese banks' direct investment in Europe conforms broadly to that of Japanese manufacturing companies. Thus, of the 371 Japanese manufacturing enterprises in Europe that responded to the eighth survey conducted by JETRO in January 1992, 253 (68% of the total) of them were capitalized 100% from Japan.[21]

4.3.3 Motivation for Presence and Expansion in Europe

A detailed analysis of the Japanese banking presence in the United Kingdom and Germany, where they have significant presence, forms part of Chapter 8. A brief account of their presence in individual European countries is given here to make an assessment of the motives for their presence and expansion in Europe.

Amongst European countries, the **United Kingdom** has attracted the largest number of Japanese banks. Concentrated mainly in the City of London, 28 Japanese banks have at least one branch there and some enjoy double representation by opening both a branch and a subsidiary. When analyzing the Japanese presence in London, one has to distinguish categorically between the desire for participating in international financial markets, for which London happens to be a major center, and the motive of undertaking an active

---

[20]On the other hand, the developing countries often treat the financial sector as a sensitive one and try to protect it from foreign invasion. See Ozawa (1989) p. 85.

[21]Japan External Trade Organization (1992).

role in the domestic financial market. The majority of Japanese banks owe their existence in London to the former but, recently, the latter is also gaining prominence. This is reflected in the increasing share of sterling-denominated assets (a proxy for domestic banking) as well as in the spread of branches in other parts of the United Kingdom. The Japanese banks' motive of functioning as funding vehicles for their domestic offices is also fulfilled primarily through London

In **Germany**, the volume of Japanese direct investment has been substantial since the early 1960s. A large number of Japanese manufacturing companies have their units in Germany, particularly in and around the industrial area of Düsseldorf. The major city banks opened their branch offices in Düsseldorf between the mid-1960s and the mid-1970s in order to serve their Japanese clients. Thus, the motive of Japanese banks' arrival in Germany fits more into the classical explanation of "bank-following-clients". In the late 1980s, there was a rush on the part of the Japanese banks to open subsidiaries in Frankfurt, which is the center of the country's capital market, so as to be able to participate in the growing securities-related business.

In **France**, Japanese banks should be treated as newcomers. Until a few years ago, only the BOT, with its Japanese consortium Banque Européenne de Tokyo, was present in Paris. After 1985, when the Japanese FDI started to increase rapidly,[22] there was a fresh interest for Japanese banks to open offices in Paris. The wave of deregulation and liberalization of the French financial markets in 1986 and 1988 gave more incentives to Japanese banks for active participation.[23] As a result, 93 percent of total Japanese FDI in finance to France (1950-90) took place between 1987-90.[24] In just a short period, the Fuji Bank has become the largest foreign bank in France in terms of balance sheet size.[25] The Japanese FDI to France is likely to increase in the future and here the Japanese banks are, in a way, leading their corporate clients. The active presence of the Japanese banks is supposed to help in removing the information barriers and boost direct investment.

---

[22]The amount of Japanese FDI to France increased from $67 million in 1985 to $1257 million in 1990.

[23]Sazanami (1991) p. 27.

[24]ibid.

[25]Schissel (1989) p. 12.

In **Switzerland**, the Japanese banking presence is guided by a very different motive. Most of them operate in Zurich through subsidiaries and are engaged in the underwriting and trading of Swiss Franc denominated bonds. The attraction of Swiss Franc denominated foreign bonds has increased for Japanese corporate borrowers because of low interest rates, relatively easy issuing procedures and the dominance of the private placement market.[26] The boom in this business sphere has attracted Japanese banks, too. However, Japanese banks are also active in fund management and, on a limited scale, in private banking. The share of Swiss banking assets held by foreign banks ranges between 10-15 percent and the share held by Japanese banks is not commensurate with the number of their subsidiary units.[27] This largely explains their active involvement in the securities business.

In a country like **Belgium**, where foreign banks with about 60 branches make up nearly half the total balance sheet of the banking system[28], the Japanese banks have a significant presence after the United Kingdom and Germany, i.e. 6 branches and 13 subsidiaries as of June 1992. Their operations are quite diversified in Belgium. While most of them are very active in money market and foreign exchange operations, playing a supplementary role to London[29], some cover other European countries from Brussels and book the loan portfolio of different countries.

In **Luxembourg**, Japanese banks at one time established offices to serve as bases for Euro-German mark transactions.[30] The importance of Luxembourg as a Eurobond center further boosted Japanese interest there. The country earns its reputation as a financial center from its liberal taxation and strong secrecy laws, absence of minimum reserve requirements and free capital movement. However, more recently, Japanese institutions have developed a strong interest in trust business and investment advisory services in Luxembourg.

The Netherlands host not only Japanese financial institutions but also the financial subsidiaries of many Japanese manufacturing and trading companies. It has been sug-

---

[26]Widmer (1989) pp. 439-46.

[27]Kitamura (1991) p. 112.

[28]Blanden (1991).

[29]Hirota (1990) p. 19.

[30]Takagaki (1986) p. 47.

gested that the arrival of Japanese banks in the Netherlands in the 1970s largely correlated with the period in which many Japanese manufacturing, trading and service firms became established there.[31] The European Option Exchange in Amsterdam and a large number of Japanese companies listed on the Amsterdam Stock Exchange are other reasons for the Japanese presence there.

In **Italy**, where 108 foreign banks from 23 countries are represented, the Japanese constitute the third largest group after EU and U.S. banks.[32] With an eye on the growth prospects in Italy after 1992, many Japanese companies are making direct investment there. With their offices clustered in the financial city of Milan, Japanese banks are so far serving their Japanese clients in Italy with 8 branches, 3 subsidiaries and 2 representative offices as at the end of June 1994.

Spain is seen by the Japanese banks as the next attractive spot within Europe. However, very little information is available about the latest moves by Japanese banks there. The obvious assumption is that growing Japanese direct investment in Spain, the stability of local currency and prospects for high economic growth are the reasons for the Japanese banking arrival there. With their presence limited to 13 branches and no subsidiaries, Japanese banks in Spain seem to be concentrating on corporate banking.

To sum up, it should be noted that the Japanese banking presence in Europe cannot be treated as a homogeneous phenomenon. The reasons for their arrival and growth in each of the European countries are so different that no single hypothesis can help clarify all of them. Table 4.7 below shows the broad classification of motives with reference to individual European countries in order of significance. Thus, the United Kingdom, Switzerland and, to some extent, Luxembourg attract Japanese banks, in the first instance, because of the international financial markets. However, in Germany, France, Italy and Spain, Japanese banks are guided by the direct investment of their corporate clients. In Luxembourg, Belgium and the Netherlands, the liberal financial regulations justify the Japanese presence.

The desire to participate in Europe's domestic financial markets should be seen as a subsequent move by the Japanese banks for enlarging their business field and for justifying their continued profitable existence in the host country. Thus, it could be argued that the reasons which motivate the Japanese banks' arrival into Europe are not

---

[31]Hart and Piersma (1990) p. 89.

[32]Graf von Pückler (1989) p. 174.

Table 4.7: Motives for Japanese Banking Presence in Individual European Countries

	Attraction of international financial markets	Following Japanese clients to overseas markets	Liberal financial regulations in host markets	Attraction of domestic financial markets
United Kingdom	I	II	...	III
Germany	...	I	...	II
France	...	I	...	II
Switzerland	I	...	...	II
Italy/Spain	...	I	...	...
Luxembourg	I	...	I	...
Belgium/ Netherlands	II	III	I	...

I Primary motive

II Secondary motive

III Subsequent motive

identical with those justifying their continued presence and expansion. Their expansion is guided more by the experience gained in the foreign markets, the degree of familiarity with the local markets and the need for survival with reasonable growth. The need for survival stems from the assumption that, in the long-run, the business opportunities arising from the influx of Japanese companies in Europe has a tendency to decline.

4.4 Operational Focus, Strategies and Performance of Japanese Banks in Europe

4.4.1 Major Activities

The activities performed by an MNB in the host country could be viewed in a two-by-two matrix as shown in Figure 4.2. Thus, an MNB has the choice of focusing on the domestic or the international markets of the host countries. Within domestic or international markets, they could concentrate on money markets or on capital markets. The choices made by Japanese banks reflect a very complex blend of administrative guidance from home regulators, banking regulations in the host countries, competence developed by Japanese banks in new areas and the profitability potentials within different market segments.

Japanese Financial Institutions in Europe

Figure 4.2: Sphere of Operations for Multinational Banks in the Host Country

| | | Market Focus | |
		Domestic Markets	International Markets
Nature of Market	Money Market	A	C
	Capital Market	B	D

A = Retail Banking, Domestic Interbank Market etc.
B = Domestic Equity and Bond Markets (Primary and Secondary)
C = International syndicated Loan Market, CDs and CPs Markets,
    Foreign Exchange Market and International interbank Market etc.
D = International Bond and Equity Market (Primary and Secondary)

The activities of Japanese banks cover, with varying degrees of emphasis, each of the four spheres of the European financial markets. Their desire to participate in the international financial markets justifies their focus on spheres C and D. The necessity of foreign currency fund raising makes their position as borrowers dominant in zone C. Japanese banks' participation in the overseas domestic markets should be viewed as an emerging pattern of the 1990s. Whereas the discussion about the involvement of Japanese banks in the foreign national markets forms part of chapter 8, an analysis of their operations in the international financial markets appears in chapter 6. The following sections explain the markets or functions which Japanese banks emphasized in the 1980s.

4.4.1.1 Funding Vehicles for the Head Office

The essential corollary of the overseas activities of an MNB is to play a supporting role for its head office.[33] This could range from helping the head office in global asset and liability management to optimizing inter-office transactions. The supporting role of

---

[33]In this sense, international banking is seen as a subset of domestic banking. See Aliber (1984) p. 661.

overseas offices was more pronounced in the case of Japanese banks while they were operating as funding vehicles for gaining access to non-yen funds.[34] The need for foreign currencies, particularly dollars, reinforced the dominant position of the Japanese banks in zone C of Figure 4.2. Three reasons account for the Japanese need for foreign currency funds:

(i)   the currency structure of Japan's foreign trade; about 60 percent of exports and 83 percent of imports were denominated in currencies other than yen at the end of 1992. Japanese banks need foreign currency funds to finance foreign trade.

(ii)   the liberalization of the Foreign Exchange Law in 1980 led to an autonomous increase in the outflow of long-term capital, most of which took the form of portfolio investment in foreign securities. This created additional demand for foreign currencies in the later part of the 1980s.

(iii) impact loans, which are foreign currency loans to business corporations, increased sizably in the 1980s. Japanese foreign exchange banks have been borrowing externally in order to meet domestic demand for impact loans.

Borrowing from foreign banks was the main method of securing funds for the financing of trade in the 1960s and 1970s, and most of funding of this nature came from the American banks. In the 1980s, because of the improved rating of the Japanese banks, fund raising in the international interbank market in the form of deposits and Euro CDs gained in prominence. The importance of fund raising through the international interbank market is amply reflected in the principal accounts of Japanese banks' overseas branches published by the BOJ. The structure of their liabilities shows that deposits remain the largest source of funding; they accounted for 67 percent of the total liabilities at the end of 1991.[35] Suzuki states that these are deposits in form only and are, in fact, short-term uncollateralized borrowing with a maximum maturity of two years.[36]

---

[34]In this context, one author comments that "the Japanese banks are torn between the disadvantage of having to fund themselves in a foreign currency and the advantage of having the relationship with (Japanese) customers." See Dufey (1990) p. 145.

[35]Bank of Japan, *Economic Statistics Annual*.

[36]Suzuki (1987) p. 188.

The importance of Japanese banks' fund raising function in Europe is emphasized by Fujita and Ishigaki (1986), too. They found out in their survey that:

> "At the London branch, fund raising is by far the most important activity (for all banks), with trade finance and loans to non-Japanese companies being next in importance ...Japanese banks raise 51 percent of funds in Europe, 35 percent in America, 9 percent through other regions and only 6 percent through head offices".[37]

Thus, focusing on the net flow of Japanese banks' international funds in London, it becomes clear that their biggest source of funds were *other banks from outside the United Kingdom*, which supplied more than half the funds.[38] Taking note of the fact that London's major financial sources are U.S. and Swiss banks, it is supposed that Japanese banks in London raised substantial funds through interbank transactions with the American and the Swiss banks.[39]

On the other hand, the dominant customers to which Japanese banks in London are lending are their own offices; of the $91 billion in net funds (outstanding) raised by the Japanese banks at the end of September 1987, $62.5 billion (69 percent) was lent to own offices and the rest to non-banks.[40] The hypothesis of funding vehicle role is sufficiently endorsed by the above-mentioned facts. The fact that 63 percent of the lending by the Japanese banks in London was in US dollars[41] suggests that the Eurodollar was the major foreign currency used by the Japanese banks for funding inter-office needs.

Figure 4.3 shows the growth of the inter-office accounts of the Japanese banks' overseas branches. The overseas branches were heavy net lenders to related offices until 1986. Since 1987, the amount of net claims on own offices has been steadily declining. One cannot rule out the impact of the JOM here, which was created in December, 1986. This has also led to an increase in the yen borrowing of overseas branches through inter-office accounts. The economics of international financial intermediation would suggest,

---

[37]Fujita and Ishigaki (1986) p. 209.

[38]Walton and Trimble (1987) p. 520.

[39]Nakao (1989) p. 43.

[40]Walton and Trimble (1987) p. 520.

[41]ibid. p. 523.

Figure 4.3: Inter-office Accounts of Japanese Banks' Overseas Branches

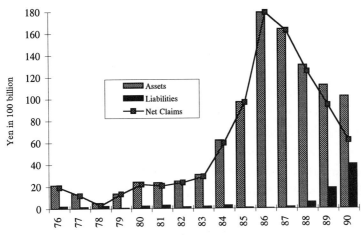

Source: BOJ, Economic Statistics Monthly

as Niehans (1983) aptly puts it, that "interbranch costs are significantly lower than interbank costs. Instead of dealing with another bank through an interbank broker, a branch in need of loanable funds may be able to obtain some of them from a branch elsewhere. By transacting with each other, they can avoid the chain of interbank transactions".[42] Thus, inter-office business is considered both efficient and cost-effective. In a survey of international interbank market, the BIS reports that:

> "Inter-office business is perhaps most intensively cultivated at those banks attempting to minimize their interbank costs...Where such banks have an extensive branch network and the size of their business is considerable, they may be able to deal between their own branches with almost as much flexibility as dealing in the wider interbank market, and inter-office flows, of course, do not inflate a banks consolidated balance sheet".[43]

---

[42]Quoted in Lewis and Davis (1987) pp. 260-261.

[43]BIS (1983) p. 17.

4.4.1.2 Focus on International Financial Markets

It has been mentioned in Section 4.3.3 that participation in the international financial markets constitutes the main motive for Japanese banks' presence in Europe. In the 1980s, they actively participated in the international interbank market, syndicated loan market, Eurobond market and international derivative products market.[44] Whereas Japanese banks excelled in the syndicated loan market and quickly gained market share, they tried to accumulate experience in other markets, too. The initial stimulus came from the general expansion of the global financial markets and their wish to take part in these markets. Later, the international expansion strategy of the Japanese corporate sector and its fund raising operations overseas, with increased emphasis on Eurocredit markets, led Japanese banks towards other market segments.

From amongst various segments of international financial markets, Japanese banks have improved their position as bookrunners in the overall Eurobond market despite the 'Three Bureaux Agreement' at home. With all other home regulations limiting their distribution capacity, Japanese banks do not figure in the international equity market. In the derivative products market, Japanese banks mostly play the role of end user or intermediary and not that of a market maker. With their massive size, they figure in the syndicated loan market as leading providers and lead managers of funds but not as arrangers.

4.4.1.3 Emerging Role in Foreign Banking Markets

A detailed discussion of this point is given in Chapter 8 with reference to the role of Japanese banks in the domestic markets of the United Kingdom and Germany. It is argued that the Japanese banks' involvement in the foreign banking markets is confined to wholesale banking; the major target being the large and medium-sized corporate sector. The difficulties and costs involved in establishing a retail banking presence has kept Japanese banks away from this market segment. Despite their financial strength, Japanese banks did not make any efforts at acquiring any local retail banking network. It may well be the case that Japanese banks did not have the required mandate from their supervisory authorities for this purpose. Conversely, the political implications of any such action restrained their expansion plans in this direction.

---

[44]For details about the performance of Japanese banks in each of these market segments, refer to section 6.1.4.

4.4.2 Business Strategy

From the issues discussed so far, several indicators of Japanese banks' strategy in Europe can be identified. The choice of forms of overseas representation, focus on international financial markets, prominent role as funding vehicles and not so significant involvement in the domestic markets of host countries convey meaningful information about the European strategy of Japanese banks. Furthermore, a sudden increase in the number of subsidiaries after the mid-1980s hints at Japanese banks' defensive strategies in response to apprehensions of market barriers likely to be created by the proposed integration of European markets. Conversely, it implies positioning for lucrative business opportunities from the emerging common market.

Although the classical explanation of following corporate clients who established overseas bases helped Japanese banks formulate their initial international strategies, participation in the recycling of petro-dollars provided them with a convenient way of entering international financial markets. The virtual demise of the syndicated loan market after the debt crisis and the increased reliance of Japanese borrowers and investors on Euromarkets augmented Japanese banks' involvement in the securities markets and in investment banking. The dire need for foreign currency funds, particularly dollar funds, obliged Japanese banks to act as funding vehicles. In this context, their strategy was unique. They satisfied the need for foreign currency funds not by liquidating their existing foreign assets but by extensive borrowing in the international interbank market.

Despite the rising tide of Japanese FDI to Europe, the business derived from Japanese corporate clients has not proved a growth area for Japanese banks. Lately, these traditional relationships have been providing fewer opportunities and banks have had to find new ways for survival and growth. This has pushed them into new strategic areas of the local banking markets of individual European countries. Now, they are focusing on areas such as project financing and lending to medium-sized companies in the host countries.

The oft-quoted Japanese banking strategy is their emphasis on market share or asset growth, with very low profit margins. One usually hints at their fast growing share of international banking assets in the 1980s to substantiate this. Their aggressive asset growth policy is also reflected by the fact that they registered average growth of about

12 percent in their assets in the 1980s.[45] Since a substantial part of Japanese banks' international assets are booked in London, their market share emphasis is equally true of their European strategy. As far as the policy of offering services at low margins is concerned, it is not a unique Japanese strategy. Low prices are a classic market entry strategy and many foreign banks built a U.S. presence this way. The Japanese differ only in their willingness to keep offering low rates in order to keep growing.[46]

However, the market share strategy of the Japanese banks is currently undergoing a slow change. They have drastically curtailed their market share ambitions since early 1990, particularly after the Japanese stock market took a downturn. This indicates that their international strategy is strongly coupled with the health of the Japanese stock market.[47] Japanese banks depend heavily on the growing stock market in three principal respects:

(i)   the substantial portfolio investment to boost net income;

(ii)   the value of their investment portfolio, which is critical to their market valuation; and

(iii)   the ability of the market to continue to absorb the massive stock and bond issues the banks need to raise capital levels and to fuel expansion.[48]

The latest strategy of Japanese banks is to focus more on return on assets (ROA). With this motive, measures such as selling existing assets, buying new and profitable assets, and increasing non-interest income business are commonly being undertaken.[49] The emphasis on non-interest income is reflected in the fact that such income accounted for 46 percent of the total income in 1990[50] in comparison with 1988 when the share of such income was only 27 percent.

---

[45]Mitsui Bank (1989) p. 7.

[46]Bellanger (1987) p. 52.

[47]Japanese banks are allowed to count 45 percent of unrealized gains on their holding of stocks as part of Tier II capital for capital adequacy guidelines of the BIS.

[48]Hanley et al. (1989) p. 29.

[49]Naruse (1990) p. 5.

[50]The Swiss and the US banks are the only ones which earn more than Japan from their non-interest income. European banks earn about 40 percent of their income from non-interest sources. See OECD (1992b) quoted in Danton (1992) p. 296.

Having tried their hands successfully in the wholesale lending markets, Japanese banks now find themselves on the learning curve of complicated financial techniques, such as derivative products and other innovations. The Japanese strategy in this regard has been to buy in the brains they need. The high ratio of local to Japanese staff in the newly created derivative products department at many Japanese banks indicates the importance assigned to this area.

If one were to identify the Japanese banks' overall strategy in Europe, it has been more evolutionary than otherwise; they have sought mostly to fit the situation and to survive unscathed. On their international strategy, Düser says that:

> "one of the main objectives of the thesis is to draw attention to the developmental situation of Japanese banks abroad...caused by their unfinished strategic evolution... so far Japanese banks have been able to succeed with their rather incremental and adaptive (strategic) behavior. They seized those business opportunities which happened to surface within reach".[51]

Although it would be inaccurate to label Japanese banks' international strategy as disjointed incrementalism, it is true that it has been more contextual than comprehensive.[52] The latest example of contextual strategy is given by Fuji Bank's comment on its European strategy:

> "Our European strategy revolves around the integration of the European Community markets. When integrated, the EC market will be almost as large as the North American market, a very attractive opportunity indeed".[53]

To sum up, in order to maintain a successful and long-term presence in Europe, Japanese banks must view their strategy on a country-by-country basis, evaluating their capabilities in relation to the strategies of host country banks in terms of market share, product development and customer relations.

---

[51]Düser (1990) p. 139.

[52]Contextual decisions are made through an exploration of the main alternatives in view of institutional goals. In such decisions, details and specifications are omitted so that overviews are feasible. See Etzioni (1968) p. 283 quoted in Walter (1983) p. 166.

[53]Shigyo (1991) p. 24.

4.4.3 Profitability of European Operations

Profitability is the rate of return on the capital employed. In the context of an MNB, overall profitability means the weighted average of domestic and international profit rates. Thus, in equational form:

$$\textbf{Overall profitability} \ = \ \textbf{aX} + \textbf{bY} \ \dots\dots\dots\dots \ \textbf{(1)}$$

Where a + b = 1

        a = Share of national banking business in total banking business
        b = Share of international banking business in total banking business
        X = National profitability rate
        Y = International profitability rate

Thus, the contribution of international banking business to overall profitability depends not only on its profit rate but also on the proportion of assets committed to it. It can be further deduced from equation (1) that the overall profitability rate improves if the proportion of low earning assets is kept under control. In other words, if a realistic assumption is made that earnings from international banking assets are lower than from domestic assets,[54] then acquiring more international banking assets implies lowered overall profitability. However, it could be argued that profitability is not always the main objective in multinational banking. Often it is the desire to establish a name which is responsible for the tendency of some major banks to countenance expansion at the expense of profitability. Mere presence in all major markets may be essential to a bank's name and image in its existing markets.[55]

Since Japanese banks acquired increasing proportions of international banking assets in the 1980s with low margins, this clearly signals their preference for market share over profitability.[56] Market share has also been the driving force of Japanese banks in

---

[54]Though, it can not be said categorically that international banking business is less profitable than domestic banking, it is generally believed that, because of acute competition and related low margins, gross profit rates are lower in international business than in the domestic sphere. See Iwami (1989) p. 105; Glüder (1988) p. 84; Krüger (1989) p. 319.

[55]Coulbeck (1984) p. 133.

[56]Danton (1992) p. 292.

the Euromarkets.[57] Except for the BOT, which has had higher international commitments, most city banks increased the share of overseas assets in total assets almost threefold, from an average of 12 percent in 1977[58] to 35 percent in 1992. Taking the average profitability rate of domestic business at 1.4 percent and that of international business at 0.68 percent for all the city banks for the year ending March 1991,[59] an extension of the previous argument is that high earning domestic assets have subsidized the international banking business of Japanese banks. Thus, with the exception of the BOT, the overseas affiliates of most of the banks actually represent a net drain on parent banks' consolidated profits.[60] Because of the non-availability of data, it is difficult to prove the hypothesis that return on the international assets of Japanese banks has reduced the variance of their total returns, which is often given as a reason for the diversification of business. Table 4.8 below provides time series data on the share of international banking profits[61] in the total profits of city and long-term credit banks for the six year period from April 1984 to March 1990.

Despite the aggressive moves of Japanese banks in the latter half of 1980s, their share of international banking profits has revolved around 20 percent of total profits. Compared to some of the MNBs from the U.S., Germany and U.K., which obtain between one-third and one-half of their profits from international business, the Japanese banks have yet to match this trend. The decomposition of international business profits of city banks shows that foreign exchange business has been the most profitable component of international banking business, the share of which in the international profits increased from 13 percent at the end of March 1984 to 52 percent at the end of March 1990. The share of interest income declined considerably from 70 percent to 28

---

[57]Iwami (1989) p. 105.

[58]Fujita and Ishigaki (1986) p. 215.

[59]Based on the data published in Kinyu Zaisei Jijo (in Japanese).

[60]Hanley et al. (1988a) p. 3.

[61]The published figures of Japanese banks' international earnings mostly comprise: (i) earnings from the loan portfolio of overseas branches, (ii) earnings on overseas loans of domestic branches, (iii) domestic foreign exchange commissions, (iv) foreign money market and foreign exchange dealing profits, and (v) fee income. Table 4.8 aggregates income from all foreign exchange business in Column B(I), all interest income in Column B(II) and all fee/commission income in Column B(III).

Table 4.8 : Japanese Banks' Income from International Banking Business

(Yen in 100 Million)

Fiscal Year	Total profits (A)	International banking profits (B)	Profits from foreign exchange business B(I)	Interest income B(II)	Commission and fee income B(III)	Capital gains from securities	(B)/(A) [in %]
All City Banks							
1984	31,208	6,325	813	4,413	1,100	..	20.27
1985	31,972	6,488	1,729	3,750	1,009	..	20.29
1986	38,374	7,327	2,129	4,224	973	..	19.09
1987	42,910	7,963	2,862	4,194	908	..	18.56
1988	45,939	8,916	2,863	4,028	2,024	..	19.41
1989	42,602	8,898	4,665	2,466	2,195	-429	20.89
Long-term Credit Banks							
1984	3,613	955	74	762	119	..	26.43
1985	4,130	1,041	153	764	124	..	25.21
1986	5,460	1,212	93	1,027	93	..	22.20
1987	5,954	1,645	167	1,332	146	..	27.63
1988	6,887	1,436	227	954	255	..	20.85
1989	5,301	1,049	358	514	275	-97	19.79

Notes: 1. Fiscal year ends in March of the following year
2. International banking profits before special deduction for bad debts and other reserves

Source: MOF, Annual Report of the Banking Bureau

percent during the same period, conveying the impact of reduced emphasis, narrow margins and strong competition prevalent in traditional commercial banking. Though fee income and commissions gained somewhat in prominence, Japanese banks have yet to make significant headway in the investment banking and securities business. Unlike city banks, long-term credit banks display a different composition in their international banking income, with interest income still accounting for the dominant share (50%) and income from foreign exchange business gradually gaining in importance.

How do Japanese banks perform in Europe? Until very recently, virtually no concrete information was available on the regional breakdown of Japanese banks' overseas assets and profitability. Japanese banks do not publish such data.[62] The only case that recently revealed information on the subject was occasioned by Mitsubishi Bank's listing of its shares on the New York Stock Exchange. The continental classification of its assets and profitability submitted by the bank in this connection is reproduced in Table 4.9. The

---

[62]Holloway (1989) p. 55.

Table 4.9: Geographical Distribution of International Assets and Revenue of Japanese Banks
The Case of Mitsubishi Bank

(Yen in Billions)

	Domestic		Foreign								Total	
	Japan	Share in %	North America	Share in %	Europe	Share in %	Asia/ Oceania	Share in %	Other Areas	Share in %	Amount	in %
Year ended March 31, 1988												
Gross Revenue	1,332	58	254	11	312	14	242	11	140	6	2,280	100
Net Income	109	91	14	12	14	12	2	1	-19	-16	120	100
Total Assets	26,978	69	3,631	9	4,458	11	3,450	9	669	2	39,186	100
Year ended March 31, 1989												
Gross Revenue	1,562	55	326	12	368	13	310	11	260	9	2,826	100
Net Income	167	92	10	6	10	6	2	1	-9	-5	180	100
Total Assets	31,819	68	4,633	10	5,289	12	4,307	9	562	1	46,610	100
Year ended March 31, 1991												
Gross Revenue	2,720	62	478	11	610	14	386	9	148	4	4,342	100
Net Income	107	105	5	5	5	5	8	8	-23	-23	102	100
Total Assets	37,717	70	5,055	9	5,761	11	4,586	9	540	1	53,659	100
Year ended March 31, 1993												
Gross Revenue	1,897	66	374	13	294	10	266	9	23	1	2,854	99
Net Income	59	106	-10	-18	3	5	11	19	-7	-12	56	100
Total Assets	37,987	76	3,675	7	4,345	9	3,353	7	265	1	49,625	100
Year ended March 31, 1994												
Gross Revenue	1,665	73	268	12	187	8	169	7	4	0	2,293	100
Net Income	27	69	4	10	2	5	5	13	1	2	38	100
Total Assets	37,131	79	3,641	8	3,886	8	2,042	4	399	1	47,099	100

Source: Hanley et al. (1989); Mitsubishi Bank, Annual Reports.

Mitsubishi Bank, being a significant player in European markets, provides a typical example of a city bank's international commitment and performance. The table brings to light the fact that Europe accounted for about 11 percent of the bank's total assets and earned about 14 percent of total gross revenue between 1988-1991.[63] This should not be understood as the higher earning capacity of assets booked in Europe but rather as the importance of assetless banking business, such as foreign exchange and other fee earning business. The scant contribution of Europe to the total net income of the bank (6%) between 1989-94 implies substantial operating costs as well as low margins in international financial markets.

Since the beginning of 1990, Japanese banks have shown tendencies to pull back from their asset-growth based strategy and this has been coupled with new emphasis on profitability, better loan pricing and cost reduction. The latest indication of growing emphasis on return on assets by the Japanese banks is likely to create a new era of Japanese banks' overseas presence and will cast the shape of international banking in the 1990s.

4.5   Japanese Banks and the Challenge of an Integrated European Banking Market after 1992

The creation of the European financial area[64], as envisaged by the European Commission, and the crucial groundwork by the European financial institutions with a view to achieving their goals in the post-1992 era have been two seminal events of European finance since 1985. The ensuing reorganization of the European financial services sector poses a unique challenge to MNBs from all the industrial countries of the world.

---

[63]According to its annual report, the Sumitomo Bank earned about 15 percent of its consolidated revenues from Europe between 1989-93. One source reported that the Fuji Bank derived 12 percent of its revenue in the year to March 1988 from Europe. It earned 14 percent from America, 7 percent Australia and Asia and the rest (67%) from domestic markets. See Holloway (1989) p. 58.

[64]The financial services sector is of growing importance to the European economy in terms of output produced (6.5 percent of total value-added) and in terms of employment (3 percent of total employment). See Emerson et al. (1990) p. 98.

Amongst the non-EU banks, the Japanese and the U.S. banks are particularly affected by these dramatic changes because of their strong presence in Europe.

4.5.1 Program and Philosophy of a Unified Banking Market in Europe

The legal framework of the EU seeks to achieve a unified financial market as a policy objective. Of all the financial services, in banking unanimity has already been reached. The leading measure adopted to secure this unison is the Second Banking Directive, which was adopted in December 1989 and came into force on January 1, 1993. It is based on three basic concepts:

-   a single community-wide passport enabling banks licensed in one Member State to open branches and provide conventional banking services in other member states;

-   permission for banks to provide a broad range of financial services, including dealing in shares and debentures, advising on takeovers, portfolio management and custodian services; and

-   harmonization of basic supervisory standards.

Related to the freedom of banks to provide services throughout the EU are:

(i)   the Own Funds Directive (adopted in April 1989) which defines capital for credit institutions;

(ii)   the Solvency Ratio Directive (adopted in December 1989) which specifies risk adjusted capital ratios[65]; and

(iii)   the Directive for the supervision of credit institutions on a consolidated basis (adopted in April 1992).

These directives set down minimum prudential standards and, together with the Second Banking Directive, provide the full regulatory framework for banks in the EU. The whole system, however, is being built on three principles, viz. home country control, mutual recognition and minimum harmonization.

For the non-EU banks in the EU, the Second Banking Directive stipulates that their subsidiaries, but not their branches, will be treated as EU enterprises and have the

---

[65]While BIS capital adequacy rules have the character of guidelines, a similar version of capital adequacy requirements is mandatory on European banks through the Own Funds and the Solvency Ratio Directives of the EU.

benefit of all rights and freedoms, including the right of extensive operations throughout the EU. After 1992, the authorization of a non-EU bank by any Member State as a subsidiary would mean simultaneous authorization for all the 12 national banking markets.

The original draft of the Second Banking Directive had caused considerable anxiety among non-EU countries. Its proposed reciprocity clause was interpreted as empowering the Commission to suspend the authorization of foreign subsidiaries or the acquisition of participation in EU banks unless the Commission was satisfied that banks from the EU enjoyed "reciprocal treatment" in the non-Member States. At that time, reciprocity appeared to mean equivalent treatment (i.e. treatment *equivalent* to that which foreign banks would have received in the EU). Fears of the restriction of access to EU markets were particularly rife in the United States and Japan. Now the main criterion is "national treatment", i.e. no discrimination in the non-Member State between domestic and foreign institutions. The term *national treatment* should be seen as an improvement over *reciprocal treatment* and should mean treatment which is *identical* to that received by domestic institutions. Where such treatment is not found to be present, sanctions can only be decided by the Council of Ministers. These sanctions could take the form of suspending authorization decisions for up to three months, with the possibility of renewal. When "national treatment" is found to hold, but the non-Member state is nevertheless considered not to provide "effective market access" comparable with that granted by the Union to non-EU institutions, the Commission can seek a mandate from the Council to commence negotiations to remedy the situation but no sanctions can be applied. It is important to note that the above-mentioned provisions do not apply retroactively and shall not be invoked against financial institutions already established in the EU.

The philosophy of a unified banking market. The project of integrating European financial markets has been perceived as an economically necessary and welfare-improving measure.[66] Among the several types of economic gains to be expected from the proposed integration, the one which is most amenable to quantitative illustration is the reduction in costs of intermediation by banks. The efforts of the EU in quantifying the gains are reflected in the research on the "Cost of Non-Europe" in financial services carried out by Price Waterhouse. The study reports an indicative price reduction of

---

[66]Grilli (1989) p. 313.

between 5-15 percent (midpoint 10%) for 8 countries through the completion of the internal markets in financial services. This amounts to estimated gains in consumer surplus of between 11 billion and 33 billion Ecu (midpoint 21 billion Ecu) and represents 0.3 percent to 1 percent (mid-point 0.7%) of the EU's gross domestic product in 1985.[67] Of the individual Member States, Spain can be expected to experience the largest price fall; in the intermediate category lie Italy, France, Belgium and Germany; the lowest price fall would be expected in Luxembourg, the United Kingdom and the Netherlands.[68]

In theory, the economic gains of integration can come either from increased competition or from economies of scale and scope in the provision of services. In the Cecchini Report, there is no clear indication as to the real sources of economic gains. While the primary logic behind the single market for the manufacturing sector is that increased efficiency can be achieved from scale economies, there is evidence that the economic gains through financial integration arise overwhelmingly from increased competition among financial institutions and not so much from economies of scale and scope.[69] The evidence from the majority of research does not seem to support the view that large banks are necessarily more efficient in cost terms.[70] Thus, if economic gains come from increased competition, the presence of foreign banks in the EU should increase competition for financial services and, thereby, contribute to increased economic gains.

4.5.2 Groundwork by European Banks Towards the Unified Banking Market

The attitude of European banks towards the unified banking market in the EU is reflected in their emphasis on two particular aspects: *Marketing and Cooperation*. European banks view marketing, including product development and market segmenta-

---

[67]Price Waterhouse (1988) Section 6 and p. 166.

[68]Emerson et al. (1990) p. 106.

[69]Shigehara (1991) p. 88 and 95.

[70]Dietrich (1990) found that there is no evidence of economies of scale in the banking operations of representative banks from all EU countries and Austria, Finland and Sweden. Clark (1988) suggested that economies of scale in financial services flatten out at size levels well below some of the larger international competitors that exist today [Quoted in Walter (1990) p. 69)] One research puts the minimum efficient scale at US$25 billion in total assets. [Benston et al. (1982)]

tion, as the most important planning issue.[71] The focus on marketing strategy conveys a transition from a seller's to a buyer's market and places greater emphasis on the selling concept. Product innovation and niche strategy are being given maximum attention in this phase of change. It is interesting to notice that, whereas many bankers expect to exploit opportunities in retail and large domestic corporate segments of the market, they do not expect competitive activity in these segments. Conversely, major competitive threats are expected in those market segments, which are felt to be relatively uninteresting to one's own bank.[72] Therefore, it is very likely that, in the home markets, the focus would be more on traditional market segments, such as mass retailing and large corporate clients and, in the foreign markets, on multinational corporations, upscale and high net worth individuals and non-traditional market segments.

The ground work by European banks is most visible in the changing structure of European banking. In the EU countries, the number of mergers and acquisitions involving financial firms has increased considerably. Thus, within the EU, between July 1984 and June 1990, there were 804 cases of joint ventures, cooperation and equity participation by banks.[73] Out of these, 598 cases occurred within the short period between July 1987 and June 1988. Of all the cases, 53 percent were within the home country of Member States, 23 percent within the EU and 23 percent were international.[74] This conveys that 1992 induced strategic transactions are taking place at all levels. Most of these alliances (60 percent) were primarily for the banking business and, within alliances for non-banking purposes (40%), the securities business proved the most attractive.[75]

Taking the case of the 50 largest European banks on the basis of capital (in which there were 10 French, 9 German, 8 Italian and 7 British banks), there were 115 cases of alliances between 1983-1990, with banks from France being the most active

---

[71]Arthur Andersen (1986) p. 59 quoted in Gardner and Molyneux (1990) p. 208.

[72]Middleton (1990) p. 24.

[73]The proportion of such transactions to all mergers and acquisitions activities rose from 14% in 1985/86 to 25% in 1989/90 See OECD (1992b).

[74]ibid.

[75]Fassbender and Leichtfuss (1990) p. 249.

purchasers group and banks from France and the UK being the most targeted group.[76] The conduct of banks differed markedly in making such alliances. The top ten banks had varying methods of planning their European strategy, e.g. Deutsche Bank appeared to be avoiding joint ventures in favor of obtaining majority shareholding and setting up new businesses from scratch. It is interesting to note that most of the cases of joint ventures and cooperation were in the category of the next 40 banks. Evidently, whereas there are signs of consolidation of strength at the top, the rest of the banks are reorganizing themselves to tighten their grip on the home market. The intent is to protect what is likely to be lost rather than what can be gained from integration.

Gardener and Molyneux find five distinct types of strategy that have emerged in the recent merger and amalgamation activity in European banking:

    (i)   alliances (non-predator minority interests);

    (ii)   strategic minority interests;

    (iii)   cross-border acquisition;

    (iv)   national merger and acquisition; and

    (v)   cross-border mergers to create supranational groups.[77]

The first two types of strategies hint at cooperation and, coupled with national merger and acquisitions, they denote a tightening of the grip on the home markets. The (iii) and (v) options imply increasing business coverage and consolidation of power.

4.5.3 The Attitude of Japanese Banks Towards 1992 and After

The overall Japanese approach towards European integration has been one of pushing into Europe. This is evidenced by the influx of Japanese companies and considerable increases in Japanese FDI to Europe. Thus, the total number of Japanese manufacturing companies in Europe increased from 117 companies in 1983 to 721 at the end of January 1992, most of which are concentrated in the UK, France, Germany and Spain.[78] Between 1985 and 1991, the stock of Japanese FDI to Europe has increased seven fold, the majority of which have been in banking, insurance, real estate and services. Unlike Japanese manufacturing companies, which are setting production facilities in Europe for

---

[76]ibid.

[77]Gardner and Molyneux (1990) p. 213.

[78]JETRO (1992).

alleviating trade friction, a sudden increase in the number of banking subsidiaries (Table 4.5) in Europe after the mid-1980s is partly a response to apprehensions of market barriers likely to be created by the proposed market integration.[79] This is more so because the benefits likely to accrue to non-EU banks from a large unified market are still grossly unclear. There is only a general attraction of the dynamics of a $5 trillion EU economy with its new financial needs.[80]

Although the arrival of increasing numbers of Japanese corporate clients provides Japanese banks with a comparative advantage in their core business, it is unlikely to prove a growth area in the long-run. Japanese banks will have to look for new market segments to survive. Their efforts at harnessing non-Japanese clients and non-Japanese business opportunities is reflected in increased lending to medium-sized local companies and project financing. So far, Japanese banks have increased their presence in Europe mostly through branches and wholly-owned subsidiaries. Other than two acquisitions in Europe (refer to Section 4.3.2) they have not opted for predator-style acquisition of banks. This cautious attitude may be aimed at avoiding political opposition in Europe. The cases of cooperative alliances between Japanese and EU banks are also few and far between and tend to focus on investment banking and innovative market segments.

4.6   Summary and Conclusions

The evolution of Japanese banks as multinationals is reflected in their growing network of overseas offices. In terms of industrial organization, this could be interpreted as the internalization of market activities. In Europe, the Japanese banking presence gathered fresh momentum in the 1980s and Europe now has more Japanese banking subsidiaries than Asia or North America. However, the heavy concentration of offices in the U.K., Germany and France hints at their limited geographical diversification within Europe. The stimulus for Japanese banks' arrival in Europe varies widely between different countries. One has to distinguish categorically between the motives of participating in international financial markets and following domestic clients abroad as opposed to the desire to take part in the domestic banking market overseas.

---

[79]As explained in Chapter 7, a part of the increase in direct investment in finance is attributable to the appreciation of yen.

[80]Yoshizawa (1991) p. 4.

In choosing the form of organization, Japanese banks initially relied on branches and, later, more on subsidiaries. Though established for the purpose of engaging in securities-related business, subsidiaries are also intended as local institutions for Union-wide operation in the integrated banking markets of Europe. In Europe, except for two cases of majority stakes in local banks, Japanese banks have not so far resorted to any outright predator-style acquisition. Instead they have minority stakes in various financial institutions.

Japanese banks' arrival into Europe was initially influenced by the Japanese FDI to Europe. Their expansion, however, has been guided by the desire to participate in international financial markets and to serve as funding conduits for their head offices. The currency structure of Japan's foreign trade, the autonomous outflow of long-term capital in foreign securities and the dramatic increase in impact loans at home forced Japanese banks to function as funding vehicles for their head offices and to satisfy the huge demand for foreign currency funds. The dominant customers to which Japanese banks have lent money were their own offices. Whereas most of the funding came in the form of borrowing from American banks in the 1960s and 1970s, because of improved rating and familiarity with the international markets, in the 1980s Japanese banks raised their funds in the international interbank markets in the form of deposits, and Euro CDs.

The operational strategy of Japanese banks throughout the 1980s was one of emphasis on market share. However, the policy of doing business at low margins is not entirely Japanese; the Japanese differ only in their willingness to keep offering services at a low rate in order to keep growing. The latest strategy of Japanese banks is to focus more on the return on assets. The limited evidence on profitability indicates that Japanese banks have subsidized their international banking business from high earnings at home. The low-earning international assets contribute only about one-fifth of the total profits, where foreign exchange business contributes the maximum. Based on the case of the Mitsubishi Bank, it can be said that Europe's contribution to the net income of Japanese banks is slightly better than that of North America.

The creation of the unified banking market in Europe after 1992 and the structural changes are going to influence Japanese banks as well. They have to postulate new strategies for the 1990s to evaluate their capabilities with reference to the behavior of host country banks in terms of product development and differentiation, market segments and customer relations.

Chapter 5

Japanese Securities Companies in Europe

Banks and securities firms differ substantially from one other in the way they obtain their funds and the types of services they provide. Some basic differences between the two are given here which justify separating the discussion about Japanese banks from that about Japanese securities companies. The internationalization of Japanese securities firms is analyzed separately because:

(i)   Securities firms traditionally act as principals for temporary periods only and their assets turn over extremely quickly. This differs from commercial banks which hold most of their loans until maturity, therefore, making asset turnover relatively slow.

(ii)   Securities firms and banks adjust to internal and external changes over very different time horizons. Securities firms have very short time horizons: trading is hour by hour, arbitrage spans several days, and underwriting spans days or weeks. These firms can adjust their risk profile quickly. By contrast, commercial banks' risk profile generally changes much more slowly.[1]

(iii) Securities firms are evaluated on a liquidation basis and their accounting is marked-to-market. Commercial banks are evaluated as going concerns and their accounting is based on original cost.[2]

(iv)   The securities firms are mostly faced with market risks whereas banks are exposed to credit risks as well.

(v)   The fundamental differences in the balance sheet composition of banks and securities firms make most performance comparisons between these two groups difficult and misleading.[3] Conventional asset-based measures, used for measuring a bank's performance, are not consistently reliable indicators of a securities firm's performance.

---

[1]Haberman (1987) p. 2.

[2]ibid. p. 3.

[3]Spindler et al.(1991) p. 191.

This chapter covers those Japanese securities companies which are major international players in terms of their network of offices. Thus, of 41 securities companies that have overseas offices, the top four account for about half of all the offices established abroad.[4] As of the end of March 1992, the top four Japanese securities companies had 62 subsidiaries, 26 branches of the subsidiaries and 38 representative offices in foreign countries. The next ten securities companies account for another 30 percent of total overseas offices. Evidently, as mentioned in Section 2.1.1, the oligopolistic character of the domestic securities market mirrors itself in the internationalization process, too.

5.1   Multinationalization of Securities Firms

Unlike commercial banks, securities firms did not internationalize their operations before 1960. The problems of communication and the lack of timely information prevented cross-border issues of, and trade in, securities from becoming a regular and profitable business. The national capital markets were very segmented before 1960 and domestic clients provided the only source of business for securities firms. However, the first group of securities firms to engage in cross-border selling were the U.S. investment banks and their history provides the earliest account of multinationalization in the securities industry.

5.1.1 A Brief History of U.S. Securities Firms Overseas

Before, 1960, most U.S. securities firms (often referred to as investment banks) relied heavily on commission splitting with foreign agents as a method of selling U.S. equity abroad, an arrangement which was similar in nature to the correspondent banking relationship in commercial banking.[5] However, the method was slow and did not provide good quality service for investors. This led to the setting up of overseas sales offices by U.S. securities firms in the early 1960s.[6] The internationalization of U.S. securities firms as underwriters starts with the emergence of the Eurobond market in London in 1963. Many U.S. securities firms moved there to service the needs of those non-U.S.

---

[4]Information obtained from the MOF.

[5]Scott-Quinn (1990a) p. 276-77.

[6]ibid. p. 278.

corporate clients who, because of U.S. government controls on foreigners, could not use the foreign dollar bond market in New York.[7] Later, in 1968, new controls on fund raising by U.S. multinational corporations who wished to invest overseas[8] forced them to raise funds outside the United States. This provided fresh impetus to the international business of U.S. securities firms.

However, the year 1980 should be seen as the start of a new and more conspicuous period of globalization and integration in investment banking.[9] The institutionalization of savings and increasing demand for international portfolios by institutional investors made the securities business more price and quality conscious. Volatility in financial asset prices made immediacy even more important both for borrowers and investors.[10] To provide sophisticated professional service, U.S. securities firms made large upstream investment in the Eurobond market in global distribution. In U.S. Treasury bonds, they made downstream investment in market making in London and Tokyo.[11] Morgan Stanley, Goldman Sachs, First Boston, Salomon Brothers rest of the major U.S. securities firms have all sought to build up a very substantial "three-legged stool" doing 24-hour trading around the globe.

5.1.2 The Internationalization of Japanese Securities Companies

Japanese securities companies began establishing their overseas presence in 1953, when one of the Big Four established its first foreign office in New York.[12] Initially, Japanese securities companies set up representative offices and conducted activities mainly designed to provide information to local investors about the Japanese economy and stocks and to collect information about the host country.[13] As investment in Japanese securities by foreign investors became a permanent commitment, these offices were

---

[7]Interest Equalization Tax (IET) had raised the cost of funds for foreign borrowers.

[8]The prominent control here was in the form of Foreign Direct Investment Rules.

[9]Scott-Quinn (1990a) p. 269.

[10]ibid. p. 283.

[11]ibid. p. 276.

[12]Viner (1987) p. 17.

[13]Nikko Research Center (1988) p. 182.

promoted to the status of overseas affiliated firms for the purpose of marketing Japanese stocks.[14] Thus, in the 1960s, Japanese securities companies' overseas posts were mainly sales offices promoting Japanese stocks.[15] This was less a response to domestic pressures than a need to increase their sales channels.[16] The first wave of securities companies' overseas expansion took place between 1971 and 1975, when 46 new overseas offices were set up, most of them by the Big Four (see Table 5.1). A second wave of opening overseas offices started in 1980, dominated by the medium-sized 'second-tier' securities companies. The overseas expansion of Japanese securities companies reached dramatic proportions between 1986-90, with a total of 197 offices (97 new subsidiaries and 100 new representative offices) opening within five years. This phase marked the arrival of even smaller 'third-tier' securities companies on the international scene.

Table 5.1: New Overseas Offices of Japanese Securities Companies

Period	Subsidiaries	Rep. Offices	Branches	Total
1960-65	4	0	0	4
1966-70	4	5	4	13
1971-75	18	25	3	46
1976-80	16	16	5	37
1981-85	21	46	..	67
1986-90	97	100	..	197
1991-92	12	18		30
Total as of Dec. 1992	161*	64	..	225*

*Overseas subsidiaries have a total of 30 sub-branches; thus the total number of overseas offices is 273

Source: MOF, Annual Report of the International Finance Bureau (in Japanese)

---

[14]ibid.

[15]The first boom of investments in Japanese securities by foreigners came in 1960-63, which comprised mainly of US individual investors as well as of other investment trusts specializing in Japanese stocks. The second boom came in 1967-69, comprising mainly of European investors.

[16]Prindl (1989) p. 31.

The period 1991-94 showed a phase of rationalization of overseas network of office. This was partly a reaction to unfavorable domestic market conditions and partly a result of restructuring in the wake of the Investment Services Directive.

The primary task of such international networks throughout the 1970s was to facilitate the introduction of foreign capital into the Japanese stock markets.[17] In comparison with foreign investment in Japanese securities, Japanese investors' purchases of foreign securities remained very limited. Thus, whereas foreign buying and selling of Japanese stocks and bonds taken together increased ten fold (from about ¥1,900 billion in 1975 to ¥19,049 billion in 1981), Japanese buying and selling of foreign stocks and bonds remained at low levels (¥3,118 billion in 1981). The emergence of Japanese securities companies as underwriters on the international financial scene began around 1975 with increasing bond issues of Japanese corporations in the Eurobond. Their role in the underwriting of yen-denominated foreign bonds also started picking up around this period. However, their involvement in managing the foreign bonds issues in foreign capital markets - a business usually referred to as "out-out" operations - was not so significant until 1975 and was limited to Asia-dollar bond issues.[18]

However, the enactment of the new Foreign Exchange Law in 1980 boosted the overseas operations of Japanese securities companies. It was further stimulated by the lifting of various controls on Japanese investments in foreign securities. In recent years, Japanese securities companies have increasingly diversified their activities, extending to underwriting Japanese issues in overseas markets and foreign issues in the Japanese markets; brokerage business of executing Japanese orders for foreign securities; dealing in Eurobonds; and various investment banking activities, such as mergers and acquisitions, corporate advisory services, offering derivative products etc. The determined efforts with which Japanese securities companies have extended and expanded their operations in Europe, and the areas in which they have developed expertise is the subject of their present position in the 1980s and is discussed in detail in the following pages.

---

[17]Stocks were the main instrument of foreign investments, with Japanese bonds becoming increasingly popular. See Tazaki (1983) p. 17.

[18]ibid. p. 20.

5.2 Organizational Characteristics of Japanese Securities Companies in Europe

In international banking, Europe and the United States have been equally attractive for foreign banks. However, for the international securities business, Europe has been a favored spot for foreign securities firms, it being the center of the Euromarkets and the hub of international securities business.[19] Like U.S. securities firms, Japanese securities companies also see their presence in Europe as the focal point of their international strategy. This is evidenced by the number of subsidiaries that Japanese securities companies have opened in Europe (Figure 5.1).

Figure 5.1: Overseas Subsidiaries of Japanese Securities Companies (End 1992)

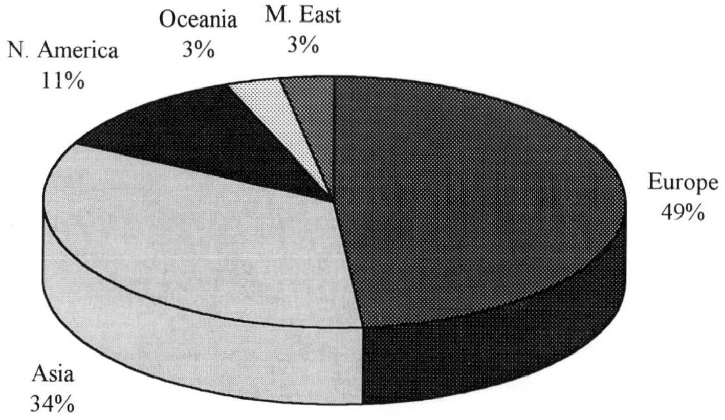

Source: MOF, International Finance Bureau

Of all the affiliates of Japanese securities companies with a stake of 50% or above, more than half were established in Europe. If the number of representative offices opened by them in Europe is added to this, the importance of Europe becomes striking. Thus, Japanese securities companies had a total of 107 offices in Europe at the end of 1992, comprising of 78 subsidiaries, 12 sub-branches of subsidiaries and 17 representa-

---

[19]The foreign sector's equity turnover accounted for 44% of the total equity turnover on the London Stock Exchange in 1991. See Patel (1992) p. 48.

tive offices). The optimism concerning future prospects in Europe manifested itself in the arrival of new and smaller securities companies until early 1991. Since then, the deteriorating conditions in the domestic stock markets have put a check on their overseas expansion. About 10 Japanese securities companies closed their representative offices in Europe between early-1991 and mid-1992 and more are scheduled to do the same in the future.[20]

Despite signs of over-capacity and declining margins in the Eurobonds market, Japanese securities companies' continuing emphasis on Europe suggests that borrowers and investors, particularly the Japanese, still place more emphasis on the nationality of the intermediary than on the brand name. Thus, nationality is still a strong factor in the Eurobond market.[21]

5.2.1 Geographical Spread of Offices within Europe

Table 5.2 provides information about the geographical spread of offices opened by Japanese securities companies within Europe. This classification illustrates two distinct facts:

Firstly, most of the Japanese securities companies in Europe are either in the United Kingdom or in Switzerland. Of the 32 securities companies in Europe, all have at least one subsidiary in London and 19 have subsidiaries in Switzerland. Apart from the importance of London as an international financial center, the geographical concentration of offices in the United Kingdom and Switzerland is strongly correlated with the Eurodollar and Swiss franc[22] as the most popular currency denominations among Japanese corporate bond issuers. With the exception of 1978, more than 75 percent of all external issues of Japanese corporate bonds throughout were either Eurodollar or Swiss franc-based issues, with the Eurodollar issues gaining and the Swiss franc issues declining in importance. A review of the growth of overseas offices in Table 5.2 shows increasing emphasis on the securities markets in the United Kingdom and Switzerland.

---

[20]Information obtained from the MOF.

[21]Balder et al. (1991) p. 27 and 32.

[22]Widmer (1989) provides five reasons for the attractiveness of the Swiss franc market: (i) the traditionally low nominal interest rates; (ii) very strong distribution power of the Swiss banks; (iii) a broader array of instruments available to issuers; (iv) strong demand for Swiss franc denominated fixed-rate instruments; and (v) the relatively low procedural burden.

**Table 5.2: Geographical Spread of Japanese Securities Companies' Offices
in Europe**

Countries	end-Dec. 1978		end-Dec. 1985		end-Dec. 1992	
	Subsi-diaries	Rep. Offices	Subsi-diaries	Rep. Offices	Subsi-diaries	Rep. Offices
Austria	..	..	..	..	..	2
Belgium	..	..	..	2	2	..
Denmark	..	..	..	1	..	1
France	..	5	2	6	4	5
Germany	4	2	4	2	5(1)	7
Ireland	..	..	..	..	0(1)	..
Italy	..	..	..	..	4	1
Luxembourg	2	..	1	..	2	..
Netherlands	3	..	3	..	4	..
Spain	..	..	..	..	3	1
Switzerland	4	..	10	3	19(10)	..
United Kingdom	4	3	14	3	35	..
Europe Total (A)	17	10	34	17	78(12)	17
World Total (B)	34	18	62	55	161(30)	64
Europe´s share (A/B) in %	50.0	55.6	54.8	30.9	8.5(40.0	26.6

Figures in parenthesis indicate the sub-branches of subsidiaries

Source: MOF, Annual Report of the International Finance Bureau (in Japanese)

Secondly, the Big Four Japanese securities companies are far more diversified than all other Japanese securities companies making them the most robust of all the Japanese financial institutions. They have wholly owned subsidiaries in all major European countries and are continuously expanding their coverage. Their moves, especially those of Nomura's, provide hints about the future strategic course of other securities companies. Over and above their presence in the United Kingdom and Switzerland, there are two more European countries where the Big Four Japanese securities companies made a simultaneous entry around 1973, i.e. Germany and the Netherlands. In the rest of western Europe, their interest is of recent origin starting from the late 1970s to the early 1980s. Thus, in France, Nomura opened its subsidiary in 1980 and the other three followed suit; Yamaichi in 1985, Nikko and Daiwa in 1987. Italy and Spain became attractive for the Japanese in the late 1980s, with the prospects of growing capital markets and strong currencies. Luxembourg, despite being the place where maximum Japanese foreign securities investment is undertaken,[23] has not attracted many securities companies; only Nomura (since February 1990) and Nikko (since March 1974) are represented there. Presumably, most of the business in Luxembourg is carried out through the London office of the securities companies.

Since 1991, Japanese securities companies have been restructuring their network of offices, Whereas some second-tier companies closed their offices, the Big-Four are centralizing their European operations in London. The restructuring has resulted in an increased focus on core business such as fixed income and equity markets and staff cutting.

5.2.2 Organizational Forms of Presence

Other than the representative offices, practically all functional units of Japanese securities companies are in the form of subsidiaries. While no specific reason can be given for their over-dependence on the subsidiary form of organization, it is believed that the phenomenon is more pronounced because of regulatory requirements and tax systems in the host countries. Further, establishing subsidiaries provides securities companies with a legal status equal to that of local institutions and has its own advantages. In some European financial markets, establishing subsidiaries under the local law is a precondition for participating in certain segments of the market, e.g., in Germany, for lead managing or participating in government bond syndicates. Japanese securities companies have no branches in Europe. Instead of opening branches in overseas markets,[24] a convention common with international banks, they have opened branches of their subsidiaries. The practice of opening branches of foreign subsidiaries was initially adopted in the United States and was later extended to Europe; it is most conspicuous in Switzerland. The branches of subsidiaries could be a likely form of expansion for them in the post-1992 era, when Europe-wide operations will be permitted by the Investment Services Directive.

---

[23]In 1989, 42 percent of total Japanese foreign securities investment, mostly in Euroyen bonds, was made in Luxembourg. See Yamasaki (1990) p. 5.

[24]Japanese securities companies initially (before 1975) opened branches in overseas markets which were later converted to subsidiaries.

Except for the Luxembourg subsidiaries of Nomura and Nikko[25], all the European subsidiaries of Japanese securities companies are wholly-owned. This shows the value attached by the Japanese to the undivided control of their business and the strategy of internalization of foreign operations within the large organizational structure. The cases of strategic alliances in Europe are few and most of them represent minority stakes in countries or business areas which are not fully covered by them so far. The Big Four differ with regard to their policy of strategic alliances overseas. Nomura takes the joint venture route for the purpose of getting established in certain market segments. Nikko has the strategy of developing its own teams, with no joint venture or cooperation with any European institution so far. Daiwa and Yamaichi are adopting the mixed policy of cooperation and internal team building for specialized activities.

5.2.3 Personnel for European Operations

A significant feature of the overseas presence of Japanese securities companies is the high ratio of non-Japanese personnel in their European staff. To take one example, the London affiliates of all the Japanese securities companies had a total of 1612 employees in August 1985 of which 76 percent were non-Japanese.[26] Two years later, this ratio was even higher with 81 percent of non-Japanese staff.[27] Understandably, most of the local staff have been hired for the trading rooms of the overseas offices. The high local content in middle level managerial positions helps Japanese securities companies to overcome many language and cultural barriers and improves their competitive position.

The increasing need for local staff can be supported by another fact also. Earlier trading in Japanese securities was the main job of securities companies, which could be handled by Japanese staff. Now, a good deal of business is related to foreign securities and often conducted with local investors, where familiarity and contacts with the market are important considerations. Recruitment of local staff has been mostly from the

---

[25]10 percent of Nomura Bank (Luxembourg) S.A. is owned by the Nomura Bank International PLC and 12.5 percent of Nikko (Luxembourg) S.A. is owned by Nikko Securities Co., (Deutschland) GmbH.

[26]Nikko Research Center (1988) p. 184.

[27]Though precise figures are not available about non-Japanese staff at the overseas offices of Japanese banks, it is believed that the ratio is lower in banks than in securities companies.

prestigious English universities but in some cases, experts from other institutions were also poached by means of lucrative offers of position and pay.

5.3 Activities, Strategies and Performance in Europe

5.3.1 Nature of Operations

The basic operations performed by a securities firm involve (i) assisting buyers and sellers of securities as broker and dealer; and (ii) raising capital for issuers of securities. The role of securities firms as investment bankers has also increased their involvement in various corporate finance-related activities, such as mergers and acquisitions, venture capital financing, leasing, factoring and portfolio management. This diversification of activities by investment bankers is indicative of attempts made by them to smooth out the income variability inherent in the business of investment banking.[28] In the following, the discussion about the activities of Japanese securities companies is focused on their role as broker-dealers and underwriters. This is because their globalization has been hastened, in the first instance, through these activities.[29] A brief reference has also been made to their emerging role as international bankers.

Japanese securities companies as broker-dealers. The need for the international diversification of portfolios by investors provides cross-border business to securities firms. In terms of the two-by-two matrix in Figure 5.2, selling domestic securities to foreigners (B in the figure) and foreign securities to domestic clients (C in the figure) are the initial and most convenient forms of entry into the cross-border securities business.[30] Indeed, foreign investors' demand for Japanese securities provided the bulk of business to the international departments and outposts of Japanese securities companies in the 1960s and early 1970s. Table 5.3 confirms the increasing amount of foreign investment in Japanese securities.

Japan's new Foreign Exchange Law (1980), which liberalized in principle all cross-border transactions, released pent-up Japanese demand for foreign securities (C in the Figure) and thus provided new business for securities companies. Assuming that Japa-

---

[28]Gardner and Mills (1988) p. 114.

[29]Yukihara (1991) p. 476.

[30]The observation is justified from the experience of U.S. investment banks in Europe. For details, see Scott-Quinn (1990a).

**Figure 5.2: A Multinational Securities Firm in Broker-Dealer Business -
Product-Client Relationship Matrix**

		Type of Securities	
		Domestic	Foreign
Type of Client	Domestic	A	C
	Foreign	B	D

A	=	Domestic securities business
B + C	=	Cross-border securities business
D	=	Foreign securities business (Out-out business)

nese securities companies have an advantageous position in Japan-related cross-border securities business,[31] it could be said that they were involved in increasing amounts of overseas business after 1980. The most dramatic increase in cross-border business for Japanese securities companies after 1984 came from the purchase of foreign bonds by Japanese investors; total trade in external bonds (sum of buying and selling) by Japanese investors increased more than twenty-fold between 1984 and 1989 (see Table 5.3). When Japanese brokers started selling foreign securities to domestic investors, proximity to the rapidly changing market and sources of information became important, justifying expansion of their overseas presence. Their acquisition of membership of various stock exchanges in Europe supports this hypothesis.

The second part of Table 5.3 shows foreign investors' involvement in the trade of Japanese stocks and bonds. The European content of cross-border trade in Japanese securities managed by Japanese securities companies is difficult to assess. The amount of buying and selling activities of European investors on all the Japanese stock exchanges provide some indications on this point. Thus, European investors were the dominant

---

[31]One securities company estimates that, in 1985, Japanese securities companies handled 75 percent of Japanese trading in American treasury bonds, and American brokers only 20-25 percent. See Economist (1986)

Table 5.3: Cross-border Trade in Securities between Japan and the Rest of the World

(Yen in Billion)

Year	Japanese Investment in Foreign Securities		Foreign Investment in Japanese Securities	
	Trade* in Stocks	Trade* in Bonds	Trade* in Stocks	Trade* in bonds
1974	126	143	719	187
75	163	26	1,090	797
76	151	36	1,866	1,311
77	60	222	1,884	2,345
78	58	1,530	2,573	4,744
79	81	5,586	2,399	3,791
80	130	10,257	4,561	5,952
81	351	2,768	9,916	9,133
82	487	6,449	7,620	12,817
83	884	8,226	14,325	18,960
84	722	20,056	18,598	28,737
85	2,482	132,539	19,542	49,238
86	6,929	536,269	37,644	82,672
87	19,261	384,818	54,194	86,824
88	20,418	359,825	43,740	74,982
89	22,909	425,540	55,208	68,360
90	21,480	397,508	38,744	54,040
91	13,075	332,666	32,272	43,709
92	9,262	267,301	23,206	39,986

* Trade figures imply the summation of selling and buying activity

Source: Tokyo Stock Exchange Fact Book

foreign investor group accounting for about half of all the stock trading by foreigners on Japanese stock exchanges between 1987-91.[32] The Japanese securities companies must have been strong contenders for this business because of their intensive research on Japanese stocks. With the acquisition of TSE membership by European securities firms, the concern arose that overseas orders for Japanese stocks would shift from overseas subsidiaries of Japanese securities companies to foreign securities firms. This created the necessity for Japanese securities companies to enhance their investment counselling and operational capabilities aimed at overseas institutional investors.[33] There has been a decline in foreign investors' interest in Japanese bonds and shares since 1990 with its adverse impact on the overseas business of Japanese brokers.

---

[32]Tokyo Stock Exchange (1992b) p. 66.

[33]Nikami (1991) p. 47.

Intermediating in the trade of foreign securities for foreign clients (D in Figure 5.2) is a difficult field for brokers. This is especially difficult when a securities firm wants to operate as a market maker in foreign stocks. A securities firm obtains this kind of business after long years of establishing its name in alien markets. In the mid 1980s Japanese securities companies' embarked on the path of diversification by market-making first in Japanese stocks in London[34] and then in European stocks.[35] As an example, one could cite the case of Nomura which, in July 1990, started market-making in 13 European stocks from Germany, France and the Netherlands in addition to more than 60 U.K. stocks in which it already makes market.[36] This type of new business could be seen as incremental business for existing ventures, where the interaction between products, clients and locations help in building a full service global investment banks.[37]

It is interesting to note that the value of Japanese shares traded in London more than doubled after 1992[38] while the number of foreign purchases in Tokyo has dwindled.[39] Even Japanese investors and companies are discovering the attractiveness of other markets. As long as Japanese financial institutions intermediate in such transactions, these developments, on balance, imply only a shift of business away from Tokyo. However, these events do add to the significance of the overseas network of Japanese securities companies.

Japanese securities companies as underwriters. The underwriting of securities in foreign markets is the other important activity which gained in prominence after 1975 and more so in the 1980s. The overseas offices of a securities firm could be underwriters for their domestic or foreign clients. The issues underwritten could, in turn, be sold to domestic or foreign investors. Of the four possible business areas, Japanese securities

---

[34]As of April 1988, 68 Japanese stock were being traded in London.

[35]Japanese securities companies participate in the 'SEAQ international system' of London Securities Exchange since its inception after the Big Bang.

[36]Nomura started market making in British stocks in September 1987.

[37]Scott-Quinn (1990a) p. 39.

[38]The shift of business from Japan to the other Asian financial centers, like Hong Kong and Singapore, has been of a higher magnitude.

[39]Baker (1994) p. 15.

companies have maximum business in the underwriting of the Eurodollar and Euroyen issues of their Japanese clients most of which are sold to Japanese clients. Notwithstanding the reasons for the popularity of this type of business, one could argue that it has resulted in the hollowing out of the domestic capital market. For Japanese underwriters, this meant additional business and not just a shift of domestic business abroad.[40] Obviously, this has given a push to Japanese securities companies' international business. Table 5.4 provides information about the external financing by Japanese corporations.

Table 5.4 : Direct Financing Activities of Japanese Corporations (1975-92)

(Yen in Billion)

Fiscal Year	Total SB [1]	External SB	Total CB [2]	External CB	Total WB [3]	External WB	Total Paid-in Equity [4]	External Equity	Grand Total*	Total External
1975	1,870	347	510	179	0	0	924	21	3,304	547 [16.6]
1984	1,884	1,134	2,839	1,227	437	434	864	49	6,024	2,844 [47.2]
1985	2,383	1,439	2,534	948	921	866	662	11	6,500	3,264 [50.2]
1986	2,619	1,639	3,953	485	2,097	1,993	633	1	9,302	4,118 [44.3]
1987	1,739	824	6,132	1,077	3,439	3,439	2,123	39	13,433	5,379 [40.0]
1988	1,592	843	8,062	1,067	4,982	4,982	4,581	17	19,217	6,909 [36.0]
1989	1,849	1,120	9,379	1,739	9,185	8,270	7,896	336	28,309	11,465 [40.5]
1990	4,364	2,298	1,425	514	3,020	2,625	664	0	9,473	5,437 [57.4]
1991	6,304	3,877	1,889	610	4,087	3,705	293	1	12,573	8,193 [65.2]
1992	7,931	4,111	815	240	1,650	1,650	NA	NA	10,396	6,001 [57.7]

SB = Straight Bonds; CB = Convertible Bonds; WB = Warrant Bonds
*Grand Total represents the summation of columns [1]+[2]+[3]+[4]
Figures in parenthesis represent the share of external issues in the total

Source: The Bond Underwriters Association of Japan, Bond Review
     Figures for 1975 and 1984 from Senda (1991) p.13.

---

[40]The sizable warrant-related bonds issued by the Japanese corporate sector overseas might not have been possible in the domestic market for various reasons.

The external means of direct financing, which accounted for 17 percent of total direct financing in 1975, increased considerably in the 1980s, accounting for 65 percent of total direct financing in 1991. The sizable increases in funds raised externally by Japanese issuers[41] should be seen as an indicator of the massive business obtained by Japanese securities companies as underwriters. The table also shows the predominance of warrant bonds[42] and straight bonds as the main instruments of fund raising in external financial markets.[43] The activity of Japanese corporations in these segments of the new issue market have helped the take-off of Japanese securities companies' overseas offices.

No accurate information is available to support the hypothesis that foreign issues of Japanese corporations are sold back to Japanese investors. However, from a scrutiny of the following facts, it could be deduced that the European offices of Japanese securities companies provide a meeting point for their domestic clients, both borrowers and investors:

(i)   Cash rich Japanese institutional investors have established offices in Europe in order to search for better investment opportunities.

(ii)   Most of the Eurobonds underwritten by Japanese securities companies are private placements.

Recently, Japanese securities companies have increased their involvement in the underwriting of issues made by foreign borrowers. This, to some extent, belittles the myth that their strength lies only in Japanese business. Although the case of Nomura may not be representative of others, of all the Eurobond issues lead managed by

---

[41]It is widely known that Japanese corporations used a part of the cheap funds raised in the overseas markets for financial investment in higher earning assets, a phenomenon that came to be known as *Zaitech*.

[42]The explanation for this is to be found in the cost of raising capital through overseas warrant bonds which were substantially below the long and short-term prime rates. Thus, as of April 1989, when overseas financing was very popular, the issuing cost of Eurodollar-denominated warrant bonds for Japanese issuers was 0.826% (after swap, yen costs) and 0.504% (yen costs with forward exchange rate contract). This was considerably below the long-term prime rate of 6% and short-term prime rate of 4.25% in Japan as of April 1989. For details, refer to Suzuki and Ishiyama (1991) pp. 45-53.

[43]Despite all the domestic reforms by Japanese authorities to get these market segments back to Japan, still over 60 percent of all straight bonds and 90 percent of warrant bonds (both figures as of November 1991) continue to be issued outside Japan. See Table 5.4 for details.

Nomura in 1989, 61 percent were for Japanese issuers and 29 percent for European issuers, the rest being for supranational bodies, Americans and Asians.[44]

Japanese securities companies as international bankers. The securities firms from those countries where commercial banking is legally separated from investment banking (e.g. Japan and the United States), bring to overseas markets an intense desire to participate in commercial banking. Japanese securities companies started their quest to enter international banking in the early 1980s when they applied to the Bank of England for a banking license. Their primary objective was to provide securities related banking services, including foreign exchange and corporate advisory services. Of all Japanese securities companies, only the Big Four have started banking operations in Europe and do so through their wholly-owned subsidiaries.[45] Nomura claims to have obtained banking licenses in five countries[46] and combines international banking with its main business as a global investment bank. In the City of London, while all of them engage in foreign exchange trading, money market operations and wholesale corporate lending, only Daiwa is involved in a broader spectrum of banking operations, ranging from trade finance, global custody, exposure management to treasury and investment management. The banking activities of Japanese securities companies in the overseas markets should be viewed as preparation for the reforms introduced in Japanese financial system, when all types of financial institutions will be eligible to participate in each other's field through fully-owned subsidiaries.[47]

5.3.2 Business Strategy

As mentioned earlier, in the beginning, the international business strategy of Japanese securities companies was to promote the sale of Japanese stocks in the European markets. This initially suited their main function as brokers very well. Later, around 1975, the regulations in the domestic corporate bond market and liberal Euromarkets stimulated them to bring their clients, both investors and borrowers, to overseas markets.

---

[44]Nomura Securities Co. (1990a) p. 16.

[45]Nomura was the first to receive a banking license from the Bank of England (1986) followed by Daiwa (1987) and Nikko and Yamaichi (both in 1988).

[46]In the United Kingdom, Germany, Switzerland, the Netherlands, and Belgium.

[47]Under the Financial System Reform Law, which came into force in April 1993, the Big-Four established trust banking subsidiaries in the domestic market in April 1994.

Around this time, Japanese securities companies began to assume the strategic role of underwriters for their Japanese clients, a role which later helped them rise to the top positions as Eurobond underwriters. The new Foreign Exchange Law of 1980 induced another phase of strategic expansion; this time to satisfy the pent up demand of Japanese investors for foreign securities.

The growing internationalization of the securities markets and advances in communications technology simultaneously made it both imperative and easy to establish a foreign presence. The favored securities firms were those which operated as integrated global entities. This explains the efforts of the Big Four at becoming 'full-line' investment bankers. However, unlike the Japanese banks, which emphasized market share in the overseas markets, securities companies adopted a determined and shielded strategy; the objective was to defend what they regarded as *their* business. Raising capital for Japanese corporations, selling foreign securities to Japanese investors and Japanese securities to foreigners has always been assumed to be the natural domain of Japanese securities companies.[48] The expansion policy employed by Japanese securities companies in Europe is based on the idea of getting closer to the product they are selling (e.g. Euro-securities), and to the customers (e.g. European investors), who still rate provision of immediacy and quality of service very highly.[49]

The focus of the European strategy has been to develop London as the main base of operations. The policy of making London a regional headquarters signifies the need for autonomy and the speed of decisions in securities business. The organization model chosen by all Japanese securities companies for this purpose has been wholly-owned subsidiaries. The limited cases in which the option of joint venture or cooperation has been exercised reveal the strategy of "growing alone". The hazy ramifications of the 'Unified Europe' after 1992 has further hastened the process of their expansion in Europe (see section 5.4). This has been guided more by the fear of being excluded from a potentially large market than by the present scale of business. The signs of a new European strategy by the Japanese securities companies started emerging when Japanese securities companies - particularly the Big Four - sought banking licenses in the United

---

[48]With the entry of foreign securities brokers on the Tokyo stock exchange in 1986, the dominance of Japanese securities companies in selling Japanese securities to foreigners may be diminishing.

[49]Scott-Quinn (1990a).

Kingdom. Not only did their efforts at internalizing all aspects of securities business become clear but also the desire to diversify across markets and products became apparent. The present trend of financial institutions turning into integrated investment bankers is amply reflected in the importance attached to banking by Japanese securities companies.

The European strategy today represents the core of the Japanese securities companies' international policy. When viewed in terms of regional performance, it has also proved to be the most successful one (see Section 5.3.3 below). Their future strategy is likely to take significant turns when Japan-related business eventually slows down. The search for non-Japanese business areas would thrust upon them new pressures to become more local in the host countries. The downturn of the Japanese stock market and the consequent temporary decline in home-related business has made this issue more urgent now than before.

5.3.3 Profitability of European Operations

It is difficult to view the overseas profitability of Japanese securities companies as a coherent whole because of notable variations in performance on different continents. Thus, the story of their U.S. operations has been a little disappointing, with most of them reporting losses there.[50] This has strengthened their networks in Europe and Asia where they have performed much better. However, of all the overseas operations, European business provides the largest single source of overseas profits, accounting for over two-thirds of the total. The prominence of Japanese borrowers and investors in Euromarkets is the main attribute of their European success. The geographical allocation of assets and revenues of Nomura in Table 5.5 provides a good case for analysis here.

The table shows two stylized facts. *First,* Nomura had almost half its assets in the overseas markets at the end of March 1990 but these assets generate only 20 percent of revenue. This hints at the thin margins and tough competition outside home markets. As in case of Japanese banks, the first stylized fact also supports the contention that domestic business subsidized the overseas expansion of Japanese securities companies. *Second,* though the proportion of assets invested in Europe at the end of March 1990 is more or less the same as the proportion invested in the United States, Europe turned out relatively better results.

---

[50]Holloway (1989) p. 55 and Nomura Securities Co. (1990a) p. 8.

Table 5.5: Geographical Allocation of Nomura's Assets and Revenue

Assets: (Share in %)

	Sept. 30, 1988	March 31, 1989	March 31, 1990	March 31, 1992	March 31, 1993	March 31, 1994
Japan	64.6	67.2	51.9	38.5	35.5	32.3
United States	9.7	10.1	19.3	29.7	34.8	32.8
Europe	15.8	15.3	20.6	27.5	25.7	30.8
Asia & others	9.9	7.4	8.2	4.2	4.1	4.2
Total	100.0	100.0	100.0	100.0	100.0	100.0

Revenue:

	Year ended September 30,		Six months ended 31.3.1989	Year ended 31.3.90	Year ended 31.3.91	Year ended 31.3.92	Year ended 31.3.93	Year ended 31.3.94
	1987	1988						
Japan	88.7	87.8	85.7	80.2	70.0	64.1	61.3	61.0
United States	1.4	2.5	2.2	4.1	6.9	9.2	14.8	16.7
Europe	7.3	7.0	9.3	12.7	19.6	24.0	21.6	19.5
Asia & others	2.6	2.7	2.8	3.1	3.6	2.8	2.3	2.8
Total	100.0	100.0	100.0	100.0	100.0	100.0	100.0	100.0

Source: Nomura Securities Co., Annual Reports

Within Europe, the geographical classification of profits in Table 5.6 brings to light the preponderance of London as the most important source. The Big Four in London increased net profits after tax from 55 percent of their European total at the end of September 1985 to 76 percent at the end of March 1989. Correspondingly, this implies that the share of continental Europe declined from 45 to 24 percent during the same period. In continental Europe, Switzerland occupied the top position contributing 16 percent of the European profits of the Big Four at the end of September 1988. The high share of London and Switzerland is explained by the Japanese boom in warrant-related Eurobond and Swiss franc denominated bonds issues. Beyond London and Switzerland, next in the ranking are Frankfurt and Paris, which contribute about the same share, i.e. 6 percent at the end of September 1988. The profitability profile of Japanese securities companies within Europe is in conformity with their organizational strategy and efforts in individual countries.

Table 5.6: Profitability of the Big Four Japanese Securities Companies in Individual European Countries

(Net profit after tax, yen in million)

Year ending	Amsterdam	Frankfurt	Switzerland Tota	Paris	Brussels	Milano	London (Bank)	London	Total		
									London	Continent	Europe
Sept.1985	1,806	1,606	4.781	1,672	0	0	0	11,996	11,996	9,865	21,861
Share (%)	8.3	7.3	21.9	7.6	0	0	0	54.9	54.9	45.1	100.0
Sept.1986	5,002	4,651	9.804	2,964	0	0	0	25,025	25,025	22,421	47,446
Share (%)	10.5	9.8	20.7	6.2	0	0	0	52.7	52.7	47.3	100.0
Sept.1987	5,024	4,479	9.827	3,078	793	0	805	24,112	24,917	23,201	48,118
Share (%)	10.4	9.3	20.4	6.4	1.6	0.0	1.7	50.1	51.8	48.2	100.0
Sept.1988	2,405	1,636	4.172	1,700	383	230	1,312	14,070	15,382	10,526	25,908
Share (%)	9.3	6.3	-6.1	6.6	1.5	0.9	5.1	54.3	59.4	40.6	100.0
Mar-1989*	958	1,591	4.031	1,583	377	924	1,630	28,541	30,171	9,464	39,635
Share (%)	2.4	4.0	-0.2	4.0	1.0	2.3	4.1	72.0	76.1	23.9	100.0

* for the six months period because of change in accounting year

Source: Nikkei Newsletter on Bond and Money (in Japanese) (1990)

The composition of the sources of profits in Europe is somewhat unclear. One could draw on the case of Nomura's London profits. Bond underwriting accounts for about one-third of Nomura's London profits and trading for a further portion,[51] after which selling Japanese equities in Europe is the next largest contributor to profits. Dealing in British Government bonds and in Euro-equities still accounts for only a small fraction of Nomura's profits.[52] In continental Europe, brokerage still provides the bulk of profits.

5.4 The Investment Services Industry in Europe after 1992 and Japanese Securities Companies

The term "investment services", the equivalent of investment banking, came into vogue from the proposed directive of the European Commission on the securities industry. As per the directive, investment services include brokerage, dealing as principal, market making, portfolio management, underwriting of securities, investment advisory, and safekeeping of securities. An investment firm, according to this directive, means any natural or legal person whose business is to provide any of the above-mentioned investment services.[53] In order to assess the response of the Japanese securities companies in the emerging European investment services industry, it would be desirable to review the present state of the securities markets in Europe. Furthermore, an appraisal of the regulatory developments is warranted in order to comprehend the emerging shape of the industry.

5.4.1 Background to the European Investment Services Industry

Taking investment services as a subset of the financial services industry, it could be said that the European evolution of the industry has been quite uneven, with the United Kingdom invariably in the lead with respect to financial innovation and deregulation, and the continental countries following along with greater or lesser enthusiasm.[54] Within

---

[51]This contrasts markedly with the domestic profit composition where brokerage forms the largest single source of profits.

[52]Rowley (1989) p. 57.

[53]Official Journal of the European Communities (1990) p. 18.

[54]Walter (1990) p. 39.

Europe, competition between various financial centers regarding market concentration, especially between London, Frankfurt, Paris, Luxembourg and Zurich, has intensified significantly. While London maintains its historic lead, Paris and Frankfurt are trying to rationalize their financial systems so as to become more attractive.[55]

Four segments of the European investment services industry constitute the core element: the new issue market, the secondary market for securities, the market for investment management services and the market for corporate restructuring. Because of the long tradition of reliance by corporations on bank financing, the *new issue market in Europe* has, in comparison with the United States, been relatively less developed. After 1985, there has been a change in the behavior of the European corporations and new issues have gained in prominence. However, most securities sold by European corporations are domestic issues in their own national markets with banking and financial companies comprising about 60 percent of all such issues in 1987.[56] The *intra-European secondary market in securities* has grown considerably since the mid-1980s, guided primarily by the upward trend in stock prices in the 1980s and securities market deregulation in various European countries. The growth of the secondary markets has stimulated considerable interest in European securities and many investment bankers have moved rapidly to expand their research coverage of continental European securities.[57]

Investment management services include asset management, investor finance, distribution of mutual funds, and custodial services. In Europe, with the increase of institutional savings and international diversification of portfolios, asset management was a major growth area in the period to 1992. For managing (a) the portfolio of European securities for non-European investors; (b) the portfolio of European and non-European securities for European investors and (c) the portfolio of European private investors, competition

---

[55]In its latest efforts (mid-January 1992), the German government has proposed sweeping reforms of the country's securities and money markets. Changes in the law to give investment trusts greater flexibility, including permission for them to issue money market funds; supervision of securities markets by a national self-regulatory authority; these are some of the main reforms likely to become law. See Parkes and Waller (1992).

[56]Walter and Smith (1990) p. 23.

[57]ibid. p. 42.

has become global and institutional investors have become more transactions oriented and price conscious.

The market for corporate restructuring. After 1985, when the European Single Market Act was announced, European corporations were compelled to adopt a broader European strategy and this has created an urgent need for corporate restructuring. The advent of the market for corporate financial advisory services has flourished in the wake of these developments as evidenced by the intra-European mergers and acquisitions. The evolving market for corporate control has been seriously constrained by the heavy concentration of shareholdings in the hands of management or banks and lack of transparency in the disclosure of information.

According to Walter and Smith, investment banking firms competing for business in different market segments in the EU fall into five strategic groups. They are:

"(a) UK and continental merchant banks such as SG Warburg, Morgan Grenfell, Kleinwort Benson, Banque Indosuez, Banque Paribas;

(b) evolving investment banking units of European universal banks such as Deutsche Bank Capital Markets, Barclays de Zoete Wedd, Midland Montegu, County NatWest, CS-First Boston and Banque Nationale de Paris;

(c) non-European 'full-service' investment and commercial banks such as Merrill Lynch, Goldman Sachs, Morgan Stanley, Nomura Securities, Industrial Bank of Japan, Citicorp, and J.P. Morgan;

(d) financial services affiliates of major nonfinancial firms such as General Electric Capital Corporation, Ford Motor Company and BP; and

(e) niche players such as Hambros, James Wolfensohn and Wasserstein Perrella."[58]

Each of these groups comes from an entirely different background and has a comparative advantage relative to the others. The largest European institutions have, over and above their dominant role in their domestic market, influential positions in intra-European business and compete directly with non-European investment firms. In contrast with the national markets, the ease of entry into the Euromarkets constitutes the first attraction for non-European firms.

---

[58]Walter and Smith (1990) p. 138.

5.4.2 Emerging Regulatory Framework

While international competition in Europe has certainly been given an impetus through the establishment of a "single passport" for EU banks in the Second Banking Directive, the local character of retail banking services means that integration in this sector will be highly limited for some time to come.[60] The securities sector, however, marked by highly standardized products and an overwhelming dominance of mobile over fixed production factors, is inherently international. The European capital market integration is, thus, being driven by international competition rather than by EU legislation.[61]

Five directives explicitly relating to securities markets are now in effect. These directives are as follows:

- Admission Directive (1979),
- Listing Particulars Directive (1980),
- Disclosure of Major Shareholdings Directive (1988),
- Prospectuses Directive (1989), and
- Insider Dealing Directive (1989).

Other than these EU directives, which aim at opening up the capital markets of the Union, there are two controversial directives which relate to the conditions under which securities firms may do Union-wide business: the Investment Services Directive and Capital Adequacy Directive. The *Investment Services Directive (ISD)*, on which a common standpoint was agreed upon by the Member States in November 1992, stipulates a regime for investment firms similar to the Second Banking Directive for credit institutions. The ISD is likely to come into force from 1996. Under the Directive, investment firms, authorized in one Member State, are free to establish and provide investment services throughout the EU without further authorization. This is often described as the 'single license' or 'common passport'. The Directive also ensures that investment firms that hold membership of stock exchanges in their home countries can have access, directly or indirectly, to membership of stock exchanges and organized securities markets of host countries. Given the importance of securities market activities

---

[60]Steil (1993) p. 1.

[61]ibid.

for major banks, the question of banks' getting direct access to the EU regulated markets was the most contentious.[62]

The Directive also provides for *relations with third countries* (i.e. non-European countries) on the subject. EU *branches* of investment firms authorized in non-EU countries will not be accorded the single passport rights under the ISD. The full *subsidiaries* of third country firms established in a Member State will be passported subject to a procedure intended to ensure that EU investment firms receive reciprocal treatment in the third countries in question.[63] Thus, the request for authorization from 'third country' securities firms to operate in the EU through subsidiaries presupposes that EU investment firms will receive effective market access comparable to that granted by the EU to investment firms from that country. Once authorized, third country firms would be subject to equal treatment with firms whose home base is in any of the Member States. The Directive further provides for periodic review of treatment accorded to EU investment firms in third countries and for negotiations with a view to obtaining comparable competitive opportunities for EU investment firms. In addition to initiating negotiations, the Directive also contemplates limiting or suspending their decision regarding requests pending at the moment of the decision or future requests for authorization for up to six months. Such limitation or suspension shall not apply to the setting up of subsidiaries by investment firms duly authorized in the EU or by their subsidiaries or to the acquisition of holdings in EU investment firms by such firms or subsidiaries.

The *Capital Adequacy Directive* seeks to coordinate the measures as regards the definition of own funds, the amount of initial capital and a common framework for the monitoring of market risks of investment firms.[64] However, the final shape of the Directive, on which agreement was reached by Member State economic and finance ministers in March 1993, sets minimum initial capital levels for EU investment firms, ranging from Ecu 50,000 (about US$ 57,000) to Ecu 90,000 (about US$ 102,000) depending upon the general scope of activities, as well as detailed additional require-

---

[62]France, Italy, and Belgium have until the end of 1996 to allow host country banks to trade directly on their exchanges, while Portugal, Spain and Greece were given time until the end of the century. Until the restrictions are lifted, banks wishing to trade directly on these exchanges will only be able to do through a separately capitalized securities subsidiary.

[63]ibid.

[64]Official Journal of the European Community (1992)

ments to cover specific categories of asset risk. The most significant of these risk categories are *position risk* (broadly defined to include market, credit and liquidity risk) and *settlement* (counterparty) *risk.*[65]

The Directive, which forms part of the wider international efforts to bring about approximation of the capital adequacy rules in force in major industrialized countries, will be implemented at the same time as the Investment Services Directive, and so is not likely to come into effect until 1996. The latest agreement in principle on international capital rules for securities firms[66] is likely to provide a boost to the adoption of this Directive by the EU in the near future.

A recent study by the Royal Institute of International Affairs suggests that flaws in EU legislation and growing protectionism in many Member States are seriously jeopardizing achievement of a singe European securities market.[67] The study particularly criticizes a provision in the EU's proposed ISD which seeks to promote the concentration of securities trading in markets which can be easily monitored by national regulators. A major conclusion of the study is that the faltering liberalization drive could inflate the cost of equity capital for European companies and depress the return to investors by perpetuating inefficient financial intermediaries and stock exchanges.[68]

5.4.3 Response of Japanese Securities Companies

In the past, Japanese investors have considered the European capital markets as too fragmented, illiquid and complex.[69] The Japanese view on European capital markets partly accounts for their preference towards U.S. capital markets. The Japanese institu-

---

[65]For details of the Capital Adequacy Directive and risk measures, see Steil (1993) pp. 19-21.

[66]On January 30, 1992, bank and securities regulators (Bank for International Settlements and International Organization of Securities Commissions) agreed in principle to the 8 percent capital requirements of the net exposure of a securities firm (that is, after taking account of a offsetting positions and other "hedges") and 4 percent of their gross positions.

[67]Steil (1995).

[68]ibid.

[69]In contrast with the Japanese view, U.S. investors see arbitrage opportunities in European fragmentation and take an aggressive approach to European markets. See Arthur Anderson & Co. (1989) p. 30-31.

tions always found that the diversity of European markets made it difficult to understand them.[70] This explains their low geographical diversification in continental Europe and concentration in the familiar Anglo-Saxon environment of the United Kingdom. The integration of the European capital market was identified by the Japanese as a prerequisite for significant Japanese institutional investment. Thus, one perception of Japanese corporations and financial institutions is that the Single European Market after 1992 would mean a harmonization of standards and regulations and this would afford chances of pursuing pan-European strategies.

A second, and perhaps more dominant, Japanese perception of the emerging shape of the regulatory framework is the uncertainty regarding the outcome. The fear that more protectionism will creep in under the guise of reciprocity[71] has considerably prejudiced the European strategy of Japanese financial institutions since 1985. Unlike American financial institutions, which have little to fear from this perception because of their longer history in Europe,[72] the Japanese fear emanates from a widespread perception that Article 7 of the Investment Services Directive is targeted at Japan. Japanese worry in this regard is also influenced by the general view in Europe that Japanese financial markets do not provide effective market access to foreign financial institutions and may have a "boomerang effect" on them. The fact that Japanese securities companies opened a total of 48 new subsidiaries (about 60 percent of the total) in Europe between 1986-90 leads to the judgement that the dramatic spurt in the Japanese presence in Europe has been principally motivated by the above-mentioned perception. The expectation is that "grandfathering"[73] will prove to be an important safeguard for them.

The extent to which the integrated European capital markets will prove a boon for the Japanese financial institutions is difficult to judge. To the extent that the Member States

---

[70]ibid. p. 31.

[71]Nomura Research Institute (1988) p. 17.

[72]Prospects for American investment bankers in a single European market look exceptionally good. In fact, American institutions are likely to be among the major beneficiaries of the removal of barriers in Europe.

[73]Grandfathering implies that institutions established before the enforcement of the Directives will not be affected by the new provisions of national treatment and relevant measures.

come closer to establishing a common currency, greater uniformity and stability in interest rates across the EU,[74] it is likely that a variety of financial services driven by the volatility factor will decline in importance. There will clearly be some tailing off of treasury and foreign exchange operations in financial centers throughout the EU.[75] In the changing environment, all types of investment banks operating in Europe, including the Japanese ones, would be faced with the strategic choice between broadening or limiting the range of services they offer. Japanese securities companies would be particularly confronted with the decision of more localization as Japan-related business shows its cyclical downturns.

In the post-1992 period, Japanese securities companies are also confronted with revising their organizational strategy in Europe. The reorganization may involve retaining only the London subsidiary and carrying Europe-wide operations through its branches. In other words, a Europe-wide presence would be ensured through the London subsidiary. At present, several rationalization schemes are being considered by Japanese financial institutions.

5.5 Summary and Conclusions

In comparison with banks, the internationalization of securities firms is a relatively new phenomenon. The growth of Japanese securities companies overseas was insignificant until the early 1970s. The real expansion process occurred in the 1980s when the majority of the new offices were opened. Within Europe, the concentration of their activities in the United Kingdom and Switzerland is strongly correlated with the Eurodollar and the Swiss franc as the main currencies used by Japanese issuers overseas. The strategy of working in Europe through wholly-owned subsidiaries explains the value attached by Japanese securities companies to growth from within.

The foreign investors' demand for Japanese securities provided Japanese securities companies with initial reasons for establishing themselves in Europe. Later, after the enactment of the new Foreign Exchange Law (1980), Japanese demand for foreign

---

[74]At the Maastricht Summit of December 1991, Member States resolved to enter the third and final stage of Economic and Monetary Union (EMU) by January 1999 and to set up the European Central Bank (ECB) by July 1998 or at least six months before a single currency comes into existence.

[75]Gamble (1991) p. 333.

securities provided renewed impetus to their foreign expansion. The surge in Japanese corporate fund raising in the Euromarkets brought securities companies into prominence as underwriters. Around 1987, the Big Four opened their banking subsidiaries in London so as to function as fully-integrated investment bankers. Their dominant position in Japan-related business explains the importance of the nationality of borrowers and intermediaries in international capital markets. The business strategy of Japanese securities companies in Europe has been to get closer to the customers (European investors) and the product (Euro-securities) they are selling. The importance of immediacy and quality of service in securities business guides their operational strategy.

In Europe, where regulatory changes are providing new shape to the securities markets, Japanese securities companies have positioned themselves for the post-1992 growth potential. The integration and harmonization of markets within the EU is likely to provide them with chances of pursuing pan-European strategies in the future.

Chapter 6

International Competitiveness of Japanese Financial Institutions

There has hardly been a topic in recent years that has attracted more public attention in economics than that of competitiveness. Whether one discusses the economics of a single firm, an industry, a country or even of a continent, sooner or later the question of its competitiveness is raised...however, the ubiquity of the term does not match the clarity of the concept.[1] Like the term wealth, the term competitiveness has a certain rhetorical appeal. Therefore, it is used quite often, sometimes in widely differing contexts.[2]

The concept of *international competitiveness* is often used in analyzing countries' macroeconomic performance. It compares, for a country and its trading partners, a number of salient economic features that can help explain international trade trends. Thus, capacity for technological innovation, degree of product specification, the quality of product involved are all factors that may influence a country's international competitiveness.[3] The term has come to be used in other contexts, too. Thus, international competitiveness is also applied to:

- the global position of a firm;
- the global success of a particular industry;
- industrial accomplishments of a particular country.

Most of the research on the subject of international competitiveness tends to focus on the manufacturing sector. Very little work has been done in the past on the competitiveness of the services sector in general and financial services sector in particular. Though the inclusion of international trade in services in the Uruguay Round inclined researchers to focus their attention on the subject, no systematic analysis is yet available on the indicators and measures of international competitiveness in the financial services sector. The recent research on the subject was stimulated by the declining share of the U.S.

---

[1]Blattner (1992) p. 9.

[2]Hellwig (1992) in Blattner (Ed.) p.42.

[3]Durand and Giorno (1987) p. 148.

financial firms in international financial markets.[4] Conversely speaking, there was a general perception that the Japanese financial institutions have gained market share in the late 1980s and become globally competitive. The present chapter examines the validity of this statement.

The international competitiveness of financial institutions can be viewed either from a macro perspective, where all institutions from one country are observed as a cohesive group, or from a micro perspective, where enterprise-specific characteristics of individual institutions are examined separately.[5] Further, the competitive position of financial institutions from one country can be examined vis-à-vis other internationally active financial institutions or vis-à-vis the local institutions in the host country. Because of the anecdotal evidence regarding Japanese banks "herding behavior" and their focus on wholesale banking, a macro analysis of Japanese banks as a group against MNBs from other countries is emphasized in this study.

To begin with, Sections 6.1 and 6.2 provide a detailed account of the global position of Japanese banks and securities firms. In the case of banks, their global position is analyzed with the help of BIS statistics, network of offices, and share of business domiciled abroad, and performance in international financial markets. For Japanese securities companies, competitive position is assessed with reference to their role as bookrunners in the Eurobond market and international equities market, and as brokers in international securities markets. Subsequently, Section 6.3 analyzes the sources of competitive advantage available to Japanese financial institutions. Of particular interest are the sources that relate to the home market structure of the Japanese financial institutions, advantage arising from low-cost capital, and advantages based on conventional measures of competitiveness. It must be noted that the present chapter does not investigate or explain the international competitiveness of Japan as a nation. Nor does it provide any value judgement about the international competitiveness of the Japanese services sector as a whole.[6]

---

[4]Federal Reserve Bank of New York (1991, 1992); Hale (1990) and Kreps (1990).

[5]The analysis of enterprise-specific competitive strengths is often constrained by the non-availability of data. Therefore, in the literature, the focus has often been on the macro analysis of international competitiveness.

[6]See Enderwick (1990) for a general discussion of the international competitiveness of Japanese service sector.

6.1 Global Position of Japanese Banks

The global position of a country's banks is sometimes measured in terms of the percentage of total deposits of the top 100 or 300 banks held by the banks of that country. Rhoades (1983), applying this measure for the period 1956-80, found that Japanese banks, which had the fourth position in 1956, with a share of 5 percent in the total deposits of the top 100 banks,[7] rose to the first position in 1979, with the largest share (i.e., 23.4%) of the world's total deposits[8]. Here one could notice the first signs of the Japanese banks' emerging international strength.

Another common, but better, measure of international strength is the number of a country's banks in the world ranking of the largest banks in terms of assets. Since it is recognized that MNBs mostly come from a group of banks that have a substantial asset base in the domestic market,[9] the increase in the number of banks from a country in the top ranks is treated as an indirect indicator of its global strength.[10] Thus, it is often used in research [Goldberg and Hanweck (1991); Dohner and Terrell (1988)] to signify the development of a country as a world banking power. Basing their research on this criterion, Goldberg and Hanweck (1991) observe that:

> "...In the 17 year period (between 1969-86), the Japanese share of assets *(in the world's top 300 banks)* has more than doubled. Japan has become the leading country not only in terms of percent of total assets but also in terms of number of banks on the list."[11]

These conclusions about the international position of the Japanese banks must be accepted with a note of caution. The statistical support for these judgments comes from the asset size and asset growth data, the majority of which are expressed in converted dollar terms. In the period of appreciating domestic currency (in this case the yen), converted dollar values invariably *inflate* the assets and *distort* the growth rate calcula-

---

[7]The top hundred reported by the American Banker.

[8]Rhoades (1983) pp. 433-35.

[9]Glüder (1988); Coulbeck (1984).

[10]Virtually all banks operating abroad were major producers of banking services in their home country prior to their investment abroad. See Terrell (1979) p. 19.

[11]Goldberg and Hanweck (1991) p. 211.

tions. Not just that, ignoring the currency denomination of assets and their respective share in the total assets also introduces a serious error factor into the estimates. The usual estimates suggest that three-quarters of Japanese banks assets are denominated in yen and the rest in foreign currencies.[12] Thus, the almost sudden increase in the value of their assets should partly be explained by the inflated dollar value of the yen-denominated assets (caused by the sharp appreciation of the yen after September 1985)[13] and partly by their market share strategy.

That the countries which have gained importance in the world banking were also the countries with the strongest currencies explains the sizable improvement in the share of Japanese and German banks in the 300 largest banks' total assets[14] and could also be used to analyze the position of the U.S. banks. The U.S. banks experienced an increase in their share from 1980 to 1984 when the dollar was strong and a decline after 1985 when the dollar weakened. This observation has the predictive value of suggesting a correlation between the international strength of a currency and the elevation of the banks from that currency area to the top group.

6.1.1 BIS Estimates

The BIS estimates of international banking assets and liabilities provide useful insights into the position of Japanese banks as multinationals. The BIS publishes two types of international banking statistics: one is based on the location of banks *(territorial basis)* and the other is based on the nationality of ownership of banks in the reporting area *(ownership basis)*. Territorial statistics provide information about the gross external assets and liabilities (i.e., cross-border positions in all currencies and domestic positions in foreign currencies) of banking offices operating in a given set of countries, irrespective of the nationality or ownership (see Table 6.1).[15]

---

[12]Kurosawa (1989) p. 2.

[13]For example, if one assumes that Japanese banks have a ratio of yen-denominated to dollar-denominated assets of 3:1 and experience no real increase in their assets, a doubling of yen value against the dollar would inflate *the current dollar value of the total assets* by 75 percent.

[14]Goldberg and Hanweck (1991) p. 213.

[15]This is in keeping with the balance of payments accounting practices which emphasize location.

Table 6.1: Japan's International Banking Assets

(Stock values at current $ in Billion)

	Gross International Position					
	Territorial Basis			Nationality of Ownership Basis		
Year	Total*	Japan's Share($)	Japan's Share(%)	Total* -	Japan's Share($)[2]	Japan's Share(%)
1973	294	17	5.78	-	-	-
74	360	20	5.56	-	-	-
75	442	20	4.52	-	-	-
76	548	22	4.01	-	-	-
77	690	22	3.19	-	-	-
78	893	34	3.81	-	-	-
79	1,111	45	4.05	-	-	-
80	1,323	66	4.99	-	-	-
81	1,542	85	5.51	-	-	-
82	1,687	91	5.39	-	-	-
83	2,108	109	5.17	2,166	457	21.10
84	2,166	127	5.86	2,272	518	22.80
85	2,574	195	7.58	2,714	707	26.05
86	3,278	345	10.52	3,460	1,121	32.40
87	4,207	577	13.72	4,387	1,556	35.47
88	4,520	734	16.24	4,615	1,765	38.24
89	5,355	842	15.72	5,387	1,967	36.51
90	6,272	951	15.16	6,239	2,121	34.00
91	6,221	942	15.14	6,163	1,936	31.41
92	6,211	879	14.15	6,042	1,678	27.77
93	6,465	919	14.22	6,260	1,683	26.88

*Total represents international banking assets of BIS reporting banks. Up to 1977, the reporting area of BIS represented G-10 countries and Switzerland. Austria, Denmark and Ireland were brought into the reporting area in December 1977. From December 1983, Finland, Norway and Spain were also added. In December 1983, the seven off-shore banking centres of the Bahamas, Bahrain Cayman Islands, Netherlands Antilles, Panama and Singapore were brought in more fully.

[2]In the case of Japan, the operations of Japanese banks' affiliates in Hong Kong and Singapore are not covered in the statistics based on the nationality of ownership.

Source: BIS; Pecchioli (1983) etc.

Though the territorial statistics show the increasing share of the banking offices in Japan in the total international banking assets, from 5.8 percent in 1973 to about 15 percent between 1989-91, it does not project a true picture of the Japanese banks' external position. This is because the business of the overseas affiliates of Japanese banks is excluded and allocated to their respective host countries. In the same fashion, it includes the business of Japanese affiliates of foreign banks also. To the extent international banking business carried out by the overseas affiliates of Japanese banks[16] is excluded in the territorial statistics, there is a gross underestimation of Japan's international banking position.[17]

As against the territorial series, the international banking statistics based on the nationality of ownership are of recent origin[18] and seek to remedy the shortcomings of the territorial series [see Table 6.1]. This series evidently provides a more accurate measure of the Japanese banks' international position because it includes the business booked by the overseas affiliates of the Japanese banks. In 1983, when such statistics were first published, U.S. banks were identified as the dominant nationality group in terms of their share in the total assets. However, they were quickly surpassed by the Japanese banks in September 1985. Japanese banks almost doubled their share in total international banking assets from 21 percent at the end of 1983 to 38 percent at the end of 1988. Though Japanese banks continue to maintain their dominant position, their share declined to 27 percent at the end of 1993 after reaching a peak of 39.4 percent at the end of March 1989.[19] The fall in the Japanese share reflects the pressures created by the sharp decline in Japanese equity prices since early 1990 and the capital adequacy guidelines proposed in the Basle Accord that came into force in 1992. However, during the period between 1983-1990, Japanese banks' claims expanded by an amount equal to $1,664 billion and accounted for 41 percent of the overall growth in international banking

---

[16]At the end of 1988, about 40 percent of the international banking business of Japanese banks was booked outside Japan. See BIS (August, 1989) p. 19.

[17]Iwami also recognizes this fact when he says that the Japanese banks' international assets figures are far smaller than their actual weight. See Iwami (1989) p. 5.

[18]The publication of ownership-based international banking statistics began in 1983.

[19]Whereas in 1991-92, the decline in the share of Japanese banks was largely owing to their reduced activity in the international interbank market, in 1992-93, the decline occurred because of the reduction in their claims on related offices. See for details BIS, Annual Reports; Bank of Japan (1991c) p. 24.

activity. It is also noteworthy that about 60 percent of the expansion of Japanese banks' international claims between 1983-90 took place after December 1986. This coincides with the opening of the JOM, which offered Japanese banks opportunities to circumvent some of the domestic regulations.

The rapid expansion of Japanese banks' international banking business must be seen in the light of certain peculiarities, which are elaborated here:

(i) Almost 40 percent of the expansion of assets between 1983-90 took the form of claims on related offices [see Table 6.2, Part (A)]. This implies that Japanese banks use their global network to supplement their huge funding requirements and also for arbitraging between domestic and international markets. It has been argued that inter-office business, when compared with interbank business, proves to be both cost-effective and efficient. However, the inclusion of inter-office business in international banking assets has considerably overstated the position of Japanese banks.[20] If inter-office claims are left out, the Japanese share in total international assets shrinks to 23.4 and 21.6 percent for 1989 and 1990 respectively.

(ii) Direct credits by the Japanese banks to non-banks expanded at an average annual rate of 28 percent between 1983-88, which was considerably higher than the rate at which overall claims on non-banks of other reporting countries increased (i.e., 8 percent).[21] The singular aspect of Japanese bank lending to non-banks is that Euroyen impact loans and foreign currency loans to residents in Japan accounted for a major part of the growth in claims on non-banks between 1983-90.[22]

(iii) Since the end of 1983, the huge expansion of the international assets of Japanese banks has been driven largely by new home office business[23] or its booking there. The share of home office in total international lending increased from 41

---

[20]This view is endorsed by the Bank of Japan too. It is believed that round-tripping operations (booked through inter-office accounts) artificially inflated Japanese banks' external assets.

[21]BIS (1989) p. 17.

[22]For details refer to Section 3.4.2.

[23]BIS (1989) p. 17.

**Table 6.2 : The International Banking Assets and Net International Position
of Japanese Banks (BIS Estimates)**

(A) International Banking Assets of Japanese Banks

(US$ billion)

Year	Total	of which vis-a-vis				
		Related offices	Non-related banks	Non-banks	Official Monetary Institutions	CDs & Securities[2]
1983	456.7	122.1	198.1	134.7	2.1	0
84	517.9	137.8	222.1	155.2	2.9	0
85	707.0	192.1	302.8	205.7	5.4	0
86	1,121.4	370.6	440.9	301.4	8.5	0
87	1,555.8	503.2	613.7	426.7	12.1	0
88	1,765.4	618.0	674.1	460.0	13.3	0
89	1,967.4	705.0	753.7	495.8	12.8	0
90	2,121.3	776.5	803.8	526.3	14.7	0
91	1,935.8	716.1	708.4	496.3	15.1	0
92	1,677.8	601.9	609.5	455.9	10.5	0
93	1,683.4	577.6	632.6	462.7	10.5	0

(B) Net International Position* of Japanese Banks

Year	Total	of which vis-a-vis				
		Related offices	Non-related banks	Non-banks	Official Monetary Institutions	CDs & Securities[2]
1983	42.0	6.2	-21.5	103.5	-15.8	-30.2
84	21.6	-1.8	-34.1	113.7	-21.4	-34.7
85	34.5	-4.0	-54.9	146.4	-25.4	-28.6
86	49.6	-35.5	-72.5	223.2	-20.1	-45.6
87	58.0	-47.0	-130.8	338.9	-35.7	-67.5
88	51.8	-53.7	-139.1	359.5	-38.7	-76.3
89	42.7	-8.6	-220.0	387.8	-37.0	-79.6
90	64.3	27.3	-226.3	380.0	-44.2	-72.5
91	107.7	20.0	-162.5	333.3	-31.9	-51.1
92	164.8	49.2	-139.4	321.0	-36.9	-29.0
93	194.5	52.2	-131.4	328.3	-32.9	-21.6

*Net position implies total assets minus total liabilities

[2]CDs and securities as assets imply banks´ holdings of these securities.
A minus net position implies banks' issues of CDs and other securities.

Source: BIS; Part (B) of the table computed from BIS statistics

percent at the end of 1983 to 61 percent at the end of 1988.[24] How much of the international business is booked at the home office depends, firstly, on the extent to which banks have built up a network of foreign offices in order to carry out international business and, secondly, on the importance of the local foreign currency business in home financial markets. On the basis of the evidence given in point (ii), the latter seems to be true in the case of Japan. However, one cannot deny the presence of some incentives in home office booking of the international banking business.

(iv) Part (B) of Table 6.2 shows the net international position of the Japanese banks between 1983-93. It becomes clear from the table that Japanese banks had a net creditor position vis-à-vis non-banks throughout, a large part of which was financed from a strong build-up of their net debtor position in the international interbank market between 1983-90. Japanese banks were also the largest issuer of international securities (including CDs) and obtained net deposits from official monetary authorities. An *overall net creditor position* implies the use of local funds for international banking. However, this overall net creditor position changed little between 1983-90 despite large Japanese savings and the huge current account surplus. The explanation is that Japanese banks, while being large external lenders of yen funds, were heavy borrowers of foreign currency funds, for financing Japanese residents' foreign securities purchases[25] as well as for hedging exchange risks.[26]

(v) The annual growth rate of Japanese banks' international assets declined considerably from 26 percent in March 1988 to 8 percent in 1990 and, in fact, turned negative between 1991-92 [Table 6.2, Part (A)]. Between January 1991 and December 1993, Japanese banks slimmed down their external liabilities by $568 billion, a large part of which amounted to reducing their dependence on the international interbank market. Thus, Japanese banks' international banking business entered a phase of contraction in early 1990, gathering force in 1991

---

[24]ibid. p. 18.

[25]ibid. p. 21.

[26]Turner (1991) p. 78.

and early 1992.[27] Just as overseas expansion was fueled by heavy reliance on the international interbank market, contraction is most visible in their diminished activity in this market segment.

6.1.2 Expansion of the Overseas Network of Offices

The global strength of a bank or banks from a particular country is also reflected in the growth of its overseas network of offices. Consistent growth in the number of overseas offices should be seen as providing valuable information about banks' emerging strength and strategies. Apparently, MNBs strive for a multinational network of offices to realize their overall operational goals. One argument is that a well-spread geographical network provides immense opportunities for efficient asset and liability management at the global level. For some types of banking business, such as foreign exchange dealing, continuous trading with the help of a branch network in different time zones enables banks to make more intensive use of market intelligence and to avoid carrying overnight positions.[28]

It is evident from Figure 6.1 that Japanese banks have continually increased their presence abroad. The expansion process, which started around 1971, was initially slow but gained momentum after 1980 and was most conspicuous between 1986-90. A total of 427 new offices (127 branches, 130 subsidiaries and 170 representative offices) were opened during 1986-90, accounting for about 40 percent of all overseas offices.[29] A growing network of overseas offices is an expression of long-term plans as well as of the aggressive strategy of MNBs,[30] the whole of which cannot be clarified by the widespread hypothesis of "following-the-clients" in overseas markets. In terms of the industrial organization theory, the Japanese banks have been positioning themselves for a competitive advantage over others through "vertical integration" and the internalization of market transactions.

---

[27]See Takeda and Turner (1992) p. 82-83 and 89-90 for details.

[28]Callier (1986).

[29]Notably, a part of the expansion in the late 1980s is explained by the efforts of the major regional banks to expand overseas. With 48 branches, 24 subsidiaries and 59 representative offices, the Japanese regional banks have 12% of the total number of overseas offices of all Japanese banks as of the end of 1990.

[30]Glüder (1988) p. 272.

Figure 6.1: Expansion of Japanese Banks' overseas Network

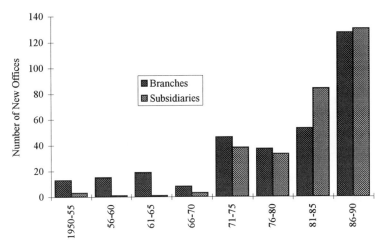

Source: MOF

When comparing the overseas expansion of Japanese banks with that of other countries, one notices that Japanese banks with 337 overseas branches at the end of June 1992 are still way behind U.S. (with 819 branches in 1989)[31] and British (1016 in 1985)[32] banks. It appears somewhat contradictory that Japanese banks should occupy first place in terms of international assets (Section 6.1.1) despite their limited foreign representation. The wisdom learned is that for conducting wholesale banking business, it is sufficient to be present in important financial centers. Except for California, where some Japanese banks do retail banking business, elsewhere in the world Japanese banks have concentrated their activities on the wholesale segment of the international banking market.

6.1.3 Share of Overseas Business in the Total Business

Yet another indicator of the global position of banks is the share of their total business domiciled overseas. Since February 1992, The Banker magazine has published the annual ranking of the global banks based on the share of business outside their home

---

[31]Danton (1992) p. 295.

[32]Jones (1990) p. 31.

base. The listing is designed to show the relative importance of overseas business for internationally active banks. The position of Japanese banks in this kind of ranking is given in Table 6.3. Since some Japanese banks did not disclose the domestic-overseas split of their assets, the income earned overseas or the proportion of loan booked overseas were taken as proxy for the purpose.

Table 6.3: Japanese Banks' Overseas Business: Share in the Total Business

	FY 1990		FY 1991		FY 1992		FY 1993	
	%	Rank	%	Rank	%	Rank	%	Rank
Asahi Bank	17.9^4	(55)	17.8^1					
Bank of Tokyo	31.3^4	(31)			28.4^1	(35)	27.3^1	(38)
Bank of Yokohama	22.9^1	(44)						
Dai-Ichi Kangyo Bank	36.0^2	(23)	39.3^1	(16)	32.0^1	(31)	33.1^1	(24)
Daiwa Bank					19.02	(49)		
Fuji Bank	37.0^3	(21)	35.0^2	(23)	35.0^2	((25)	33.0^1	(25)
Hokkaido T. Bank	23.3^4	(43)	22.0^1	(37)				
Industrial Bank of Japan					22.9^2		23.4^2	(44)
Long-term Credit Bank	16.0^4	(58)	21.8^1	(38)	19.2^1	(48)	19.7^5	(48)
Mitsubishi Bank	34.8^1	(26)	26.2^1	(34)	20.7^1	(43)	21.1^1	(47)
Sakura Bank	39.2^2	(17)	29.7^1	(30)				
Sanwa Bank	33.8^3	(28)			24.2^1	(38)	24.1^1	(40)
Sumitomo Bank	35.0^2	(25)	32.0^2	(27)	35.0^2	(26)	32.0^2	(30)
Sumitomo Trust & Banking	28.5^2	(35)	31.7^2	(29)	20.2^1	(46)		
Tokai Bank	33.7^4	(29)			35.5^2		29.2^2	(36)
Yasuda Trust & Banking	26.8^4	(38)			26.0^2	(36)	21.8^2	(46)

The table shows the importance of overseas business in the consolidated business of the Japanese Banks

1 = Assets Overseas
2 = Income from overseas business
3 = Revenue generated overseas
4 = loans made overseas
5 = Gross business profits overseas

Source: The Banker

The table shows that top Japanese banks have more than 35 percent of their assets domiciled outside Japan. The average overseas assets for Japanese banks appearing in the listing was 29 percent for the fiscal year ending March 1991 and has declined to 26 percent for the fiscal year ending March 1994. By way of comparison, the top global banks from other countries have over 60 percent of their business outside their home country. In terms of ranking in the top 50 global banks, the Japanese banks *do not* figure in the first 20. However, a total of 10 banks (most of them city and trust banks) consistently appeared in the list between 1991-94. Thus, whereas Japanese banks are considerably large in terms of total asset size, their international involvement (assets or revenue generated abroad) is not high when compared with banks from Switzerland, the U.K. and France. Japanese banks' overseas assets are set to increase further with the proportion of assets domiciled in Asia expanding more rapidly.[33]

6.1.4 Performance in International Financial Markets

This section assesses the position of Japanese banks in Eurocredit, derivatives and foreign exchange markets. These markets are highly integrated across national trading centers and come closest to constituting a "level playing field" for institutions from different countries. As such, these markets provide a means of highlighting the factors associated with competitiveness in a truly international setting.[34]

The Eurocredit Market consists of the Eurobonds and Euro syndicated loans market denominated in any currency. Despite the potential for banks and securities companies to participate in most sectors of the Eurocredit market, a high degree of segmentation is evident. While commercial banks dominate the Euroloan market, securities firms control the Eurobonds market. The position of Japanese banks in the Eurocredit market can be judged from Euromoney's league tables of top financial institutions in different segments of the international financial markets.[35] Though the league tables published by Euromoney vary in their coverage from year to year, they provide useful information on the position and share of leading financial institutions.

In the **overall Eurobond market**, as shown in Table 6.4, Japanese banks have displayed a better position in each year after 1983. They have steadily risen to higher positions in the Eurobond bookrunners' league tables, increasing their share from 0.6 percent in 1983 to 10 percent in 1990. The number of banks in the top 50 bookrunners

---

[33]Connors (1994) p. 69.

[34]Hirtle (1991) p. 39.

[35]Though BOJ regularly publishes statistics about the "Assets and Liabilities of Overseas Branches of All Banks" in its Economic Statistics Monthly, this source does not help much in assessing the role of Japanese banks in international capital markets, where mainly overseas subsidiaries, and not branches, of Japanese banks are active.

Table 6.4: Japanese Banks' Position as Bookrunners in the Eurobond Market

	Number of Banks in the top 50	Share in Eurobonds under-written by the top 50 (%)
1983	1	0.60
1984	2	0.90
1985	4	2.30
1986	4	4.23
1987	7	7.59
1988	6	6.20
1989	8	7.50
1990	8	10.00
1991	5	3.17
1992	6	5.31
1993	6	5.16

Source: Compiled from Euromoney, Annual Financing Report, various years.

also increased from 1 in 1983 to 8 in 1990. The share of Japanese banks started dwindling after the downturn of Japanese stock markets in December 1989. The economic recession in Japan that began in early 1991 led to a steep decline in real investment and reduced the overseas financing activity of Japanese corporate sector. As a result, in 1993, the share of Japanese banks as bookrunners in the Eurobond market declined to about 5 percent of the total.

Their performance as bookrunners in the Eurobond market should be interpreted as remarkable, not only because they have Japanese securities companies as their main competitors but also because they are bound by home regulations in this regard. For example, the "Three Bureaux Agreement" of the MOF banned Japanese banks from lead managing the public issues of external bonds by private Japanese corporations.[36] In this particular respect, the competitive advantage of their ties with Japanese clients was not available to the Japanese banks in the Eurobond market. Thus, when Japanese banks acted in the capacity of bookrunners or lead managers, they did it mostly for:

---

[36]"Three Bureaux Agreement" (*Sankyoku-Goi*) was reached by the three bureaus (Banking, Securities and International Finance) of the MOF in 1975. Under the agreement, Japanese banks were expected to maintain a lower profile in the international securities markets than the Japanese securities companies. This was probably because of the orthodox belief that securities business is inherently riskier and exposes commercial banks to additional risks.

(i)   public external bond issues of non-Japanese clients;

(ii)   public external bond issues of Japanese public utilities; and

(iii) private placements of both Japanese and non-Japanese clients.

The restrictions imposed on Japanese banks in this regard were abolished in April 1993, which is likely to improve their competitive position in the future.[37] Thus, the reforms designed to dismantle the barriers between banking and securities business (Section 2.3) started feeding through to the Eurobond market where the London-based securities arms of five Japanese banks launched a spate of deals for Japanese clients.

From amongst the sub-sectors of the Eurobond market, Japanese banks obviously have a competitive advantage in managing the bond issues denominated in Japanese yen. They have also improved their performance in U.S. dollar denominated bond issues. However, one must admit that, in the bond markets for Ecu and other European currencies, Japanese banks face stiff competition from French, American and English financial institutions and hence do not appear in the Euromoney league tables. In fixed rate and convertible bonds markets, as well as in sovereign and supranational issues, they lag behind Japanese securities companies and only the IBJ appears to be making headway.[38]

The **international syndicated loan market** is the natural domain of banks and most of the Japanese banks, with their massive size, figure in this market as significant providers of syndicated loans.[39] This belittles, to some extent, their position as the arrangers of syndicated loans, where the American and the English banks have an edge. Thus, Japanese banks provided 25 percent of the loans in the syndicated loan market in 1990 in the top 50 financial institutions but were arrangers only for 8 percent of the loans. In 1991, they arranged 11.8 percent of the loans and provided 16.2 percent of the

---

[37]The MOF introduced a five-year transition period for deregulation during which restriction would be eased gradually. The overseas subsidiaries of Japanese banks would be allowed to lead manage small amount bond issues (less than ¥10 billion for the time being), and for companies with net assets over ¥500 billion.

[38]Contrary to their position in the Eurobond market, Japanese banks do not figure in the **international equity market** league tables, probably because of the infancy of the market and its slow take-off after the October crash of 1987.

[39]It is interesting to note that, unlike the British or the French banks which syndicate international bank loans in foreign currencies domestically, the Japanese banks' syndicated loan business is conducted from their foreign branches. See Lewis and Davis (1987) p. 247.

total.[40] Guided by their experience in the Latin American debt crisis, the Japanese banks have shifted their attention to the western world and now focus more on the OECD area. The Japanese banks' medium and long-term foreign lending to OECD countries increased from 39 percent of the total outstanding at the end of 1983 to 67.4 percent of the total outstanding at the end of 1991.[41] This also led to an increase in the share of western Europe in the total.

Table 6.5 provides information about the position of Japanese banks in the international syndicated loan market. Whereas the figures for 1983-85 are not directly comparable with those of 1986-87 and 1988-1990, they do provide grounds for assessing the increase in the number of Japanese banks (2 banks in 1983, 6 in 1984-85, 10 in 1986-87 and 13 in 1990) that figure in the top 50 banks. Their growing influence on the market, which is not directly reflected in the market share, is confirmed by the absolute amount of funds provided by them in the market.

Table 6.5: Japanese banks' Position as Lead Managers* in the International Syndicated Loan Market

	Number of Banks in the top 50	Share of the Market (in %)
1983	2	3
1984	6	4.6
1985	6	4.7
1986	9	7.39
1987	10	6.77
1988	NA	NA
1989	12	NA
1990	13	NA
1991	NA	NA
1992	5	NA
1993	7	3.1

*figures for 1989 and 1990 show Japanese banks as loan providers and not as loan arrangers
Between 1983-85, figures show the combined performance in Euroloans and Euronotes market

Source: Compiled from Euromoney, Annual Financing Report, various years

---

[40]Estimates based on the International Financing Review's ranking of top 50 banks.

[41]There has been a simultaneous reduction in the exposure of Japanese banks to Latin American countries from 37% at the end of 1983 to 8.3% at the end of 1991. See Ministry of Finance, Japan, Annual Report of the International Finance Bureau.

The syndicated loan market after the debt crisis of 1982 has a new face with numerous innovative devices such as note issuance facilities (NIF) and multi-option facilities. Nowadays, the competitive edge in this market is possessed by those financial institutions that have developed skills in these areas.[42] As NIF underwriters, the Japanese banks do figure in the league table with some of them in the top ten in 1985-86. However, in the market for multi-option facilities, only the BOT appeared in 9th position in 1986 but lost ground to the English banks in 1987 and was relegated to 26th position. It would be apt to say that, in the innovative FRN and Euro CPs markets, Japanese banks are still on the learning curve. Unlike the U.S. markets, where Japanese banks enthusiastically participated in the financing of Highly Leveraged Transactions (HLT),[43] in Europe they have not displayed interest in this area. It is probably more because of the low stature of the HLT market in Europe.

The Derivative Products Market. From amongst the various derivative products used in the financial markets, swaps are among the most international for a variety of reasons: the major swap dealers operate from more than one financial center; they market their products to a multinational client base; and they denominate their product in several currencies.[44] The market specialization between banks and securities firms in swap business is not so conspicuous as in the Eurocredit market. Practically all large and internationally active banks and securities companies have swap dealing units. However, banks tend to develop strength in the area of interest rate risk management and securities firms in securities financing related swap business.

Very little information is available about the competitive position of major financial institutions in this market. The general perception is that some U.S. banks and securities companies are the strongest competitors in the market. Japanese banks are considered to be developing their skills in this area. According to a survey by the Bank of England, Japanese banks in London accounted for about 15 percent of the outstanding notional value of interest rate swaps at the end of 1986.[45] Recently, they have made increasing

---

[42]Métais (1990) p. 171.

[43]Estimates suggest that Japanese banks held over half of the highly leveraged transactions loan exposure attributable to non-U.S. banks in 1989. For details on the subject, see Borio (1990b).

[44]Aderhold et al. (1991) p. 42.

[45]Walton and Trimble (1987) p. 522.

use of currency swaps. This has been stimulated by the yen-denominated bond issues of non-Japanese and sovereign clients, which have mostly been linked to a currency swap agreement.[46] However, the role played by the Japanese banks in London is that of an end-user or an intermediary and not that of a market maker.[47] An interesting fact about Japanese banks' involvement in the swap market is that their subsidiaries do not act as counterparties in swap agreements because of the parties' preference to deal with the branches of Japanese banks. Evidently, it is assumed that the parent bank's credit rating is applicable to its branch and not to its subsidiary.[48]

The Market for Foreign Exchange is the most international and competitive of all financial markets; probably, the only barrier to entry into this market is imposed by the initial investment in equipment and staff for an efficient dealing room.[49] The foreign exchange market is a vehicle for four main activities: trade, investment, exposure management, and position taking.[50] The transactions relating to trade and investment represent a small fraction of foreign exchange transactions. The bulk of activity in the foreign exchange market reflects position management activity of foreign exchange dealers.[51] The volatility of exchange rates in the 1980s has increased the importance of this activity as a source of profit for all major financial institutions.

Because a bank's international network of branches serves as an internal source of information, there is evidence to the effect that profitability in the foreign exchange business may depend upon the network of offices that a bank has established.[52] The Japanese banks' attempts at completing their network of offices in major financial centers might have been targeted at reaping this benefit. Within treasury operations, Japanese banks now put a lot of emphasis on foreign exchange dealing, which is not only recognized as off-balance sheet business for capital adequacy guidelines of the BIS

---

[46]ibid.

[47]ibid.

[48]ibid.

[49]Giddy (1983) p. 216.

[50]Holmes et al. (1991) p. 65.

[51]ibid. p. 69.

[52]ibid.

but is also profitable. As an example, one could cite the case of Fuji Bank, where foreign exchange dealing and money market activities contributed 30 to 40 percent of the revenue generated by its international divisions.[53]

Euromoney publishes regular surveys of corporate treasurers and their opinion about financial institutions active in foreign exchange markets. These surveys suggest that the U.S. based institutions have a strong position in the market. In Euromoney's survey, only two Japanese banks figure in 1989 (the BOT and the Dai Ichi Kangyo Bank), which together accounted for a paltry 2.5 percent of the market share.[54] In the yen-dollar market, other than the above two banks, the Sumitomo Bank, the IBJ and the Fuji Bank occupy prominent positions. The competitive position of Japanese banks in this currency segment derives from their information edge over others with regard to their home currency. The BOT and the Sumitomo appeared in first and eighth position respectively in the yen-German mark market in 1990.

In other market segments of international financial markets, such as **merger and acquisition** (M&A), Japanese banks have thus far had a low profile. In a separate survey of M&A advisers conducted by Euromoney, three Japanese banks occupied 28th, 30th and 37th position out of 40 advisers in terms of total number of deals worldwide for the year 1989. The Sanwa Bank with 41 deals, the IBJ Group with 38 deals and the Long-Term Credit Bank with 22 deals were the banks that appeared in the league table. The survey makes a further interesting revelation that almost all the deals done by the Japanese banks were for Japanese clients.[55]

6.2   Global Position of Japanese Securities companies

Other than the international syndicated loan market and foreign exchange markets, where internationally active banks have predominance, in all other segment of international financial markets, major securities firms occupy prominent positions. This section analyses the global position of Japanese securities companies in the Eurobond market and international equity market as lead manager and as international brokers.

---

[53] See Shigyo (1991) for details.

[54] Lewis (1989) p. 79.

[55] Euromoney (1990a) pp. 45-52.

6.2.1 Position in the Eurobond Market

The international position of securities firms could be assessed with reference to their performance in the Eurobond market. The frequently quoted Eurobond league tables published by Euromoney provide the ranking of the top performers in different segments of the market. The share of top performers in the market further helps in surveying their relative strengths. Table 6.6 furnishes the rank and share of the Big Four Japanese securities companies as *bookrunners in the overall Eurobond market* for the period 1983-91.

On the face of it, the table suggests that the Big Four figure in the top 10 and raised their share from a bare 4.6 percent in 1983 to 38 percent in 1989.[56] However, from 1984 to 1989, the increase in the market share of the Japanese securities companies was strongly correlated with the increase in Japanese issues of corporate securities.[57] Corresponding to this increase, the decline in the market share of the U.S. bookrunners was correlated with the decline in issues by U.S. firms. This information appears to confirm the importance of national ties in the Eurobond market.[58]

The dramatic increase in the share of Japanese securities companies was particularly supported by the rise in Japanese equity-warrant bond issues in the 1980s (see Table 5.4), most of which were issued overseas. In 1989, when the Big Four together achieved peak market share, Japanese borrowers accounted for 94 percent of all equity warrant issues and, as shown in Part (E) of Table 6.7, 93 percent of these issues were managed by the Big Four. If Japanese equity warrant bond issues are excluded from the reckoning, their share of the market slips to 12.8 percent.[59] Since 1990, the share of the Big Four has been declining rapidly. In 1993, their market share declined to 11 percent. This is largely in response to the drop in Japanese equity warrant issues. However, the revival of this market segment in 1991[60] and the improvement in the share of the Big

---

[56]Taken together, Japanese banks and securities companies were bookrunners for 45.8 percent of all Eurobond issues in the year 1989.

[57]Balder et al. (1991) p. 33.

[58]ibid.

[59]Frank (1990) p. 24.

[60]The equity warrant-related bonds issued externally totaled ¥3,502 billion between April 1991 and February 1992 against ¥2,625 billion in the fiscal year ending March 1991. See Table 5.4 for details.

Table 6.6: Position of Japanese Securities Companies as Bookrunners in the Eurobond Market

	1983		1985		1987		1989		1990		1991		1992		1993		1994*	
	[1]	[2]	[1]	[2]	[1]	[2]	[1]	[2]	[1]	[2]	[1]	[2]	[1]	[2]	[1]	[2]	[1]	[2]
Nomura	9	2.3	8	3.7	1	13.6	1	15.1	1	9.2	1	7.8	2	7.11	7	4.26	9	3.31
Daiwa	25	1.1	12	2.2	5	5.3	2	7.9	4	4.7	3	6.7	9	3.65	14	2.55	11	3.12
Nikko	27	0.9	25	1.4	4	5.3	4	7.2	7	3.7	8	4.0	11	2.87	13	2.6	13	2.86
Yamaichi	48	0.3	20	1.6	6	4.9	3	7.7	11	3.1	7	4.3	10	3.01	25	1.63		
New Japan					64	0.2	50	0.3	44	0.4								
Total		4.6		8.9		29.2		38.3		21.1		22.9		16.6		11.0		9.3

[1] = Rank; [2] = Share of the Market (in %)

* for the period January to June 1994

Source: Compiled from Euromoney, Annual Financing Report, various years

Four in that year shows the vulnerability of the Japanese securities companies' competitiveness outside this segment of the market. Coupled with their waning influence in fixed-rate and convertible issues, their competitive position in the Eurobond market should be construed as fragile. The competitive position of Japanese securities companies in other segments of the Eurobond market is shown in Table 6.7.

Since its take off in 1985, when the Euroyen bond market was liberalized to include foreign corporate issuers, the Big Four have maintained their lead in this market segment.[61] Though their total share has declined from three-quarters to one half, they still dominate this market. This validates the belief that financial institutions possess a competitive advantage in their home currency related securities business. Experts on the subject hint that, in contrast with the dollar denominated bond sector, where the nationality of the intermediary and issuer are strongly correlated, in the non-dollar bond sector, the nationality of the bookrunner is strongly correlated with the home country of currency.[62] However, it is now believed that the growing significance of swaps in international securities markets will make the "currency-clientele effect" somewhat weaker in the future. Other than Euroyen bond issues, the Big Four excel in dollar denominated issues, capturing well over 40 percent of the market between 1987-89. However, besides these two currencies, they are conspicuously absent from other currency segments of the Eurobond market. Unlike the Japanese banks, such as IBJ and BOT, who occupied 17th and 18th position in the top 20 lead managers of all Ecu-Eurobond issues between 1985-90, Japanese securities companies did not figure in the league table.[63] In 1990, Nomura appeared in the Ecu-Eurobond league table and signaled its intent to participate in yet another segment of the market.

6.2.2 Position in the International Equities Market

This is the second major market in which Japanese securities companies operate. The market is of recent origin and started only in the early 1980s. Consequently, Japanese investors have less diversification across global equities than global bonds. Valued at

---

[61]Much of the market is swap driven and used for dollar arbitrage. By far the largest demand for yen-denominated securities comes from the Japanese investor base, who hold these securities until maturity.

[62]Balder et al. (1991) p. 27.

[63]Lee (1991) p. 40.

Table 6.7 : Position and Share of Japanese Securities Cos. as Bookrunners in Selected Segments of the Eurobonds Market

Market Segment	1986 [1]	1986 [2]	1987 [1]	1987 [2]	1988 [1]	1988 [2]	1989 [1]	1989 [2]	1990 [1]	1990 [2]	1991 [1]	1991 [2]	1992 [1]	1992 [2]	1993 [1]	1993 [2]
(A) Dollar Issues																
Nomura	5	5.9	1	16.6	1	19.5	4	23.8	2	15.8	5	10.9	7	7.88		4.89
Daiwa	7	4.5	5	6.9	3	9.6	6	11.9	6	5.9	13	6.2	13	3.12		2.14
Nikko	11	3.2	3	8.7	5	7.8	4	12.2	4	6.5	18	4.7	14	1.17		1.81
Yamaichi	14	2.4	4	8.4	4	8.6	>20		9	4.2	12	5.8	19	3.27		1.23
Total		16.0		40.6		45.5		47.9		32.4		27.6		15.4		10.1
(B) Euroyen issues																
Nomura	1	42.4	1	38.7	1	20.8	1	20.7	1	20.8	2	27.8	1	29.86	1	19.3
Daiwa	2	19.6	3	10.9	2	17.0	2	16.7	2	18.0	1	28.7	2	17.57	3	12.82
Nikko	4	8.1	4	9.9	7	6.8	5	3.7	5	7.9	3	14.2	3	15.65	2	17.39
Yamaichi	3	8.4	5	6.8	5	7.5	3	7.7	3	10.5	4	13.2	4	12.23	4	9.94
Total		78.5		66.3		52.1		48.8		57.2		83.9		75.3		59.5
(C) Fixed-rate issues																
Nomura	1	10.7	1	9.8	3	5.8	1	7.2	1	9.3*						
Daiwa	3	6.5	11	3.1	10	3.2	5	4.5	8	4.2*						
Nikko	6	3.8	13	2.8	>20		3	1.0	10	3.2*						
Yamaichi	11	3.2	16	1.8	>20		>15		>15							
Total		24.2		17.5		9.0		12.7		16.7						
(D) Convertible issues																
Nomura	5	4.0	5	4.4	14	2.1					8	2.5	2	13.65	4	7.75
Daiwa	>10		>15		>15						12	2.1				
Nikko	>10		12	1.7	>15										8	3.73
Yamaichi	>10		11	2.0	12	2.5							7	6.02	6	5.09
Total		4.0		8.1		4.6						4.6		19.7		16.6
(E) Bonds with Warrants																
Nomura	1	17.7	1	31.3	1	36.7	1	35.0	1	41.7*						
Daiwa	2	15.5	4	15.0	4	19.3	4	16.9	2	22.8*						
Nikko	3	14.5	2	19.3	2	17.5	2	21.0	3	17.3*						
Yamaichi	4	12.4	3	18.8	3	19.4	3	20.5	4	6.3*						
New Japan	>10		10	0.7	>10	1.8	7		7	1.6*						
Total		60.1		85.1		94.7		93.4		89.7						

[1] = Rank; [2] = share (in %) in each segment   *Figures are for six months ending July, 1990

Source: Compiled from Euromoney, Annual Financing Report, various years

market prices, the foreign equity holding of Japanese investors at the end of 1991 is estimated at $42.5 billion, of which about one-third represents U.S. dollar denominated warrants of Japanese companies issued in Europe.[64] Thus, the true value of Japan's foreign share holdings was only about $28.7 billion at the end of 1991, of which two-thirds was obtained in the European markets.[65] The lower preference of Japanese investors for global equity explains, to a considerable extent, the insignificant role played by Japanese securities companies until 1986 in the international equity market. Thus, only Daiwa scored a 7th position in 1987 as lead manager in this market, capturing about 5 percent of the market.[66] In 1988, Nomura and Yamaichi made their mark on the market and secured 2nd and 7th position, both lead managing 16 international equity issues and seizing 20 percent of the market.[67] It must be noted here, that until 1988, the Japanese managed to make inroads into the market mostly by lead managing the issues of western privatization programs. In 1991, the total share of Japanese securities companies as lead managers amounted to 6 percent.[68]

However, Japanese efforts at winning a position in the international equity market is more visible in their performance as co-lead managers, which displays their placing power as well as the Japanese investors' gradual shift in preference towards European equity markets. Nomura, Daiwa and Yamaichi obtained 3rd, 11th and 14th position respectively as lead and co-lead managers in 1990.[69] With greater signs of portfolio reshuffling by Japanese investors, who favor non-U.S. equity, Japanese securities companies are likely to improve their competitive position in this market in the 1990s. Their innovative efforts, such as Daiwa's pioneering a system of public offering without listing (Powl) in 1990, might provide them with a competitive edge in lead managing the Japanese tranche of most international equity issues.

---

[64]Japan Securities Dealers Association (1992).

[65]ibid.

[66]Jones and Barrett (1988) p. 32.

[67]Lee (1989a) p. 32.

[68]Euromoney (1992) p. 28.

[69]Euromoney (1991b) p. 24.

6.2.3 Position as International Brokers

Since very few quantified facts are available on this point, the position of Japanese securities companies can be evaluated through the limited number of polls or surveys on the subject. Thus, in a poll carried out by Euromoney where the respondents were mostly institutional investors, foreign investors rated Nomura as the top broker for Japan related business followed by Baring, Yamaichi, Daiwa and Salomon.[70] The response of foreign investors highlights the division between those brokers who are able to offer a comprehensive service outside their domestic location and language and those who cater for national investors.[71] Nomura's top rank comes from its excellent research on Japanese equity, fixed income securities and the Japanese economy. It is very natural that Japanese houses have a competitive edge over others in Japan-related research because they get the details much earlier. However, in Japanese warrants and derivatives, foreign brokers perform better than the Japanese, thus showing their competence in advanced financial engineering techniques. In the survey of brokers for national markets across Europe, there is only one niche, i.e., U.K. equities research, in which Nomura appeared in the fifth place in 1991 amongst international brokers.[72] In many surveys of investors, the choice of a Japanese house is guided by an individual broker's skills, especially for non-yen products.[73]

It would be relevant here to assess the competitive position of Japanese securities companies in *value added activities* in Europe such as mergers and acquisitions (M&A). Looking at the disclosed cases of M&A by Japanese bidders in the EU, which increased from 36 cases in 1987 to 113 cases in 1990[74], it is expected that Japanese financial institutions must have been increasingly involved in these transactions. It is noteworthy that Japanese banks show a better record than securities companies as advisers in cross-

---

[70]Euromoney (1990b) p. 75.

[71]ibid.

[72]Euromoney (1991b) p. 6.

[73]Euromoney (1994) p. 94.

[74]A total of 404 M&A transactions were completed by Japanese bidders in the European Union between January 1987 and March 1992. [Information obtained from Yamaichi Securities Co., Ltd.] The sharp rise in M&A activity by the Japanese may indicate a change in the Japanese attitude to takeovers and a desire to supplement the traditional practice of setting up greenfield sites or investing in existing plants.

border deals for Japanese clients. Amongst the securities companies, Yamaichi is ahead of the other Big Four with its own large team of specialists in Europe for M&A business.

6.3 Sources of Competitive Advantage for Japanese Financial Institutions

In Section 6.1 and 6.2, the competitive position of Japanese banks and securities companies during the 1980s has been assessed with the help of numerous indicators. The rapid expansion of their international operations, particularly in the second half of the 1980s, warrants an assessment of the sources of competitive advantages. It is contended by some authors that this expansion was derived mainly from factors with no immediate correlation to the improvement in their international competitiveness.[75] Evidently, the statement was made to emphasize the impact of various macroeconomic factors in the Japanese economy and the developments at the international level on the growth of Japanese financial institutions overseas.

In the following section, various sources of Japanese financial institutions' international competitiveness are elaborated upon under five main categories: advantages from home market characteristics, the advantage of strong ties with domestic clients, the advantage of low-cost capital, the advantage of home currency, and advantages based on conventional measures. The starting premise of the present section is that the primary source of a firm's international competitive advantage lies in its home market; foreign sources of competitive advantage can supplement national sources but cannot be a sufficient substitute.[76]

6.3.1 Advantages from Home Market Characteristics

In his detailed study of the competitive advantages of ten important trading nations[77] Porter analyzed a total of 100 leading industries over a period of four years and came to the following conclusion regarding the importance of the home market of companies:

---

[75]Japan Center for International Finance (1991) p. 5.

[76]Hu (1992) p. 118.

[77]Denmark, Germany, Italy, Japan, Korea, Singapore, Sweden, Switzerland, the United Kingdom, and the United States. Together, these ten countries accounted for 50 percent of total world exports in the year 1985.

"Companies gain advantage against the world's best competitors because of pressure and challenge. They benefit from having strong domestic rivals, aggressive home-based suppliers, and demanding local customers...Ultimately nations succeed in particular industries because their home environment is the most forward-looking, dynamic and challenging."[78]

What Porter says about the competitive advantage of industries should be true for the services sector as well. He further stressed the importance of home market when he said:

"The home base is the nation in which essential competitive advantages of the enterprise are created and sustained. It is where a company's strategy is set, where the core product and process technology is created and maintained, and where the most productive jobs and most advanced skills are located.[79] ...Unless the critical underpinnings of competitiveness are present at home, companies will not sustain competitive advantage in the long-run. The aim should be to upgrade home-base capabilities so that foreign activities are selective and supplementary only to overall competitive advantage."[80]

In this section, those characteristics of Japanese financial markets are discussed that apparently afford Japanese banks and securities companies a competitive edge over their rivals.

Market Structure. When compared with other industrialized countries, the Japanese banking industry is not highly concentrated. In the deposit market, 20 major Japanese banks have a dominant position. Thus, taken together, they account for 38 percent of the market. In the loan market, they contribute 42 percent of thc funds.[81] Contrary to this, the Japanese capital markets have an oligopolistic character dominated by the Big Four securities companies. Entry in the financial market has been relatively restricted in the past and foreign competition played a limited role in altering the market structure. With a strong domestic market base, Japanese financial institutions find it easier to

---

[78]Porter (1990) pp. 73-74.

[79]ibid. p. 85.

[80]ibid. p. 92.

[81]Refer to Section 2.1.1 for details.

expand overseas. This, in turn, helps them pursue the overall strategy of supplementing and reinforcing their competitive position at home.

However, an assured domestic market share should not be interpreted as a lack of competition. Though Japanese financial markets are relatively free from foreign competition, the presence of strong local rivals has been a powerful stimulus for remaining competitive. Until the Financial System Reforms Law was implemented (in April 1993) and time deposit interest rates were fully liberalized (in June 1993), the products offered differed very little and price competition was virtually non-existent. In this environment, the financial institutions' rivalry mostly took the form of non-price competition. After the recent phase of liberalization, the institutional structure is less segmented across products and price competition is gaining ground. "Local rivalry" has started creating pressures to innovate and improve; local rivals push each other to lower costs, improve quality and service. Among all the determinants of international competitiveness mentioned by Porter, domestic rivalry is arguably the most important because of the powerful stimulating effect it has on all the others.[82]

Nature of Local Demand. Some authors view international competition as an evolutionary process, which begins with firms investing in organizational and technological resources that correspond to the cultural and demand characteristics of the immediate local environment. It has been suggested that, given the development of skills, the international competitiveness of a firm is determined by the characteristics of demand and of oligopolistic rivalry in different national markets.[83] Thus, firms gain a competitive advantage where the home demand gives them a clearer or earlier picture of emerging buyer needs and where demanding buyers pressure companies to innovate faster and achieve more sophisticated competitive advantage than their foreign rivals.[84]

---

[82]Porter refers to the four basic attributes of a nation that individually and as a system constitute the diamond of national advantage. These four factors are: (1) Factor conditions, such as skilled labor and infrastructure; (2) Demand conditions, the nature of home-market demand for the industry's product; (3) Presence of internationally competitive supplier industries; and (4) Firm strategy, Structure and Rivalry. See Porter (1990) for details.

[83]Kogut (1988) p. 316.

[84]The size of home demand proves far less significant than the character of home demand. Porter (1990) p. 79.

In the heavily regulated and segmented Japanese financial markets, local demand has not been a very strong determinant of competitiveness in the past. The clients' demand for financial products was more skewed towards capital gains, tax-advantages, and cross-ownership considerations. Even the institutional investors were not accustomed to sophisticated financial engineering products until recently. The use of financial products for liquidity and risk transformation in Japan is of recent origin; most of them introduced in Japan after their success in the western world. Thus, unlike the Japanese manufacturing sector where local clients force companies to innovate products that are light, thin, short, small[85] and internationally accepted, domestic demand does not seem to have rendered Japanese financial institutions more competitive.

Nature of the Capital Market. Corporate goals and strategies reflect the characteristics of the national capital market. In countries such as Japan and Germany, where financial institutions have a substantial part of the national shareholding, most of the shares are held for long-term appreciation or strategic considerations and are rarely traded. Companies from such countries do well in those industries where ongoing investment in R&D and new facilities is essential but the returns may be only moderate.[86] Financial institutions from such countries do well in the foreign markets where immediate return for shareholders is not a decisive factor. This factor is supposed to have influenced the pricing of financial products by Japanese financial institutions in the foreign markets. Thus, institutionalization of share ownership and cross shareholding are some of the features of Japanese capital markets that indirectly, but positively, influence the competitiveness of Japanese firms.

Government-Industry Cooperation. The Japanese financial institutions operate in a regulatory environment that is cautious and supportive of the long-term interests of the domestic financial system. Unlike financial institutions from other countries, Japanese banks and securities companies may only do what is expressly permitted by law. Three powerful bureaux within the MOF, viz., Banking Bureau, Securities Bureau and International Finance Bureau supervise the activities of banks and securities companies. In addition to written laws, they have to abide by a host of directives, often summed up as administrative guidance, issued by the MOF. The regulatory authorities hesitate to permit the introduction of innovative, and perhaps risky, products from outside the

---

[85]in Japanese *kei-haku-tan-sho*.

[86]Porter (1990) p. 81.

domestic market.[87] Thus, inefficiencies in the Japanese financial sector threaten the competitiveness of Japanese institutions.[88]

However, supervision of, and cooperation with, the financial institutions go hand in hand in Japan. The advantages arising from this kind of cooperation are evident. No Japanese financial institution has been allowed to fail in the past because of the concerted efforts of the MOF and BOJ in this regard. It is also believed that Japanese banks maintained low capital/asset ratios in the past because they could count on the implicit guarantee of the regulatory authorities.

6.3.2 Advantage of Strong Ties with Japanese Clients

The existence of an established customer base can be an extremely important competitive advantage for financial institutions in both the international and overseas domestic markets. On the one hand, strong customer ties can provide a natural clientele for a bank or securities firm wishing to enter new markets. On the other hand, an established and secure customer base can also serve to deter potential competitors, both foreign and domestic, from entering existing markets.[89] Relationships with domestic customers also shape the strategies used by foreign banks and securities firms seeking to enter overseas domestic markets. Frequently, the overseas affiliates of business organizations from the home country are targeted as potential customers when a niche strategy is adopted.[90]

That banks go overseas to serve their multinational clients is the typical explanation of the behavior of the MNBs. There is a tendency in the literature to use the same explanation for demonstrating the growth of Japanese banks.[91] The evidence given in support of this is grossly inadequate. It still needs to be checked, on the one hand, whether ties with domestic clients are a strong consideration for the Japanese financial

---

[87]The gradual liberalization of Japanese financial markets, particularly after 1984, was allowed by the authorities as a result of outside pressure. See section 2.2.2 for a list of measures aimed at deregulating the financial markets.

[88]Kreps (1990) p. 78.

[89]Hirtle (1991) p. 48.

[90]ibid. p. 49.

[91]Fujita and Ishigaki (1986); Iwami (1989); Ozawa (1989); Düser (1990) and Dufey (1990) etc.

presence overseas and it has to be proved, on the other, whether this constitutes a source of competitive advantage.

There is no gainsaying the fact that Japanese industry maintains close and long-term ties with financial institutions *at home*. The institutional structure of Japanese business exhibits strong alliances between industry and financial institutions. The bank-centered enterprise grouping (known as *Kinyu Keiretsu*) is representative of the larger pattern of the investor-manager relationship. Domestic corporations and financial institutions usually have interlocking shareholding which is evidence of a stable financial relationship. A listed company usually has a "main bank" with which it has close financial and business ties,[92] and also a close relationship with one or more of the leading securities companies, known as its *kanji shoken gaisha* or "lead underwriter".[93] The importance of home-related business in the overseas activities of Japanese financial institutions derives its strength from these domestic relationships. However, in foreign markets, the relationship between Japanese corporations and financial institutions should be influenced by a multitude of external considerations, too. The wider choice of direct financing methods and the ease of raising funds through international capital markets should affect the funding behavior of the overseas affiliates of Japanese corporations. This should, in turn, affect the degree of their dependence on home banks.

The surveys on Japanese firms' overseas investment by Japanese Ministry of International Trade and Industry (henceforth MITI) provide useful information in this connection. Table 6.8 shows the composition of long-term funds obtained by overseas ventures of Japanese corporations. Overseas affiliates of Japanese companies borrowed worldwide about 50 percent of their total long-term funds in the year ending March 1987 and 39 percent in the year ending March 1989 from local financial institutions in foreign markets. Of this, about half was from the overseas offices of Japanese banks.[94] Japanese ventures overseas rely on local financial institutions more for their short-term

---

[92]For details on the subject of main bank system, see Hodder and Tschoegl (1985), Sheard (1989) and Horiuchi (1989). For an analysis of the changes in the relationship between banks and corporations after mid-1980s, see Bank of Japan (1992a).

[93]Sheard (1992b) p. 22.

[94]In Europe, the dependence on the overseas offices of Japanese banks has increased from 37 percent in the year ending March 1987 to 65 percent in the year ending March 1990.

Table 6.8: Sources of Long-term Financing for Japanese Ventures overseas

(% values)

Sources	Worldwide		N. Americ		Europe		Asia		L. America	
	87	90	87	90	87	90	87	90	87	90
Bonds	11.3	18.5	18.5	22.7	7.5	24.7	6.9	7.6	1.9	12.8
Equity	39.3	18.0	25.0	16.5	44.3	9.9	47.6	21.9	43.7	42.5
Borrowing from local banks	49.3	39.0	56.5	46.2	48.2	35.3	45.5	49.5	54.4	19.6
of which Japanese banks overseas	[51.9]	[52.5]	[71.6]	[50.5]	[37.3]	[65.2]	[46.7]	[47.7]	[58.7]	[32.4]
Others	0.1	24.5		14.6		30.1		21.0		25.1
Total	100	100	100	100	100	100	100	100	100	100

Figures in brackets show the percentage of borrowing from local banks

Source: Compiled from MITI, Kaigai Toshi Tokei Soran (Statistics on Overseas Investment) 3rd & 4th Survey

than for long-term funding needs. In the year ending March 1984,[95] more than 90 percent of short-term funds were obtained locally and the share of Japanese banks' overseas offices was considerably higher.[96] Thus, Japanese banks' close ties with their clients overseas are reflected more in financing the short-term needs of their ventures overseas. It must be pointed out here that overseas affiliates of large sized Japanese companies (with a capital stock of ¥1 billion or more) are more dependent upon the local markets for their funding needs than small and medium-sized companies. This implies that Japanese banks' overseas offices rely more on these large-sized customers for business.[97]

The principal accounts of the overseas branches of all banks published by the BOJ disclose additional information on this point. The asset structure of overseas branches shows the nature of business conducted and hints at the importance of domestic ties.

---

[95]The data about short-term funding sources overseas for Japanese ventures was published by MITI only once in 1986.

[96]MITI (1986) quoted in Ozawa (1989) pp. 64-65.

[97] For details, refer to the survey conducted by Export-Import Bank of Japan (1991) on the subject.

Thus, loans extended by overseas branches constituted only 45 percent of their assets at the end of 1991[98] In comparison, loans make up almost two-thirds (59% at the end of 1991)[99] of Japanese banks' total assets in the domestic markets. Though this fact neither proves nor disproves the hypothesis of strong ties with Japanese clients, it suggests that there are activities other than traditional commercial banking in which Japanese banks employed their funds. The item 'cash and deposits' appears as the second largest asset item on the balance sheet of overseas branches of all Japanese banks, implying perhaps the importance of the treasury function and interbank operations. It could be inferred from above that, to conduct international treasury business, Japanese banks draw upon sources of competitive advantage[100] other than their close ties with Japanese clients.

Japanese financial institutions' ties with their domestic clients are more conspicuous in investment banking activities overseas. Both Japanese banks and securities companies enjoy the confidence of their clients in the provision of corporate advisory services, guarantee business[101] and in underwriting securities issued overseas. In comparison with the MNBs from other countries, Japanese financial institutions naturally have a competitive edge in securing this kind of business. The language and cultural affinities, often reinforced by cross-shareholding interest, make it very difficult for non-Japanese institutions to entice away Japanese firms. However, as mentioned before, Japanese banks were somewhat constrained by the "Three Bureaux Agreement" in underwriting the issues of Japanese corporate clients until April 1993, Thus, regulations at home hindered them from using these links to their advantage.

To conclude, attributing the international success of Japanese banks in the 1980s *to close ties with Japanese clients* is only one of the many explanations. There were other factors, such as low-cost capital, which contributed to their success story.

---

[98]BOJ, Economic Statistics Annual, various issues. In the absence of segregated data for loans to Japanese and non-Japanese clients, it could be assumed that Japanese clients are the main borrower group.

[99]BOJ, Economic Statistics Annual.

[100] In the 1980s, Japanese banks benefited from high ratings as a source of competitive advantage in their international treasury operations.

[101]The main banks or banks of parent companies guaranteed around three-quarters of the straight and warrant bonds issued by Japanese companies overseas. See Horiuchi (1989) p. 274.

6.3.3　Advantage of Low-cost Capital

On the basis of the twin assumptions of segmented capital markets and fairly integrated goods markets, it is often argued that the cost of capital differences have considerable competitive effects. The argument of lower capital costs in Japan has been used mostly in U.S. studies to indicate towards a macroeconomic handicap for American business. The earliest studies compared the cost of capital in particular industries across countries[102] and later the focus shifted to nationwide comparisons.[103] The debate on the subject gained in importance in the late 1980s and many empirical comparisons supported the belief that U.S. firms face higher capital costs than their counterparts in Japan.[104]

The cost of capital advantage is treated as an important factor in the ability of financial institutions to maintain a continuing presence in highly competitive markets.[105] Loopesko (1992) asserts that the importance of the cost of capital to bank competitiveness is shown to vary both over the product cycle and with respect to the choice of product mix by banks. A lower hurdle rate provided by a lower cost of capital reduces the losses incurred in the initial marketing of new products. As the product approaches maturity, economic rents are reduced by new entrants in the market. Banks with lower capital costs still earn positive results whereas others decide to exit the market. The cost of capital advantage is often mentioned as one of the main considerations for the

---

[102]Chase Manhattan Bank (1980) and Flaherty and Itami (1982) compared U.S. and Japanese firms in the semiconductor industry to conclude that cost of capital was lower for the Japanese firms.

[103]Hatsopoulos (1983) compared the U.S. and Japanese cost of capital from 1961 to 1981. A study by the U.S. Department of Commerce (1983) concluded that the weighted average cost of capital to industry in the United States was higher than in France, Germany or Japan in 1981 and that the gap had widened over the decade.

[104]The most widely cited studies are from Hatsopoulos and Brooks (1986), Bernheim and Shoven (1987), Friend and Tokutsu (1987), Ando and Auerbach (1990) and McCauley and Zimmer (1989). Though not perfectly comparable because of differing methodologies, they all suggest that, in the years 1961 to 1988, capital costs in the U.S. exceeded those in Japan by anywhere between 2 percent and 6 percent. See Poterba (1991) for a survey of the methods used in international comparisons of the cost of capital. Kester and Luehrman (1992) point out the pitfalls in using the myth of Japan's low-cost capital.

[105]Hirtle (1991) p. 51.

Japanese financial institutions' success and aggressive behavior in the 1980s.[106] In the following sections, the validity of this argument is analyzed separately for Japanese banks and securities companies.

6.3.3.1 Cost of Capital Advantage for Japanese Banks

The fact that Japanese banks maintained lower equity ratios and had access to cheaper equity is said to have substantially reduced their capital costs and helped them to offer competitive prices for their products and services. Thus, in comparison with Swiss, English and American banks, which had average shareholder equity ratios (shareholders equity as a percentage of total assets) of 6.16%, 5.13% and 4.83% respectively between 1985-89, the average ratio for Japanese banks was 2.46%.[107]

Since banks are more highly leveraged than commercial firms, a legitimate question should be whether Japanese banks have had the *cost of funding advantage* both in the deposit and capital markets? In the first instance, the comparatively high price-earning ratio (72 in 1989) and low dividend yield ratio (1.3% in 1989)[108] of Japanese banks

---

[106]Mullineux (1987); Cohen (1989); Aliber (1984, 1989) etc.

[107]Only France has a ratio lower (2.19%) than that of Japan. It must be mentioned here that factors such as state ownership (as in France) and implicit state guarantee (as in Japan) provide banks with safety mechanisms. This allows banks from some countries to maintain lower equity ratios.

[108]**P/E and Dividend-yield ratio of banks from Major countries** (at the end of 1989)

Country Composites	P/E ratio	Dividend-yield ratio
Japan*	72.1	1.3%
British Clearing banks	6.5	6.2%
U.S. Money Center banks	8.3	4.8%
French banks	9.4	2.1%
Swiss Big banks	16.2	3.7%
German Big banks	19.8	2.4%

*Japanese composite includes BOT, DKB, Fuji, IBJ, Mitsubishi, Sanwa, and Sumitomo Except for Swiss and German banks, where the figures represent average values, all other figures are median values.

Source: Hanley et al. (1990) pp. 147 and 149

explain the capital market advantage available to them.[109] The comparative market to book value ratios of the banks' stock from major countries is another measure of the ease with which funds can be obtained; Japanese banks also had an edge over others in this regard with a median ratio of 750.4% at the end of 1989.[110] Furthermore, in the deposit market, regulated deposit rates in Japan provided Japanese banks with cheaper sources of funds. The cost of funding advantage available to Japanese banks could also be seen with reference to their credit rating. Their high credit rating, mirroring their domestic strength, during most of the 1980s eased the process of obtaining funds in the international interbank market at cheaper rates. Hu points out that, in banking, the home nation's performance affects its banks' ability to raise funds in international markets and the price they have to pay.[111]

Zimmer and McCauley (1992) recently calculated comparable estimates of the cost of capital for banks[112] from Canada, Germany, Japan, Switzerland, the U.S., and the U.K. for the period 1984-90. Focusing on the period averages, they found out that, for 1984-90 as a whole, equity markets in the U.S., U.K. and Canada burden banks with a required return of around 10 percent. German and Swiss banks face moderate equity costs in the 6 percent range, while Japanese banks enjoy very low equity costs of 3

---

[109]Aliber (1989) found that since 1980 Japan has consistently had the highest P/E ratio and, since 1983, it had the lowest dividend-yield ratio amongst the G-7 countries. (pp. 210-215) However, he suggests that the argument of dividend yields is less compelling because of the differences in the dividend payout ratios across countries (p. 210).

[110]The French, English, Swiss, American and German banks had a comparative market to book value ratio of their stock of 81.8%, 117.2%, 153.2%, 157.8% and 185.9% respectively at the end of 1989. [Data Source: Hanley et al. (1990) p. 148] Taking market to book value ratios of banks as a measure, which brings the analysis closer to Tobin's Q-ratio, was attempted earlier by Aliber (1984).

[111]Hu (1992) p. 119.

[112]For making the reported profits of banks comparable across countries, they made four separate adjustments to stated profits: an adjustment for the differential treatment of developing country debt by banks, an adjustment to equity, accounting for shares held by Japanese and German banks, an adjustment for the interaction of growth and inflation with banks' net nominal asset position, and an adjustment for discrepancies between stated depreciation charges and economic depreciation. See Zimmer and McCauley (1992) for the banks included in the sample and other details.

percent.[113] The differences in the cost of equity for banks appear to arise primarily from differences in household savings behavior, macroeconomic stability, and differences in relations among banks, corporations and government.[114]

On the basis of their cost of equity estimates, Zimmer and McCauley calculated the required spreads and fees on three financial products, viz. a standard corporate loan, a commitment to lend and a 10 year interest rate swap over the period 1984-90. The required net spread on a corporate loan showed substantial variations across countries. A U.S., Canada, or U.K. bank needs spreads of 60 to 80 basis points while a Japanese bank needs only 10 basis points.[115] If a U.S. bank has to allow 25 basis points for expected loan losses and another 25 points for providing and serving the loan, then the bank will need a gross spread of about 130 basis points on the loan. While the pattern of required fees on a commitment to lend in the different countries follows the pattern of spreads on the corporate loan, the results for the interest rate swap merits particular attention. The required annual net fee on this item is between 5 and 10 basis points for banks in the U.S., U.K. and Canada. Since the interest rate swap spreads can dip below 5 basis points , U.S., U.K. and Canadian banks cannot even earn enough on swap to cover the cost of Tier 1 equity.[116]

The cost of funding advantage available to Japanese banks during the 1980s has been severely affected by three recent developments:

(i)   The capital adequacy guidelines, agreed to by the major industrialized countries in Basle (in July 1988), require all internationally active banks to raise their capital ratio to 8 percent of their risk-weighted assets by the end of 1992[117] (of which the Tier 1 capital element should be at least 4 percent).[118] The guidelines

---

[113]ibid. p. 180.

[114]ibid. p. 191.

[115]ibid. p. 188.

[116]ibid.

[117]31 March 1993 for Japanese banks. For a comparative study of the differences in approaches adopted by banking supervisory authorities in the U.K., the U.S. and Japan regarding the implementation of BIS guidelines, refer to Hall (1992).

[118]For details of the international convergence of capital measurements and capital standards, see BIS (1988).

fixed an interim target of 7.25 percent which was required to be achieved by the end of 1990. This meant that internationally active Japanese banks had to raise their core capital to 3.25 percent by the end of 1990.[119] These guidelines have introduced a level playing field and made a dent in the cost of funding advantage emanating from the low shareholders' equity ratio of the Japanese banks.[120]

(ii)   Since early 1991, the average stock price index in Japan has been fluctuating at levels which is 50 to 60 percent below its peak level in December 1989. The Japanese banks have become the worst victims of this downturn; the market to book value ratio of the Japanese banks' stock has declined substantially and now it has become increasingly difficult for Japanese banks to raise fresh equity.[121] This has further contained their asset growth because of the limits imposed by the BIS ratio.[122] Since June 1990, Japanese banks have been allowed to issue subordinated debt (counted as Tier 2 capital). Though this has helped them to overcome the difficult situation and has provided them with an additional channel for improving their worsening capital ratio,[123] it has proved to be a more costly method.

---

[119]From 1986 to 1990, the Tier 1 capital of Japanese banks increased at an annual rate of 21%. This implies that huge sums were raised by the issue of equity capital on the TSE between this period. See Frankel and Morgan (1992) p. 588.

[120]As of March 1992, a total of 92 Japanese banks (banks which either maintain overseas offices or have voluntarily chosen to adopt these rules) have opted to be covered by the BIS guidelines. Information obtained from the Federation of Bankers Associations of Japan.

[121]Just before the downturn of the TSE started, eight major Japanese banks had raised a total of 2,643 billion yen (US$19.6 billion) between January 1988 and June 1989 (split approximately 60%-40% between equity and convertible bonds). See Hanley et al. (1989) p. 24.

[122]It has been common recently to estimate the stock market price level at which Japanese banks would meet the BIS guidelines. Mattione (1992b) points out that, with the Nikkei 225 index at 17000 level, most banks would be able to meet the BIS requirement without extraordinary measures. Among other things, the estimates take into account the fact that Japanese banks are allowed, under the BIS Accord, to count up to 45% of their unrealized gains on securities holdings as Tier 2 capital.

[123]As of March 1992, the city banks had issued nearly $45 billion of subordinated debt. See Frankel and Morgan (1992) p. 590.

(iii)   Because of the accelerated process of interest rate liberalization in Japan, the ratio of market rate funding to total funding increased from 17 percent (at the end of March 1980) to around 70 percent (at the end of 1990) for city banks.[124] This, in turn, has strengthened the linkage between funding costs and market rates and resulted in higher funding costs for banks.[125] Furthermore, since the Japanese banks are 'liability-sensitive', i.e., the price of liabilities for them tends to change sooner than the price of assets,[126] the cost of obtaining funds tends to increase faster during periods of rising interest rates. The cheap money policy of the BOJ between February 1987 and May 1989 was reversed in December 1989 after which the official discount rate was gradually raised from 3.75% to its peak of 6% in August 1990. This tough instance continued until the end of June 1991 and had an obvious impact on the term-structure of interest rates in Japan.

Thus, under the changed domestic environment, in which Japanese banks' asset quality has deteriorated considerably, they have additional pressures on overall profitability. The credit rating of Japanese banks has been severely affected since 1990. During 1990, Moody's made downward adjustments the long-term rating of 10 Japanese banks which reflects the banks' weakening profitability and changing risk-profile.[127] This has adversely affected the cost of capital advantage that Japanese banks enjoyed throughout the 1980s. As a consequence, the aggregate worldwide assets of Japanese city banks declined by 5 percent in 1991 - the first yearly asset decline since before World War II. The total assets of the overseas branches of Japanese city banks fell by 13 percent in 1991.[128] Takeda and Turner believe that the hectic pace of Japanese banks' expansion in international markets seen in the second half of the 1980s seems unlikely to recur in the foreseeable future.[129]

---

[124]Bank of Japan (1991a) p. 11.

[125]Bank of Japan (1991b) p. 1.

[126]Kinzer (1992) p. 3.

[127]See Moody's Inc. (1991).

[128]Frankel and Morgan (1992) p. 590.

[129]Takeda and Turner (1992) p. 90.

6.3.3.2   Cost of Capital Advantage for Japanese Securities companies

The cost of capital advantage through the capital market, which accrued to all types of Japanese institutions (both financial and non-financial) in the 1980s, was available to Japanese securities companies also. No estimates of the extent of this advantage have been available so far. A recent study of the cost of capital for securities firms in the United States and Japan[130] provides an interesting insight into the subject. Thus, when seen in terms of the required return on equity capital, Japanese securities companies (with the Big Four as the sample) had an average cost of equity of 5.1 percent between 1982-91 as against 7.8 percent for the U.S. securities firms.[131] It has been suggested that the advantage of Japanese securities firms is smaller than that enjoyed by Japanese banks (3.1 percent compared with 11.9 percent for U.S. banks) or Japanese industrial firms (4.5 percent with 11.2 percent for U.S. industry).[132] Excluding debt costs from the computation of cost of capital under the assumption that internationally active securities firms face similar borrowing costs, it could be shown how the cost of equity is translated into cost of capital for the securities firms.

The cost of capital for securities firms further depends upon the capital requirements (i.e., required equity-to-asset ratio) imposed upon them by the authorities. Unlike the internationally active banks, which are supposed to observe agreed capital adequacy guidelines, internationally active securities firms face no similar compulsion so far. Thus, with lower capital requirements outside their home and lower cost of equity at home, Japanese securities firms need to earn less on their assets. To take the example given by McCauley and Zimmer, if the equity-to-asset requirement in Japan is 10 percent, a cost of equity of 5 percent for Japanese firms means that they need to earn only ½ percent on their assets. In comparison, a U.S. securities firm, with 10 percent cost of equity, has to earn 1 percent on assets in Tokyo. To extend the example, if the equity-to-asset ratio in the U.S. market is 2 percent then, with above cost of equity, the U.S. firm needs to earn 20 basis points on its assets while the Japanese firm can get

---

[130]McCauley and Zimmer (1991) pp. 14-27.

[131]The cost of equity is computed by making various adjustments to the ratio of reported profits to the market value of equity of firms in each group. Refer to McCauley and Zimmer (1991) for details.

[132]ibid. pp. 17-18.

away with 10 basis points of return on its assets.[133] This also illustrates the point why Japanese securities companies could manage with a lower margin on their transactions than other internationally active securities firms.

It needs to be examined whether Japanese securities companies still retain their cost of capital advantage. Various deregulation in the Japanese securities markets (e.g., gradual reduction in brokerage commission) and the financial system (e.g., repeal of Article 65) are likely to affect the profitability of securities companies. In part, Japanese investors bear a risk of lower earnings of Japanese securities companies in a deregulated environment, and this risk boosts their measured cost of equity.[134] In addition, Japanese securities companies' distance from corporate networks of mutual support may render their shares more risky than the shares of firms which are secure within such networks.[135] Indeed, in the fiscal year ending March 1992, major Japanese securities companies reported huge after-tax losses and have been badly hit by the decline in stock exchange turnover.[136] This suggests that the smaller cost of capital advantage, which Japanese securities companies enjoyed until the end of 1990, is likely to be eroded much earlier than that available to Japanese banks and other non-financial firms.

6.3.4   International position of the home currency

In the literature, the international position of the home currency is seen as a factor influencing the competitiveness of MNBs.[137] The internationalization of the U.S. banks is often associated with the dominant role of the dollar as a vehicle currency. In the case of the Japanese financial institutions, it is known that their global expansion has not been accompanied by a sufficient internationalization of the yen.[138] Thus, if Japanese banks

---

[133]ibid. p. 19.

[134]ibid. p. 27.

[135]ibid.

[136]Of the Big Four, three reported after-tax losses for the fiscal year ending March 1992. The 10 second-tier securities companies fared even worse. See Thomson (1992) p. 12.

[137]Aliber (1984); Damanpour (1990); Fujita and Ishigaki (1986) and Swoboda (1982).

[138]Fujita and Ishigaki (1986) p. 197.

could report tremendous growth overseas despite limited home currency advantage, it could be deduced that the use of domestic currency as a vehicle currency may not be a necessary condition for the competitive success of the banks from that country.

It can be argued further that if the cost of funds in domestic currency is equated with Eurocurrency rates through arbitrage, and if everyone has free access to both types of currencies, then the currency advantage would be negligible or non-existent. With the first condition already fulfilled and the second partly fulfilled in the case of Japan, it is understandable why Japanese banks did not rely heavily on home currency support for overseas growth. However, an indirect impact of the home currency in the case of Japanese banks has been that, with their capital base in a currency which was appreciating and easy to obtain, Japanese banks could support their Euro-business book with a growing capital base in yen.

6.3.5   Advantages based on Conventional Measures of Competitiveness

Over and above the cost of capital advantage and ties with Japanese clients abroad, very little is known about other facets of Japanese financial institutions' international competitiveness. One has to depend upon the conventional measures of industrial competitiveness to find other sources of their competitive strength. These measures include size, productivity, innovativeness, etc. Depending upon the availability of data, a systematic analysis of various measures appears over the following pages for Japanese banks and securities companies.

6.3.5.1   Japanese Banks

The **size** of an internationally active bank is an important indicator of its competitive strength. The attainment of a "critical mass" and the opportunities for risk diversification afforded by size may confer an important advantage in international banking.[139] In Dunning's "Ownership-Location-Internalization" paradigm, the size of a bank could be seen as an ownership advantage and, as such, may be a prerequisite to multinationalization. As already mentioned in Section 6.1, Japanese banks constitute a formidable group in terms of their size. At the end of March 1990, there were five banks in the

---

[139]Spindler et al. (1991) p. 174.

world that had assets exceeding $300 billion and all of them were Japanese banks.[140] Usually the total assets and total revenue of a bank are taken as two indicators of size. However, because of the increasing importance of off-balance sheet business in total business, total assets are no longer a sufficient indicator of competitive strength.

Related to asset size, asset growth rate is another indicator of growing competitive strength. Thus, with the real average annual growth rate of assets of 12.6 percent for the period 1985-89, eleven Japanese banks[141] were the fastest of any national group, followed by German (5.5%), British (3.61%), French (3.09%), Swiss (3.06%), and U.S. (2.2%) banks.[142] Analyzing the growth of the assets of the MNBs, Dohner and Terrell find that in the period since year end 1986, the performance of Japanese banks has changed considerably as their asset growth has exceeded the growth of their home country GNP by a far greater margin than any other sample of banks.[143] In respect of total revenue (net of interest expense), Japanese banks are not in the top ten revenue producers. They experienced the fastest growth in revenue, with the average annual growth rate of 16 percent between 1986-89 followed by British (5.67%), German (5.6%) Switzerland (4.87%), French (4.32%) and U.S. (4.26%) banks.[144]

The **productivity measures** in banking are more sensitive yardsticks of competitive strength.[145] These measures show the efficiency of banking operations and, consequently, help in gauging a bank's ability to compete under changing market conditions and over the long-run.[146] Several measures could be applied for the analysis of productivity in banking:

---

[140]These Japanese banks are Dai-Ichi Kangyo, Sumitomo, Fuji, Mitsubishi, and Sanwa. It is interesting to note that, other than these banks, there are only five banks in the US$200 to US$300 dollar range (2 Japanese, 1 French, 1 American and 1 British). See Spindler et al. (1991) p. 174.

[141]Included here are the DKB, Mitsubishi, Fuji, Sumitomo, Sanwa, BOT, IBJ, LTCB, Mitsubishi Trust and Banking, Sumitomo Trust and Banking and Mitsui Trust and Banking.

[142]Spindler et al. (1991) p. 176.

[143]Dohner and Terrell (1988) p. 9.

[144]Spindler et al. (1991) p. 177.

[145]Cohen (1989) p. 43.

[146]Spindler et al. (1991) p. 181.

(i)   the ratio of total revenue to non-interest expense; this explains the amount of
        revenue generated by each unit of currency spent on salaries, systems and non-
        interest expenses;

(ii)   total operating expenses as a percentage of operating income or earning assets,
        which signifies overall cost efficiency;

(iii)   per employee growth in average assets, operating profits and operating expenses.
        Growth in assets and operating profits per employee reflects upon the efficiency
        of human resources and growth in operating expenses per employee shows the
        cost management and cost containment efforts of an institution.

Table 6.9 provides a comparative analysis of the productivity measures of MNBs
from the major industrial countries.[147] Japanese banks, as a group, produced between
1985-89 on average ¥2.06 of revenue for every yen spent on non-interest expense and
provided the best productivity results. Because interest expenses are not included in this
ratio, it could be said that Japanese banks have a competitive edge which goes beyond
the low cost of funding. With total operating expenses of 59 percent of operating
income, they are second only to Swiss banks. Not only that, they were able to
accumulate substantial assets with the lowest operating expenses of 0.87 percent of
earning assets. The growth of operating expenses per employee of Japanese banks
between 1982-86 is similar to that of U.S. banks, but higher than that of Swiss and
German banks. Taking into account the fact that total number of employees at major
Japanese banks declined by 5 to 10 percent in the 1980s[148], the 38 percent growth in
operating expenses implies heavy investment, both at home and abroad, in expensive
advanced technology. However, the growth in operating costs is more than compensated
for by the growth in assets and operating income denoting the higher productivity of
Japanese bank personnel. At the end of 1988, the productivity measures for Japanese
banks did not change significantly.[149]

---

[147]The data given in the table may not be fully comparable because of various
differences in accounting practices between countries.

[148]Hanley et al. (1989) p. 42.

[149]Hanley et al. (1989) p.43. The non-availability of data beyond 1988 does not
allow analysis of the recent changes in the productivity of MNBs.

Table 6.9: Selected Productivity Measures for Multinational banks# from Major Industrial Countries

Bank from	Total revenue/ Non-Interest Expense (1985-89)	Total Operating Expens [1986] As a % of Operating Income	Total Operating Expens [1986] As a % of Earning Assets	(For 1982-86, in %) Per Employee Growth in Average Total Assets	(For 1982-86, in %) Per Employee Growth in Operating Expenses	(For 1982-86, in %) Per Employee Growth in Operating Income
Japan	2.06	59.0	0.87	63.4	38.4	65.8*
United Kingdom	1.52	69.1	4.16	NA	NA	NA
United States	1.51	NA	NA	6.4	38	39.4**
France	1.46	67.0	2.65	NA	NA	NA
Germany	1.44	66.5	2.24	0.7***	10.8***	9.6***
Switzerland	1.36	52.2	1.42	22.4	21.7	33.8

#the sample banks include the 3 largest banks each from Switzerland and Germany, 4 clearing banks from the United Kingdom, the 7 largest banks from Japan, the 8 largest from France and all money center banks from the United States. (The sample banks for the second column differs from that of the rest of the table; refer to the sources for the details of sample institutions)

    *the figure represents operating profits (Eigyo-Rieki)

  **the figure represents net income

*** figures are for the period 1983-86

Sources : Hanley et al. (March 1988) p.83, 88, 91, 98, 107, 117
        Total Revenue/Non-interest Expense ratio is quoted from Spindler (1991)

Innovativeness shows the ability of a bank to answer the new demand from clients by providing many permutations and combinations of risk and return, often supported by new technological devices. The innovativeness of an MNB is difficult to quantify. Therefore, most of the evidence on this point is anecdotal. The general perception about MNBs from industrial countries is that major U.S. banks have excellent skills in developing innovative financial products.[150] Although there are indications of some Japanese banks building capacities in new products and markets, on the whole, they do not have the image of strong innovators. To overcome this shortcoming, the Japanese

---

[150]It is said that Citicorp's considerable experience in swaps and options in foreign exchange transactions allows it to introduce, on average, about one new foreign exchange product per month. See Hanley et al. (1987) p. 7.

approach has been to form strategic alliances or to buy in the brains they need. However, the problem with financial products and innovations is that they do not lend themselves to the sort of incremental enhancement which is common in the field of mass manufacturing.[151] In any case, few would deny that the Japanese possess both the technology and the distribution skills to use the information technology successfully[152] and to innovate.

6.3.5.2   Japanese Securities Companies

As mentioned in chapter 5, because of fundamental differences in the balance sheet composition of banks and securities firms, not all conventional measures of performance provide clear-cut comparative results. For example, asset-based measures are not reliable indicators of a securities firm's performance because a large portion of its business does not involve the generation or holding of assets.[153] Therefore, instead of absolute size, in this study the emphasis has been placed on asset growth rates. Because of similarities ensuing from the statutory separation of commercial and investment banking in the United States and Japan, most of the international comparisons draw on U.S. securities firms for evaluation of the relative performance of Japanese securities companies.

In terms of **size**, Japanese securities companies, particularly the Big Four, possess a distinct advantage. With average shareholders' equity of $8.52 billion at the end of March 1991,[154] the Big Four have a strong base to start with.[155] The size provides a natural ownership advantage in global expansion and coverage. Judged on the basis of

---

[151]Economist (1989) p. 80.

[152]Dufey (1990) p. 151.

[153]Spindler et al. (1991) p. 185.

[154]The average shareholders' equity of the top 6 U.S. investment banks (Salomon Brothers, Merrill Lynch, Shearson Lehman, Goldman Sachs, Morgan Stanley and First Boston Corp.) was US$2.84 billion as of December 1991. See Moody's Investors Service (1992).

[155]Nomura professes to be the largest financial institution in the world when measured according to shareholders' equity. At the end of March 1994, it had shareholders' equity of ¥1.83 trillion (approximately US$17.72 billion at the exchange rate of $ = ¥103.15).

real asset growth, the Big Four clearly outperformed many international securities firms. Thus, taken together, their assets grew at an average of 37.1 percent annually over the period between 1986 through 1989.[156] In contrast, the assets of the U.S. securities firms rose by an average of 7 percent annually.[157] Looking at total revenue and revenue growth as other measures of size, it could be said that the Big Four do not dominate in terms of revenue generation but show an impressive revenue growth rate of 22.1 percent annually compared to the U.S. average of 11.7 percent between 1986-89.[158] The high revenue growth rate derives from the brisk brokerage business done by the Big Four on the fast growing domestic stock market up to December 1989. It is one of the main assertions of this study that the growth in domestic assets and revenue has substantially supported and subsidized the rise of Japanese financial institutions to prominent positions in the international financial markets. The downturn of stock prices and low stock market turnover in Japan since early 1990 and financial scandals of 1991 have had serious effects on the performance of the Big Four. All this is likely to influence their overseas business growth and competitive performance.

Profitability measures should gauge the competitiveness from another angle. Taking again the case of the Big Four, they achieved an average return on assets (ROA) of 1.83 percent for the period 1985 through 1989[159]. The oligopolistic character of the Japanese securities industry, the dominant position of the Big Four and the prevalence of fixed commissions are some of the reasons for the domestic earning driven performance of the Japanese securities companies. The average return on equity for the Big Four was 19.6 percent between 1985-89, which was roughly twice that of the U.S. firms.[160]

The **productivity** of Japanese securities companies, measured in terms of the total revenue generated per unit of non-interest expense, is higher than that of their U.S. counter-parts. Thus, the Big Four produced a revenue to non-interest expense ratio of

---

[156]Spindler et al. (1991) p. 186.

[157]ibid.

[158]ibid. p. 187.

[159]The corresponding figure for the U.S securities firms is 0.33 percent for the same period.

[160]ibid. p. 188.

2.16 for the period 1985 through 1989, whereas the ratio for U.S. firms was 1.12.[161] The higher ratio in the case of Japanese securities companies is partly because of the lower denominator caused by salaries expense item in the Japanese securities industry, which is low by Western standards.[162] It is relevant to note that the Big Four also improved their productivity over the period, with the above-mentioned ratio being 1.92 in 1985 and 2.23 in 1989.[163]

The **innovativeness** of financial institutions is difficult to measure. The reputation of financial innovators is based largely on anecdotal evidence and, usually, clubs all leading institutions from a country into one group. Thus, as against the Japanese, the U.S. financial institutions are generally considered more innovative in the marketing of new financial products. Japanese securities companies, particularly the Big Four, have improved their image by successively bringing new instruments into the primary Eurobond market.

In October 1985, Nomura introduced the 'Heaven and Hell' type of Eurobonds issued for IBM Credit Corporations, which involved multiple interest rate and currency swaps.[164] The yen and dollar bonds with principal repayment amounts linked to the spot yen/dollar exchange rate were also initiated by Nomura. *Sushi bonds* were developed by Yamaichi to satisfy the portfolio needs of Japan's trust banks and insurance companies.[165] Deferred interest bonds were devised by Japanese securities companies to suit the unique needs of Japanese institutional investors.[166] In 1990, Daiwa pioneered a system of making a public offering without listing (Powl), in its lead managing of the Japanese tranche of the U.K. water companies privatization.

---

[161]ibid. p. 189.

[162]Hakim, (1986) p. 50.

[163]Spindler et al. (1991) p. 189.

[164]The offering was designed to yield high premiums if the dollar were to rise significantly before maturity ('heaven') and a diminution of principal in the event of a major appreciation of the yen against the dollar ('hell').

[165]Since MOF restricts the funds invested in foreign bonds, a market developed, within the Euromarket, in foreign currency bonds issued by domestic institutions which are not classified as foreign bonds by the MOF.

[166]The deferring of interest for some years helped the institutional investors in selling the bonds at a premium on the basis of unpaid interest and secure capital gains.

In order to cater to the complex needs of investors, Yamaichi recently introduced a number of integrated systems, developed jointly with Global Advanced Technology Corporation (GAT), which are used by institutional investors worldwide. The Integrative Asset Allocation System (IAS) covers stock indices of 13 countries, bonds in nine countries, and convertible bond markets in Japan and the United States, as well as short-term money markets. The Integrative Stock System (ISS), based on the capital asset pricing model, and the Integrative Bond System (IBS), based on the Arbitrage free fate movement model and the Capital Asset Pricing Multiple Dimensioned Model (CAPMD) are other examples of the innovations based on advanced financial theories introduced by Yamaichi.

The Competitive Advantage of Placing Power. The typical explanation given for the relatively quicker success of Japanese securities companies, both in Eurobonds and international equity markets, is that they have *enormous placing power*[167] in the home market. It is believed that Japanese securities companies and Swiss banks have been able to dominate the market because of the ease with which they can distribute securities. In the words of Scott-Quinn:

> "The firms that were able to generate revenues were of two types - those which lead managed the issue and therefore received *precipium* on the issue (i.e. a payment out of the spread before any other member of the syndicate is paid) and those who had access to price-insensitive clients. These include the Swiss banks with non-resident discretionary clients and the Japanese securities houses with their domestic client base....in the case of Japanese clients, social relationship between investors and securities houses count for more than in the west and seem to allow a reward for services given rather than a pure free competitive return."[168]

While there is an element of truth in the above observation about the social relationship between investors and securities companies, it can not be said categorically that Japanese investors are price-insensitive. The fact that a considerable part of Japanese investment in foreign securities is made by, or on behalf of, yield conscious institutional

---

[167]Placing power, in this context, implies the ease or capacity of distributing the underwritten securities.

[168]Scott-Quinn (1990a) p. 285.

investors,[169] rebuts the price-insensitivity hypothesis. The dominant placing power of the Big Four comes, to a great extent, from their extremely large clientele concentration in the home market as well as from their efficient information production and accumulation. The oligopolistic position of the Big Four and their ability to set prices in the domestic securities market has earned them sustained business relationship with clients. Their formidable domestic client base has thus been fostered equally by the economic priorities of corporate clients and institutional investors.

In fact, the distribution capacity of Japanese banks in the home market is better than that of Japanese securities companies because of their extensive domestic network of branches. However, in practice, their capacity has been constrained by regulations at home. Thus, for example, Japanese banks are allowed to conduct securities business with institutional investors but not with private individuals and corporate clients. Further, they can not take orders from their overseas clients because they are not members of the TSE and hence have no direct access to Japanese stocks. These limitations seriously narrow the scope of business for Japanese banks as securities brokers and dealers.

Thus, to sum up the section, in most of the Japan-related securities business, Japanese securities companies still have a competitive edge over others. The finding that home-country market conditions continue to play a crucial role in the competitive success of large internationally active financial institutions suggests that the process of true internationalization is still incomplete. Despite the opportunities that international markets present for competition on a level playing field, segregation along national and institutional boundaries remains a significant factor in the competitive environment.[170]

6.4   Summary and Conclusions

Any investigation of international competitiveness should provide an assessment both of competitive position as well as of the factors that contribute to that position. The analysis in this chapter draws on several indicators for reviewing the international

---

[169]Japanese financial institutions and other institutional investors account for over three-quarters of all Japanese investment in foreign securities.

[170]Hirtle (1991) p. 25.

position of Japanese banks and securities companies and evaluates the sources of competitive advantage available to them.

The case of Japanese Banks. Because of the sharp appreciation of the yen after 1985, Japanese banks' international position measured in terms of total assets at current dollar price does not provide a true picture of their competitive strength. The BIS estimates of the international banking based on nationality of ownership afford a better insight into the subject. However, the rapid expansion of the Japanese banks' international banking assets must be seen in the light of certain peculiarities. Thus, a large share of the expansion took the form of claims on related offices or on other banks, and it has been driven heavily by new home office business. Furthermore, the overall net creditor position of Japanese banks has changed little over time despite the huge current account surplus and savings.

In addition to the above indicators, the expansion of the overseas network of offices and performance in various segments of the international financial markets offer further information for assessing the competitive position of banks. Japanese banks figure in the international syndicated loan market as significant providers of funds. With all the restrictions from home authorities, which hindered them from actively participating in the Eurobond market, they have performed reasonably well in this market.

Until recently Japanese banks had both capital and deposit market advantages, which reduced their overall funding costs and provided them with a competitive edge in foreign markets. In the changed environment at home since the early 1990s, these advantages have been drastically diminished. Japanese banks' strong ties with their domestic clients do provide an argument for going overseas but prove insufficient for continued profitable expansion in the long run. However, Japanese banks' large size, high productivity and cost-efficiency advantages, as traditional measures of competitiveness, provide new grounds for assessing their overall strength.

The case of Japanese Securities Companies. Japanese securities companies improved their international position in the latter half of the 1980s and captured prominent positions as bookrunners in the Eurobond league tables.. The dramatic increase in their market share was supported by the spurt in Japanese equity-warrant related bond issues. They also occupied dominant positions in the Euroyen bond market, suggesting the competitive advantage arising from home-currency business. The lower preference of Japanese investors for international equities explains the subdued role of the Japanese securities companies in this market. Japanese efforts at winning a position in the international equities market is more visible in their performance as co-lead managers, which displays their placing power as well as Japanese investors' gradual shift in preference for European equity market. As international brokers, Japanese securities companies, particularly the Big Four, show a strong competitive position in Japan- related business.

In searching for the sources of the Japanese securities companies' competitive strength, one often dwells upon their placing power and dependence on home-related business. This is a source of both strength and weakness for them. The recent decline in home-related business showed that their international position is somewhat fragile. Their success during 1986-89 is also justified through the cost of capital advantage which was available to all types of Japanese institutions. However, this advantage was smaller for Japanese securities companies than for Japanese banks and is likely to be eroded sooner than that of banks. An analysis of their competitiveness through traditional measures shows that their monolithic size, huge domestic profitability and high productivity provides additional evidence for their rise to prominent positions.

Other than the cost of capital advantage, strong ties with Japanese clients and traditional measures of strength, Japanese financial institutions draw upon some home-market characteristics (such as home market structure, the nature of the domestic capital market and government-financial industry relationship) for supporting their growth overseas. However, because of the slow pace of the yen's internationalization, Japanese banks did not get the benefit of home-currency effect, which is supposed to have played a major role in the international success of U.S. financial institutions.

To sum up, during the 1980s, Japanese banks and securities companies displayed improvements in their competitive position in traditional commercial banking and investment banking respectively. This shows that financial institutions specialize in international markets according to their traditional lines of business and that progress towards free movements across products and markets is still limited.

Chapter 7

Determinants of the Japanese Banks' Overseas Expansion - Evidence from the European Union

Apparently, the decision by an MNB to establish offices in overseas markets is a managerial one. It comes about when management recognizes international business as a significant variable in its strategic planning. However, in reality, the internationalization of a financial institution is the outcome of a multitude of factors, many of which are macroeconomic and exogenous in character. Volume of foreign trade, economic growth rate, the magnitude of cross-border capital flows, term structure of interest rates, and long-term movements in the exchange rate are some of the macroeconomic variables that have a bearing on the internationalization of financial institutions.

For the sake of argument, it could be said that macroeconomic changes should have equal influence on all the economic agents in an economy and this should lead to *convoy behavior* on their part.[1] Extending this view to financial institutions, when many financial institutions from a country decide to go overseas *en bloc*, it is assumed that the phenomenon has more to do with the exogenous and macroeconomic variables than with the endogenous variables peculiar to some institutions. The dramatic increase in the number of offices opened by all major types of Japanese financial institutions in Europe in the 1980s endorses the convoy behavior hypothesis. However, it still remains to be proved that the explanation for this behavior lies in macroeconomic factors. In this chapter, an attempt has been made to delineate those determinants that are macroeconomic in character and explain the *en bloc* internationalization of Japanese banks. The main intention is to evaluate those factors which are responsible for their growth in the EU. An econometric model has been developed whereby the significance of each determinant is tested with the help of a regression analysis. An investigation into the key determinants of Japanese banking expansion in the EU will possibly expand our understanding of the globalization of banking firms.

---

[1] However, in reality, economic agents react differently to economic events, depending upon their risk-return preferences. Some economic agents, particularly large and influential ones, react to macroeconomic changes earlier than others.

7.1   Factors Influencing the Japanese Financial Presence Overseas

Most of the macroeconomic factors that influence FDI in the industrial sector are also relevant to the multinationalization of financial institutions. This is why Aliber (1984) concludes that, "Most of the approaches to the theory of international banking are extensions of the theory of foreign direct investment." The following pages present a brief explanation of those factors which are believed to have encouraged the growth of Japanese banks in the overseas markets.

The dramatic growth of Japanese FDI to Europe is the first factor that is assumed to have influenced Japanese banking expansion. This factor is taken to support the hypothesis that banks follow their multinational clients into overseas markets.[2] The explanation given in the literature to support the hypothesis ranges from the defensive strategy of not losing clients in the overseas markets to the informational advantages available to banks that move with their clients.[3] The published data in Japan provides evidence in support of this hypothesis. In Table 7.1, an attempt has been made to determine the degree of correlation between the number of Japanese banking offices in Europe with that of Japanese manufacturing firms in Europe for the period 1982-91.

Table 7.1: Two Related Measures of the "Following the Client" Hypothesis

Description	Period Covered	Correlation Coefficient
1. Relation between the number of Japanese Manu- facturing firms and banking offices* in Europe	1982-91	0.968
2. Relation between the total amount (stock values) of foreign direct investment by Japan and the total number of Japan´s banking offices* in Europe	1980-90	0.924

*include all branches, subsidiaries and representative offices

Source: Computations from data published by JETRO; MOF etc.

---

[2]The hypothesis has become a cornerstone of the theory of international banking. Practically every author on the subject has endorsed this view point. A brief review of the hypothesis is given in Section 1.1.1

[3]Refer to Section 6.3.2 for details on how far close ties with home clients constitute a competitive advantage for Japanese banks in Europe.

The data shows a high correlation coefficient between the two variables and provides evidence in favor of the hypothesis. When the number of offices opened by Japanese banks is compared with the volume of Japanese FDI to Europe, the correlation coefficient is equally significant.[4] However, the results, when seen in isolation, overemphasize the importance of FDI in explaining the Japanese banking expansion in Europe and must be interpreted with caution.

Exchange value of the home currency. A recent survey of Japanese business activities abroad reveals that, of 3,408 manufacturing affiliates of Japanese companies located overseas, 52.1 percent were established after the fiscal year 1985.[5] Since 1985 marks the beginning of the period when the yen started appreciating, the exchange rate seems to have been a significant factor in motivating Japanese investment overseas. It has already been mentioned in Chapter 4 that Japanese banks exhibited a dramatic increase in their FDI to Europe after 1985. Thus, after the yen started appreciating, all types of Japanese multinationals increased their presence overseas.

Theoretically, the relationship between the exchange value of the yen and expansion by Japanese banks should depend upon whether the initial outlay or the anticipated gain from foreign investment is the focal point in their decision-making. If initial outlay guides decision-making, the relationship between the exchange value of the yen and foreign investment should be positive, i.e., appreciation of the yen should make foreign investment cheaper and encourage it. On the contrary, the relationship would be negative if expected gains from the investment guide the decision to invest, i.e., appreciation of the yen would produce lower earnings in yen terms and discourage investment.

At this juncture, the feasibility of segregating the effect of exchange rates on Japanese FDI must be analyzed. Since the stock price boom in Japan is roughly contemporaneous with the appreciation of the yen, both factors may be working together to give Japanese institutions an edge in financing their overseas investment.[6] Thus, it may be very diffi-

---

[4] Since Japanese FDI in Europe includes a sizable proportion of FDI in financial sectors, the correlation may be overstated to that extent.

[5] MITI (1992) p. 2.

[6] Froot (1991) p. 19.

cult to isolate the impact of the yen's appreciation on Japanese banks' decision to invest in new establishments overseas, particularly after 1985.[7]

Foreign trade is the third factor that influences foreign banking activity. Various authors have found that a strong relationship exists between international trade and foreign banking activity in the U.S. [Terrell (1979), Khoury (1980) Zimmerman (1989), Terrell et al. (1989) etc.].[8] Referring to Japanese banks in the U.S., Khoury (1980) identifies the volume of trade between Japan and the U.S. as an important determinant. Similarly, Terrell et al. (1989) find a statistically significant trade variable in their analysis of Japanese banks in the United Kingdom. However, the authors find it difficult to interpret their results because of the evidence that Japanese banks in London are more involved in treasury business and funding for their head offices.

The price-earning ratio of bank stocks provides an additional explanation for the growth of foreign banking activity. Conceivably, a high price-earning ratio of home bank stocks means a cost of capital advantage[9] for Japanese banks. In contrast the low price-earning ratio of host country bank stocks provides incentives for bank acquisitions in the host country.[10] Thus, the expansion of Japanese banks overseas in the 1980s should be positively related to their own price-earning ratio and inversely related to that of host country bank stocks. Since Japanese banks have not made any outright acquisition of European banks despite lower price-earning ratios in Europe, the price-earning ratio of european banks can be treated as irrelevant in the European context.[11]

Regulation and deregulation of the domestic financial markets both seem to influence the multinationalization of banking. While regulations lead to the flight of business to

---

[7]A BOJ report also attributes the rapid overseas expansion of Japanese banks from the middle of the 1980s to such exogenous factors as the rise of the yen and higher stock prices. Quoted in Japan Center for International Finance (1991) p. 21.

[8]For unexplained reasons, Hultman and McGee (1989) and Thornton (1991) did not include this variable in their analysis.

[9]For details on the advantage of low-cost capital for Japanese financial institutions, refer to Section 6.3.3.

[10]High (low) ratio would increase (decrease) the cost of acquiring host country banks. See Hultman and McGee (1989) p. 389.

[11]In the U.S., the lower price-earning ratio of the U.S. firms is seen as one of the factors in the acquisitions made by Japanese firms.

offshore markets, deregulation provide legitimate freedom to go overseas. In the case of Japan, domestic regulations and controls have been held responsible for the growth of Japanese banking in the U.S.[12] and U.K.[13] In this context, deregulation in the domestic markets are seen as a sufficient reason for repatriating back home those types of business which were previously prohibited. In contrast, the new Foreign Exchange Law of 1980 and the Banking Law of 1982 are cited as examples of deregulation that liberalized international banking.[14] On the whole, the deregulations in Japan seem to be an important factor in the expansion of banks in the 1980s and are treated as a dummy variable in the proposed model.

Foreign banking activity of a country's banks may be stimulated just as much by the *prevailing or expected economic conditions in the home and host countries.* Perpetuating economic optimism in the home country (as in Japan between 1986-90) or an expected economic boom in the host economy become a strong determinant of the expansion strategy. The economic optimism (pessimism) provides latitude (restriction) for undertaking risky business such as international banking. Table 7.2 provides three indicators of economic boom in Japan that boosted the morale of all types of economic institutions.

As is evident from the table, economic optimism in Japan was initiated by booming stock prices and supplemented by the current account surplus around 1983. The increase in the real economic growth after 1984 characterized this optimism. In the period 1987-89, all indicators show bursting economic confidence and it is in this period that the Japanese banks' overseas expansion was most dramatic. Thus, a positive functional relationship could be postulated between economic activity and the growth of foreign banking. Since increasing FDI from Japan to a region reflects growth prospects there, changes in Japanese FDI to Europe should concurrently reflect expected economic conditions in the host country.[15] Thus, it would suffice if only home market economic conditions are incorporated as a determinant in the analysis.

---

[12]Poulsen (1986).

[13]Terrell et al. (1989).

[14]For details on deregulations that boosted cross-border banking business, refer to Section 2.2.2

[15]Hultman and Ramsey (1975) noted that changes in FDI in the U.S. are highly correlated with changes in U.S. GNP.

Table 7.2: Three Indicators of Economic Optimism in Japan

Year	Stock Price Index (Topix)[1]	Current Account Balance[2]	Real Economic Growth (%)
1975	323.43	-0.7	2.7
76	383.88	3.7	4.8
77	364.08	10.9	5.3
78	449.55	16.5	5.2
79	459.61	-8.8	5.2
80	494.10	-10.7	3.6
81	570.31	4.8	3.6
82	593.72	6.9	3.2
83	731.82	20.8	2.7
84	913.37	35.0	4.3
85	1,049.40	49.2	4.9
86	1,556.37	85.9	2.6
87	1,725.83	87.0	4.3
88	2,357.03	79.6	6.2
89	2,881.37	57.2	4.7
90	1,733.83	35.8	5.6
91	1,714.68	72.9	4.4
92	1,307.66	117.6	0.7
93	1,439.31	131.5	NA

1 End of period values; January 4, 1968 = 100
2 Current account balance in billion of US dollars

Source: Tokyo Stock Exchange for the stock price index
          BOJ for other statistics

Japan's current account surplus, which is the mirror image of the excess of savings over investment, is widely held as a cause of the expansion of Japanese banks overseas. It is implied that banks from a country are best placed to intermediate the recycling of its current account surplus. However, in the 1980s, Japan's current account surplus was recycled primarily through portfolio investment. Hence, non-bank financial intermediaries, and not banks, were the main vehicles for this purpose. Thus, presumably, current account surplus has had only a minor influence on Japanese banks' expansion process. It may have been one of the indicators of economic optimism and indirectly contributed to the expansion process.

The attractiveness of international financial markets, particularly of Euromarkets, could be brought in as another variable influencing rapid expansion. In Europe, particularly in the U.K., Switzerland and Luxembourg, the gravitational pull of the international financial markets has been an important factor. It gave rise to a new approach of external network deployment of Japanese financial institutions where, in an increasing number of cases, one bank had other subsidiaries in addition to its branch office.[16] It is difficult to locate an indicator that captures the overall attractiveness of Euromarkets for Japanese financial institutions.

It must be noted here that any modeling of this type is constrained by the non-availability of data or the absence of an appropriate indicator for a functional relationship which appears to be influencing the model. For example, it has often been emphasized that the strategy of establishing a global network of offices is pursued because of the special advantages inherent in doing so. It is very hard to quantify the advantages arising from a global network of offices into a single variable. Similarly the 'pull effect' of European financial markets for foreign banks is difficult to capture through a single indicator.

Furthermore, though it may be difficult to segregate conclusively the influence of each factor on the Japanese banks' decision to establish offices in Europe, it is correct to say that no single factor is a necessary condition for such decisions. Even the significance of each factor would differ from bank to bank depending upon its size, market position, management philosophy, nature of clientele. Moreover, it needs to be emphasized that most internationalization patterns [*in banking*] are unique and fit into a specific set of historical events which are often unrepeatable.[17]

7.2   Modeling the Determinants of Japanese Banks' Expansion in the EU

7.2.1 Review of Empirical Research on the Subject

This section focuses only on those studies that have empirically tested the determinants responsible for the growth of foreign banking. It is interesting to note that most comprehensive studies on the subject have dealt either with banks coming to the U.S.

---

[16]Kitamura (1991) p. 95.

[17]Scholtens (1992) p. 22.

or U.S. banks entering overseas markets.[18] This is largely because of the greater data availability in the U.S.

The first work that initiated empirical testing of this kind was by Fielke (1977). His work examined the growth of American banking abroad and covered ten countries. A tradition of systematic investigation of U.S. banks overseas and foreign banks in the U.S. has been established by Goldberg. In association with several other authors, he has concretized the theoretical foundations on the subject over the years. Goldberg and Saunders (1980) assessed the causes of U.S. bank expansion in Great Britain, where the focus was on the effects of regulatory variables on the growth of banks across borders. Goldberg and Saunders (1981a) examined the determinants of aggregate foreign bank growth in the United States between 1972-79. Later, Goldberg and Johnson (1990) re-examined the determinants of U.S. banking activity abroad, extending the period of analysis to 1972-85. Recently, Grosse and Goldberg (1991) altered their methodology and studied foreign bank activity in the U.S. by country of origin. Other authors who have empirically tested U.S. banking abroad are Cho (1985), Sagari (1986), and Nigh et al. (1986). Among those that have examined foreign banking in the U.S. the studies done by Khoury (1980), Cooper et al. (1989), Hultman and McGee (1989) and Heinkel and Levi (1992) are noteworthy.

The independent variables taken in the above-mentioned studies differ according to the focus of inquiry. Yet some common variables have been tested by practically every author on the subject. Thus, the following can be regarded as major explanatory variables in most models.

1. foreign direct investment from home country to host country (indicator of the 'following the client' hypothesis);
2. foreign trade (signifying the role of trade financing in foreign banking);
3. the currency exchange rate between home and host currency (impelling investment decision by banks);
4. short-term interest rate differentials (influencing the cost of short-term funds);
5. price-earning ratio of bank stocks (proxy for cost of capital);
6. the GNP growth rate (indicating economic optimism); and
7. dummy variables for the influence of regulations in home country.

---

[18]Goldberg and Johnson (1990) p. 125.

The dependent variable in most studies is either foreign banks' total assets or their share in total banking assets of the host country. In some of the studies [Goldberg and Saunders (1981a), Hultman and McGee (1989), Goldberg and Johnson (1990) and Grosse and Goldberg (1991)] the number of offices opened by foreign banks has also been taken as a dependent variable.

The studies that test empirically the determinants of the Japanese banking presence overseas are limited. In studying the determinants of bank multinationalization, Khoury (1980) took the case of Japanese banks in the U.S. for the period 1972-77. Hultman and McGee (1989) basically developed a general model of foreign banking in U.S. for the period 1974-86 but extended their model to Japanese banks to suggest that the explanatory variables[19] used in the general model can also be applied to Japanese banks.

There are only four exclusive studies that empirically test the determinants of Japanese banks' overseas presence. The first study was by Terrell (1979) in which he investigated U.S. banks in Japan and Japanese banks in the U.S. As per this study, while growth in trade explains, to a considerable extent, the lending of Japanese banks in the U.S., local loan market conditions and the tightness of the Japanese banking system explain the position of U.S. banks in Japan. The second study by Poulsen (1986) traces the impact of Japanese bank regulations and loan market conditions for the period 1974-86 on the activities of Japanese banks' U.S. offices. The main contention of this work is that tight credit conditions caused by various controls in Japan resulted in a greater use of the U.S. market. The third study by Terrell et al.(1989) analyzes the U.S. and U.K. activities of Japanese banks for the period 1980-88 to suggest that Japanese banks appear to have adjusted to their domestic regulatory environment by using their London branches as a flexible funding source, and their branches and agencies in the U.S. as a substitute for their head office in extending commercial and industrial loans to Japan-based companies.[20] The policy implication of their work is that continuous deregulation in Japanese finance should lead to some repatriation of international banking business back to the domestic market. The fourth study by Thornton (1991) is the latest on the subject and covers Japanese banks in London for the period 1975-89. Selecting price-

---

[19]The independent variables included in their general model were foreign direct investment, exchange rate, price-earning ratio and a dummy variable for deregulations in the U.S.

[20]Terrell et al. (1989).

earning ratio and dividend-yield as proxies suggested by Aliber (1989) he empirically reinforces the cost of capital advantage available to Japanese banks.

To the knowledge of the author, no study has so far covered the expansion of Japanese banks in the EU. Furthermore, there is no empirical evidence of the changes in the Japanese financial markets after 1989 on the European presence of Japanese banks. The present work seeks to fill this gap in the literature by taking the expansion of Japanese banks in all the Member States of the EU as a collective whole.

7.2.2 The Model and Data Sources

The model follows the tradition of Goldberg and Saunders (1980, 1981a) and builds upon other empirical work on the subject. Thus, to determine those factors that have a bearing on the growth of Japanese banking in the EU,[21] the basic model is as follows:

$$\mathbf{Yn = a + \beta_1 FDI + \beta_2 TRDE + \beta_3 XRATE + \beta_4 PER + \beta_5 DUM + \epsilon} \quad ..Eq.(1)$$

Where

Yn	=	Annual increase in the number of offices of Japanese banks in the EU *(the dependent variable)*.
a	=	Intercept of the regression model.
FDI	=	Annual change in the foreign direct investment from Japan to the EU (in US dollars).
XRATE	=	Market rate index of the exchange value of the yen (period averages).
TRDE	=	Annual trade between Japan and the EU (total of exports and imports in US dollars).
PER	=	Price-earning ratio of Japanese banks' stocks.
DUM	=	Dummy variable for various deregulations relating to cross-border financial transactions in Japan (1976-82 = 0 and 1983-91 = 1).
β_i	=	Estimated regression parameter of the ith variable.
ϵ	=	The stochastic disturbance with mean zero and variance δ_ϵ.

[21]Since the network of offices opened by Japanese banks in Europe is concentrated in the Member States of the EU, the model should be seen as representative of the behavior of Japanese banks in the whole of Europe except Switzerland where the distinct reasons for the Japanese banking presence demand separate modeling.

Dependent Variable. The choice of the dependent variable deserves explanation. As mentioned in the review of the literature, most of the studies take the total assets of foreign banks or their share in the total banking assets in the host country as a dependent variable. However, the non-availability of this kind of information rules out the possibility of using this dependent variable in the analysis.[22] Instead of total assets, the annual change (increase or decrease) in the total number of banking offices in the EU has been taken. The total number of offices includes all branches, subsidiaries and representative offices in the EU. The reason for including representative offices in the total is to incorporate the significance of liaison work undertaken by them in obtaining international banking business as well as to capture the value attached by banks to the geographical area where more representative offices are opened. Though growth in the number of offices may not be a substitute for the growth of assets or business volume, it does capture the effect of growing business opportunities and business volume. The data for this purpose has been obtained from the Annual Reports of the International Finance Bureau (in Japanese) of the MOF.

Independent Variables. The explanatory variables in the model are the macroeconomic factors specific to the Japanese economy. The first variable is the FDI from Japan to the EU. The annual change (flow data of FDI) in foreign direct investment from Japan to the EU has been taken for the purpose. Here it would have been desirable to exclude the foreign direct investment in banking from the total to obtain the net foreign direct investment. Unfortunately, figures for the total could not be adjusted because of the non-availability of data and, to that extent, are slightly inflated. The source of this data is the BOJ's Balance of Payments Monthly.[23] The second variable is the annual foreign trade (TRDE) between Japan and the EU. The data represents the total of exports *plus* imports and has been taken from the BOJ's Annual Economic Statistics. To capture the effect of changes in the exchange rate (XRATE) of the yen, the period average index of the value of the yen has been used. The base year for the index is 1985 and it shows the dollar per 100 yen. The data has been taken from the IMF's Interna-

---

[22]The Japanese Ministry of Finance collects detailed information from all banks on their overseas involvement. However, the data is not published. There is no evidence that the Financial Institutions Group of the EU in Brussels collects any such information.

[23]The FDI statistics published by the BOJ differs from those of the MOF. The BOJ figures are the net actual flow of FDI and, as such, are more realistic than the MOF figures which are based simply on notification basis.

tional Financial Statistics. The price-earning ratio (PER) represents the year-end average of price-earning ratios for 29 major Japanese banks' stocks on the TSE.[24] The ratio has been compiled from the data supplied by the TSE. The last independent factor is a dummy variable, which is supposed to show the effects of the deregulation relating to cross-border financial transactions. It is assigned a value of 0 between 1977-82 and 1 thereafter.

The statistical characteristics of the variables used in the model (see Table 7.3) provide three important hints. *First*, the mean and standard deviation of the variables vary widely because of the differences in the units of measurement. This signifies that the relative importance of the variables in the model cannot be interpreted simply by looking at the size of regression coefficients.

Table 7.3: Statistical Characteristics of the Variables in the Regression Model

Variable	Mean	Standard Deviation	Maximum	Minimum
Yn	10.933	6.088	25.000	3.000
FDI	3.057	3.763	11.027	0.149
TRDE	42.609	26.758	90.950	12.930
XRATE	128.040	34.694	184.900	88.400
PER	42.723	14.809	66.930	19.260
DUM	0.600	0.507	1.000	0.000

Correlation Matrix of the Variables in the Model

Variable	Yn	FDI	TRDE	XRATE	PER	DUM
Yn	1.000					
FDI	0.805	1.000				
TRDE	0.781	0.960	1.000			
XRATE	0.660	0.860	0.926	1.000		
PER	0.565	0.639	0.708	0.853	1.000	
DUM	0.731	0.609	0.670	0.609	0.631	1.000

---

[24]The banks included are the city banks (11), long-term credit banks (3), trust banks (6) and regional banks (9).

Second, the correlation between the dependent variable and each independent variable (see the correlation matrix in Table 7.3) shows the individual strength of each independent variable in explaining the changes in the dependent variable. Thus, whereas FDI, TRDE and DUM appear as very strong factors in the growth of Japanese banks, XRATE and PER also have significant influence. The signs of correlation coefficients also provide provisional support for the hypotheses where all independent variables are expected to have a positive relationship with the dependent variable. *Third,* the correlation coefficient for the independent variables hints at the presence or absence of multicollinearity for each pair. Because of high correlation coefficient between some variables, there is evidence of multicollinearity, particularly that of the TRDE and XRATE variables with other factors. When multicollinearity is present, the net regression coefficients are said to be less reliable measures of the effects of their associated independent variables.

7.2.3 Hypotheses of the Model

On the basis of the theoretical considerations mentioned in Section 7.1, the following hypotheses are suggested for the model:

(i) *The expansion of foreign banking activity from a country is positively related to its foreign direct investment.* Thus, increasing the amount of foreign direct investment from Japan to the EU should lead to the opening of new banking offices by Japanese banks to service the needs of their multinational home clients.

(ii) *Increases in bilateral trade between two countries lead to an increase in foreign banking activity.* Thus, the increase in total trade between Japan and the EU should lead to growth in the Japanese banking activity in the EU.

(iii) *The expansion of foreign banking activity is positively related to the exchange value of the home currency.* The appreciation in the exchange value of the Japanese yen should encourage the opening of new offices by Japanese banks. To begin with, it is presumed here that the initial outlay, and not the yen value of the return on investment, has guided Japanese financial FDI to the EU.

(iv) *The higher price-earning ratios of a country's bank stocks (a proxy for the cost of capital advantage) should lead to growth in its banking activity overseas.*

(v) *Deregulation of cross-border financial transactions should stimulate foreign banking activity.*

7.2.4 Methodology and Results

The study covers a total period of 15 years between 1977-91 and the frequency of the data is annual. Multiple regression analysis has been used for the present model. A linear relationship has been assumed and the method of Ordinary Least Squares (OLS) has been applied for the purpose of estimating the model. The software package MicroTSP (Micro Time Series Processor, Version 5.0) has been used for obtaining the results of the multiple regression model. The empirical results of the model are shown in Table 7.4. Column I(a) presents the results of the regression equation with the TRDE variable and Column I(b) without it.

Table 7.4: Regression Results of the Model on Japanese Banking Expansion in the EU

(Dependent Variable: Annual growth in the network of offices opened by Japanese banks in the EU)

(Sample period: 1977-91)

Independent Variables	Column I(a)	Column I(b)
Constant term	13.3582	12.6999
	[3.2496]	[3.3316]
Foreign Direct Investment (FDI)	1.1745	1.4606
	[1.7489]	[4.2055]
Foreign Trade (TRDE)	0.0700	...
	[0.5105]	...
Exchange Rate (XRATE)	-0.1493	-0.1251
	[-2.0262]	[-2.2370]
Price-earning Ratio (PER)	0.1812	0.1671
	[2.0175]	[1.9996]
Deregulations (DUM)	4.4433	4.8436
	[2.811]	[3.6210]
AR(1)	-0.5618	0.5394
	[-2.2725]	[-2.3295]
Degrees of freedom	8	9
R^2	0.8650	0.8607
Adjusted R^2	0.7638	0.7833
Durbin-Watson statistic	2.3395	2.3402
F-statistic	8.5440	11.1226

AR(1) error specification uses a two-stage iteration suggested by D. Cochrane and G.H. Orcutt, "Application of Least Squares Regression to Relationships containing Autocorrelated Error Terms"

Taking the results from Column I(a) first, the coefficient of foreign direct investment from Japan to the EU is positive but significant only at the 10 percent level. This implies that the 'following the clients' hypothesis is true to some extent and FDI from

Japan does contribute to the expansion of Japanese banks in the EU. The exchange value of the yen is significant at the 5 percent level. However, contrary to expectations, but consistent with the results of Hultman and McGee (1989) and Thornton (1991), it has a negative sign. This may suggest that appreciation of the yen made a negative contribution to the expansion of Japanese banks because the expectation of reduced return from the foreign direct investment dampened the investment decision. This conclusion contradicts the surge of FDI undertaken by Japanese institutions after 1985. However, due to the high multicollinearity between the exchange rate and the other variables in the model (see Table 7.3), the sign of the XRATE variable is likely to have been confounded with the effects of other variables related to it. Thus, the sign of the XRATE variable may be inconclusive. The price-earning ratio of Japanese banks' stock is also significant and has the expected sign. This provides support for the fact that Japanese banks have had a cost of capital advantage for the most part of the 1980s. The coefficient of the DUM variable is equally significant and captures the positive impact of the series of deregulations of cross-border financial transactions on the growth of Japanese banks. The only variable that proved to be statistically insignificant was trade between Japan and the EU. It could be that trade financing has not been an important activity for Japanese banks in the EU. This also appears to hint at the increased role of Japanese banks in the cross-border securities business during the 1980s.

The regression equation was re-run without the TRDE variable to see whether the regression results improve as a consequence. Column I(b) of Table 7.4 provides the results of the alternative regression equation. Except for the FDI, the coefficient and statistical significance of all other variables changed only moderately. The regression coefficient of FDI increased in size and its T-statistic improved considerably passing the 1 percent critical value. As evident from the adjusted R^2, the explanatory power of the model also improved somewhat. The F-statistic also benefited from the dropping of the TRDE variable. Thus, *the results in Column I(b) should be treated as the final version of the model with the FDI, XRATE, PER and DUM variables,* all of which are statistically significant at the 5 percent level.

The use of the term AR(1) in the model needs explanation. When disturbances of a linear regression model are correlated, the coefficient estimates of OLS are inefficient. The AR(1) specification provides a method to obtain efficient estimates when the disturbances display first order serial correlation. (There was no evidence of serial correlation of higher order in the disturbance.)

As indicated by the results, the regression model has reasonably good explanatory power in both cases; the adjusted R^2 shows that about 75 percent of the changes in the number of offices opened by Japanese banks in the EU can be accounted for by the factors mentioned in the model. All the tests in the model are quite satisfactory. The F-statistic, which is a test of the null hypothesis that all of the coefficients in a regression are zero, exceeds its critical level at 1 percent level of significance. The Durbin-Watson statistic, which is a formal test for the serial correlation of the first order, is close to its upper limit and, thus, serial correlation does not pose any problem in the estimation.

Attempts were made to include, one by one, the other relevant macroeconomic determinants in the model to evaluate their impact. All efforts to include an indicator of economic optimism in Japan (e.g., nominal GNP, GNP growth rate or stock market index) and the 'pull effect' of Euromarkets (e.g., a dummy variable for the Single Market Act of 1987 or the fund raising by Japanese corporations on Euromarkets) did not improve the overall explanatory power of the model. In most cases, these variables were highly collinear with others and obscured the regression coefficients and signs of other variables. Even the TRDE variable had to be dropped in the final analysis to guard against multicollinearity.

7.3   Prognostic Value and Limitations of the Model

In the foregoing discussion, an attempt has been made to show that the multinationalization of Japanese banks has been guided by the interplay of a set of macroeconomic conditions in the domestic market. These macroeconomic conditions at home constitute the business environment of the financial institutions in which banks have their natural domain. Thus, the high price-earning ratio of bank stocks provided a cheaper means for overseas expansion of Japanese banks. The appreciation of the Japanese yen, another symbol of economic strength, lubricated the expansion process. The whole process gathered momentum through the chain of deregulation. Thus, the growth of Japanese banks overseas has replicated their domestic strength earned through a conducive domestic environment. The Japanese FDI in the EU and Japanese trade with the EU are the factors that initially attracted Japanese banks. However, they did not justify the dramatic and continued growth in the second part of the 1980s.

The prognostic value of any model depends upon the perpetuation of the given set of conditions. If the interpretation that cheaper equity capital and less demanding shareholders afforded Japanese banks a chance to formulate a long-term expansion strategy is correct, the cooling of the Japanese stock market after 1989[25] and the consequent changes in the behavior of Japanese shareholders will slow the penetration of Japanese banks overseas. The proposition that the appreciation of the yen has induced Japanese financial FDI is unique to a period after the Plaza Accord of 1985. If a re-emergence of a steeply higher yen is unlikely, the prognosis of the model should be that expansionary trend of Japanese banks overseas will slow down in the 1990s.

Since the anecdotal evidence suggests that trade financing was an important business for the European offices of the Japanese banks in the 1960s and early 1970s[26] and securities-related business has gained in importance thereafter, trade should be a less significant variable in the latter half of the 1970s and 1980s. Regarding the "following-the-clients" hypothesis, the impact of Japanese FDI on banking expansion would be more pronounced in those countries where Japanese arrival is in its early stages. Implicit in this observation is the viewpoint that FDI provides initial business to banks but does not help in maintaining a continued profitable existence in the long run.

Looking at deregulation as a determinant, it is difficult to make a firm judgment. Some believe that ever since the liberalization of international financial transactions by Japan gathered pace, the likelihood of the repatriation of international banking business back to Japan has increased.[27] Others perceive that the expansion of Japanese banking overseas is unlikely to be at the same pace because the liberalization of international financial transactions has run its course.[28] The growing integration of international financial markets leads to the judgment that deregulation both at home and overseas would be a significant determinant of the future strategy of all internationally active financial institutions, including Japanese banks.

Limitations of the model. The model covers the expansion of Japanese banks in the EU. The focus is primarily on traditional commercial banking activity. The model does not take into account those determinants that influence the overseas growth of securities

---

[25]Litan (1990) p. 343.

[26]In the U.S., trade financing continues to be a significant activity for Japanese bank branches.

[27]Terrell (1989) p. 35.

[28]Japan Center for International Finance (1991) p. 21.

business of Japanese banks or securities companies in Europe. A different set of determinants should explain the expansion of financial institutions in the securities business. In any theoretical analysis of the multinationalization of banking, macroeconomic factors provide only part of the explanation. Considerations of industrial organization furnish yet another part of explanation. Thus, the results of the above model provide only a partial understanding of the process and the model must be combined with other explanations to make the analysis complete.

The post-bubble developments in the Japanese economy have left their impact on the overseas activities of Japanese banks. Not only did the expansion process of the overseas network slow down, the international assets of Japanese banks also registered a negative growth after 1991. The less favorable macroeconomic conditions in Japan are even forcing smaller Japanese banks to withdraw their overseas expansion. The findings of this chapter are being reinforced through the present position of Japanese banks.

Chapter 8

Two Case Studies on the
Japanese Financial Presence in Europe

The vast differences between the financial systems of different European countries make it very difficult for non-European financial institutions to adopt common strategies when operating in Europe. The distinct economic organization in each country and the nature of Japan's relationship with each European country has led to the adoption of a variety of country-specific models of operations by the Japanese financial institutions. The establishment of a unified financial area within the EU is likely to reduce the deeply ingrained differences in financial systems of individual countries in the near future. This might manifest itself in the behavior of financial institutions from non-EU countries. In this chapter, two representative case studies of the Japanese financial presence in Europe are presented, viz. the United Kingdom and Germany. Both are significant beachheads of Japanese financial institutions in the EU. However, both differ significantly in their reasons for attracting Japanese financial institutions. The United Kingdom presents the case of a country which, because of its unique position in international finance, attracts major foreign financial institutions from all over the world. In sharp contrast, Germany is host to many Japanese financial institutions, in the first instance, because of the early arrival of Japanese trading and manufacturing enterprises there. The details of each case study aim at identifying the peculiarities of the Japanese financial presence in these two countries.

8.1   Case Study I: Japanese Financial Institutions in the United Kingdom

The City of London's preeminence in the international financial system dates from the end of the Napoleonic wars when the Dutch lost their grip on international finance. Throughout, the strength of London was very much bound up with the unique role of sterling in financing world trade and Britain's extraordinary long record as the world's chief creditor nation.[1] However, World War I brought an abrupt end to Britain's status

---

[1]Plender (1987) p. 41.

as a creditor nation and the United States thus emerged as an economic power with the dollar as the main international vehicle currency.[2] Therefore, up to 1914, it was the international trading aspect of the City which became dominant and also governed the shape taken by finance.[3]

This dominance was lost after the Second World War, but the finance functions of the City took on a new lease of life, especially as a result of the developments of the Euro-markets in the 1960s and the changing nature of international banking.[4] London was able to survive the dollar hegemony due to the innovation of the Eurodollar banking market and is still surviving the growth of Japanese and German capital exports because of the Eurobond market.[5] Today, the combined effect of London's historical impor-tance, a regulatory framework which is sympathetic to the pursuit of cross-border financial business and time zone advantages has convinced the world's largest banks, and even many of medium and small size, of the value of a presence in London.[6] With a liberal and well-established capital market, London has also been predominant in the Euro-securities business, attracting most of the new issues of international bonds, most of the Eurobond transactions in secondary markets and a substantial volume of transac-tions in foreign stocks.[7]

Though London's share in the international banking market declined from 27 percent in 1980 to about 15.8 percent at the end of September 1993[8], it still retains its leading position in markets in foreign currencies, securities and derivatives. London also hosts

---

[2]The contraction of London's position as an international financial center after the First World War was due largely to Britain's economic problems and only secondarily to the rise of New York. Rose (1994a) p. 23. Rose provides a narrative history of London as an international financial center.

[3]ibid. p. 29.

[4]ibid.

[5]Lewis (1987) p. 29.

[6]Lamb (1986) p. 367.

[7]Kitamura (1991) p. 109.

[8]Based on BIS statistics. The BIS data shows the decline in London's share to involve, in part, a drop in the UK's share of European external claims. The available data does not make it possible to estimate the effect of changes in exchange rates on London's share. See Rose (1994a) for details

the largest number of foreign financial institutions. At the end of February 1994, 520 foreign financial institutions with a total of 523 offices were based in London.[9] The geographical origins of the foreign banks in London are very wide,[10] but institutions from the European Economic Area countries (168), other European countries (55), North America (62) and Japan (53) are the major participants, and comprise about 70 percent of all institutions present.[11] In addition to this, London hosts over 160 foreign securities firms[12] which undertake investment banking related business.

Any case study of financial markets in the U.K. has to recognize the coexistence of international and domestic financial markets. In this dualistic system, whereas international financial markets are sophisticated wholesale markets and concentrated in the City of London, domestic financial markets are traditional and spread throughout the country. In the literature, the former are given greater emphasis at the expense of the virtual exclusion of the latter. The fact that most foreign financial institutions are attracted by the huge international financial markets in London does not belittle the significance of domestic markets.

8.1.1 Indicators of the Bilateral Economic Relationship between Japan and the United Kingdom

The domestic economy of the U.K. provides attractive ground for FDI from all over the world. The Japanese financial presence in the U.K. is equally fostered by the domestic economy of the U.K. The mutual economic dependence of the two countries is amply reflected in their growing foreign trade and direct investment. Table 8.1 provides some indicators of the bilateral economic ties between Japan and the U.K.

In absolute terms, total trade between Japan and the U.K. has increased threefold in the last 10 years and the U.K. now accounts for 20 percent of Japanese exports to the

---

[9]Of these, 256 were overseas incorporated banking institutions with UK branches, 76 were UK incorporated subsidiaries of overseas banks and non-banks, 11 were UK incorporated joint-ventures involving overseas institutions and 180 representative offices of overseas institutions. See Bank of England (1994) p. 42 for details.

[10]Banks from 72 countries (with banks from 10 countries having only representative offices) are represented in the United Kingdom.

[11]Bank of England (1992), p. 35.

[12]Noel Alexander Associates (1991b).

Table 8.1: Selected Indicators of the Economic Relationship between Japan and the United Kingdom

	1980	1993
Japanese exports to the United Kingdom (US$ million)	3,782	12,017
UK's share in Japanese exports to EU (%)	22.7	22.0
Japanese imports from the United Kingdom (US$ million)	1,954	4,030
UK's share in Japanese imports from EU (%)	24.9	15.6
Outward FDI in the UK(cumulative total in US$ million; 1951-)	2,010	31,661
UK's share in Japanese FDI to Europe (%)	44.9	37.9
Inward FDI from the UK (cumulative total in US$ million)	NA	518[2]
UK's share in European FDI to Japan		17.2
Number of Japanese manufacturing Units in the UK	15*	195**
Number of British affiliated companies in Japan	NA	75°

[2]For the period 1950-88
*as of January 1983; ** as of January 1992
°as of March 1990

Source: MOF, Bank of Japan, JETRO etc.

EU and about 15 percent of Japanese imports from the EU. In addition to trade, the U.K. accounts for the largest share of Japanese FDI to Europe, Though a considerable part of Japanese FDI to the U.K. is in the financial sector, the FDI in the manufacturing sector has been equally significant. The U.K. hosts the largest number of manufacturing affiliates of Japanese companies and the number of such units increased from 15 in 1983 to 195 as of January 1992. For the Japanese, the move into the U.K. market was based initially on a need to move production closer to the marketplace after the yen's appreciation in 1985. Visions of a more dynamic European market emerging after 1992, combined with fears of growing European protectionism, further spurred on the rush to build production facilities inside the EU.[13] However, the continued enthusiasm of the British authorities, and their willingness to stand for the interests of Japanese corporations, has played no small part in bringing the lion's share of Japanese investment in Europe to the U.K.[14]

---

[13]Nakamoto (1991).

[14]ibid.

8.1.2 Various Dimensions of Japanese Financial Presence

When measured in terms of the size of balance sheet assets, Japanese banks are the largest foreign banking group in the U.K. They began setting up offices in London between 1952 and 1956, when six of the city banks established branches in London. However, the most important period of Japanese banking expansion was in the early 1970s, when they were allowed by the MOF to participate in the international syndicated credit market. Figure 8.1 shows the growth of Japanese financial institutions in the City of London between 1965-92. As the figure confirms, their presence was modest until 1970. After that it started picking up and the network of offices expanded significantly during the period 1980-90. The period after 1985 saw the most dramatic increase and was characterized by the arrival of smaller Japanese banks and securities companies in London.

Figure 8.1: Growth of Japanese Financial Institutions in the UK

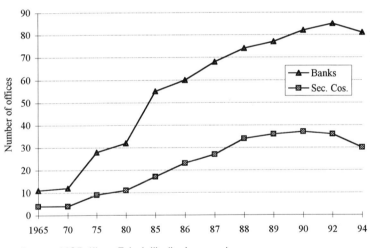

Source: MOF; Kinyu Zaisei Jijo (in Japanese)

In sharp contrast with the banks, the arrival of Japanese securities companies in the U.K. was slow and until 1970 only the Big Four were represented in London. It was only after 1980 that the issue boom of Japanese companies in the Euromarkets and increased portfolio investment by Japanese institutional investors attracted second-tier companies into London. The period between 1980-90 witnessed an increase of 25 new subsidiaries and representative offices opened by them. Table 8.2 provides an overview of the present network of offices of Japanese financial institutions in the U.K.

Japanese Financial Institutions in Europe

Table 8.2: Japanese Financial Presence in the UK (as of June 1994)

Type of Institution/Presence	Sub-total	Total
A.1 Banking branches of all banks	28	
A.2 Banking subsidiaries of securities cos.	4	
Total of banking units		32
B.1 Securities subsidiaries of all banks	32	
B.2 Subsidiaries of securities cos.	30	
Total of securities business related units		62
C.1 Representative offices of all banks	21	
C.2 Representative offices of securities cos.	0	
Total of representative offices		21
Total number of Offices in the UK		115

Source: Kinyu Zaisei Jijo (in Japanese)

As of June 1994, they have a total of 115 offices, with banks having a larger number of offices (28 branches, 32 subsidiaries and 21 representative offices) than the securities companies.[15] It should be implicit in the large presence of Japanese banks and securities companies in London that they are contenders for the same type of business in London and often compete intensely with each other.[16] As mentioned in Section 4.3.2, the organizational form chosen by Japanese banks in London reflects a clear demarcation of business lines. Thus, all city banks have both a branch and subsidiary in the City of London; the branches engage primarily in traditional commercial banking and the subsidiaries in investment banking.

---

[15]There is a difference in the total number of offices opened by Japanese banks in the U.K. and the one reported by the Bank of England. The explanation lies in the treatment of investment banking subsidiaries of Japanese banks which are not included in the list of authorized institutions under the Banking Act of 1987. However, the BOT International and IBJ International are the only two investment banking subsidiaries of Japanese banks which are included in the list.

[16]In comparison with the significant and dominant Japanese banking presence in London, banks from the United Kingdom have so far (as of April 1992) opened a total of 20 offices (7 branches, 1 subsidiary and 12 representative offices) in Japan [Information obtained from the MOF].

8.1.3 Activities of Japanese Banks in London.

The U.K. is the third largest host market for Japanese banks after the U.S. and Hong Kong.[17] Initially, their activities were confined to financing trade with Japan. Although trade financing still continues to be their main activity in New York, in London both the form and scale of the main activity have undergone vital change in the last twenty years. From the early 1970s, the Japanese banks participated in the syndicated credit market boom, which provided major impetus to their growth in that decade. Despite the slow-down in syndicated lending after the debt crisis, Japanese banks in London continued to expand.[18] This time the focus of their activity was participation in the international interbank market in London. A related aspect of their interbank activity in London was to function as suppliers of funds for their head office[19] and to related offices overseas through inter-office transfers. The justification of borrowing in London for the head office was to be found in the cheaper dollar funds in London than in Tokyo.[20] The inter-office business of Japanese banks started slowing down partly as a result of the opening of the JOM in 1986. The opening of arbitrage opportunities with far eastern offshore centers in Hong Kong and Singapore led to first cutbacks in their foreign currency business in the London interbank market in 1987 and 1988. In addition, the tightening of monetary policy in Japan in 1989 and attempts by Japanese banks at maintaining the BIS capital adequacy ratio has further led to significant cutbacks in their interbank activity.

The Japanese banks' international banking activity in London. Foreign banks in London have retained a largely international orientation[21] and this applies to Japanese banks as well. The fact that 95 percent of the Japanese banks' total assets in London relate to international banking business[22] explains the driving force behind the Japanese

---

[17]Kitamura (1991) p. 108.

[18]Walton and Trimble (1987) p. 519.

[19]A detailed reference to this point has already been made in Section 4.4.1.1

[20]For an analysis of the background of the Eurodollar borrowing by Japanese banks through the London financial markets, see Nakao (1989).

[21]Tickell (1994), p. 296.

[22]International banking business in London implies foreign currency and sterling business with non-residents of UK and foreign currency business with residents of UK.

banking presence in London. The importance of London for Japanese banks is further reflected by the share of their total international banking business booked in London. Thus, as early as 1983, they were booking almost 40 percent of their international business in London. In mid-1988, the share of business booked in London had fallen to about 26 percent reflecting the growth of domestic foreign currency business in Japan.

In the London international banking market, they raised their share from 13 percent in 1975 to a peak of 38.4 percent at the end of 1988 before falling to 32.2 percent at the end of 1990.[23] A closer look at the different components of international banking business undertaken by Japanese banks in London shows the predominance of the treasury function, which includes participating in the interbank market (both as supplier and borrower) and foreign exchange market. A number of large Japanese banks undertake international treasury business for their head office as well as for their corporate clients. The business has been highly profitable and was boosted by the strength of the yen and the expansion of the Euroyen market. The second major component of international business for Japanese banks has been lending. After the Latin American debt crisis, the exposure of Japanese banks is now more concentrated in Europe. Lending to non-banks has registered significant growth from $0.5 billion at the end of 1983 to $7.4 billion in 1987. Project financing and real estate financing are the two areas in which Japanese banks have, of late, participated with greater vigor. The third component of the Japanese banks' international activities in London, and a less known one, is their heavy reliance on Certificate of Deposits (CDs) issues in Sterling and other foreign currencies. The CDs issued by Japanese banks in London accounted for nearly half the CDs issued by all banks in London and held by overseas residents in 1988.[24] Of all outstanding Euroyen-CDs issued by Japanese banks world wide at the end of March 1991, 99.3 percent were issued in London.[25]

---

[23]Bank of England Quarterly Bulletin, various issues.

[24]Though 1990 saw a reversal in the trend as the stock of outstanding Japanese banks' CDs held by overseas residents fell by $8 billion. See Bank of England (1991) p. 238.

[25]The rest is accounted for by Hong Kong (0.2%) and Singapore (0.5). See Ministry of Finance, Japan, Annual Report of the International Finance Bureau, No.15, (1991) p. 127.

The Japanese banks' business with U.K. residents.[26] It is often said that Britain has not been one of those countries where foreign banks have made much headway into the domestic retail banking environment.[27] However, there has been a tendency to underestimate the significance of overseas banks in lending activities.[28] The involvement of foreign banks in the national banking markets overseas reflects upon their willingness to become local financial institutions and show their competitive strengths.

Until recently, doing business with the residents of U.K. had been a secondary motive for Japanese banks. Even within this business segment, they confined themselves to wholesale corporate banking where they lend in sterling and foreign currencies to the U.K. corporate sector. Contrary to their retail banking experience in California, Japanese banks have completely abstained from retail banking in the U.K. for the obvious reason of its being cost-prohibitive and difficult. So far, no outright acquisition has been made with this motive.[29]

Table 8.3 provides some indicators about Japanese banks' lending to U.K. residents. Their share of lending to U.K. residents in both sterling and foreign currencies has not been a growth sector in the recent past. Though increased in absolute terms from £8 billion to £34.7 billion between 1987-90, their share in outstanding lending amount has revolved around 8 percent during this period. Taking all the overseas banks in the U.K. as a collective group, Japanese banks were providing around 20 percent of the total lending by all overseas banks to U.K. residents. Theoretically, when foreign banks based in London make sterling loans to U.K. residents, it is domestic banking. Thus, Japanese banks' lending in sterling constitutes about half their total lending to U.K. residents. In this market segment, Japanese banks slightly increased their share from 3 percent of the total sterling lending by all U.K. banks at the end of August 1987 to 5 percent at the end of May 1990.

---

[26]It is worth noting that UK residents also include the local affiliates of foreign companies.

[27]Despite the considerable activity of foreign banks in the U.K. banking market, only one foreign bank has established a significant branch network. Several other foreign banks, however, have pursued alternative entry strategies by attempting to establish product niches, particularly in the credit card market.

[28]Tickell (1994) p. 296.

[29]Bank of Yokohama acquired Guiness Mahon, which is a merchant bank.

Table 8.3: Japanese Banks' Lending to UK Residents

(Sterling billions)

	Aug.87	May 88	May 89	May 90
Total Japanese bank lending to UK residents (in sterling and other currencies)	8.00	19.35	28.21	34.67
As % of lending by all UK banks	8.0	7.2	8.1	7.9
As % of lending by all overseas banks		21.1	23.0	23.6
Total lending by all overseas banks	**NA**	**91.709**	**122.44**	**146.85**
Japanese bank lending in Sterling	NA	8.61	13.54	18.15
As % of sterling lending by all UK banks	3.0	3.9	4.9	5.0
As % of Total Japanese bank lending		44.5	48.0	52.3
As % of sterling lending by all overseas banks		15.6	19.6	21.0
Sterling lending by all overseas banks	**NA**	**55.19**	**68.99**	**86.47**

Source: Bank of England

The sectoral composition of Japanese banks' lending to U.K. residents is given in Table 8.4. It provides more information about the business interests and risk-complexion of their involvement in the domestic economy. Thus, lending to the U.K. financial sector, which includes lending to securities dealers (covering the U.K. affiliates of Japanese securities companies) and building societies, has been the dominant item, accounting for around 45 percent of total outstanding loans at the end of May 1990. The wholesale distribution sector has been another major outlet (accounting for about 20 percent between 1987-89) for Japanese banks' lending to non-banks, which includes lending to the U.K. offices of large Japanese trading companies.[30] Whereas the respective share of all bank lending to the financial services and distribution sector was about 17 percent and 10 percent, the Japanese banks were over-represented in both these sectors.[31] In a nutshell, Japanese bank branches in the U.K. have tended to concentrate on sectors where Japanese firms have achieved a high degree of penetration.

---

[30]Walton and Trimble (1987) p. 523.

[31]The bulk of lending to the wholesale distribution sector was to the Japanese trading companies, which facilitate Japanese trade. See Tickell (1994) for details. Thus, Japanese banks were indirectly involved in trade financing.

Table 8.4: Sectoral Composition of Japanese Banks' Lending to UK Residents

Sector	Share of each sector in the total outstanding as of			Total* (Sterling in billions)
	Aug. 87	May 89	May 90	May 90
Manufacturing industry	5.8	9.9	10.9	3779
Energy	3.1	1.7	1.3	441
Water supply	1.1	0	0	0
Construction	2.1	3.8	5.6	1924
Securities dealers etc.	23.0	9.7	9.8	3379
Building societies	6.8	6.6	4.2	1470
Other financial services	17.3	29.7	30.7	10625
Wholesale distribution	20.4	17.3	10.6	3690
Retail distribution		1.9	3.1	1088
Transport and communication		1.4	2.3	784
Property companies	2.6	8.2	10.5	3635
Central and local government services	2.1	2.4	1.8	624
Other services		4.9	6.7	2334
Miscellaneous	15.7	2.9	2.5	880
Total	**100**	**100**	**100**	**34653**

*Total represents outstanding lending as of May 1990

Source: Bank of England

Their lending to the manufacturing sector has also increased, from 6 percent to 11 percent of the total, partly reflecting the growing moves by Japanese manufacturers to set up operations in the Midlands, Scotland and Wales, and the efforts of the Japanese banks to do business with these local firms. Within the manufacturing sector, there has been a marked rise in lending to motor vehicle manufacturers and to the electronics sector. Since Japanese direct investment in Britain has been most marked in these industries, it seems likely that Japanese banks in Britain are facilitating Japanese direct investment in the country.[32]

A similar increase is to be observed in their lending to property and construction companies in the U.K. With a total of £38 billion outstanding loans in the U.K. property sector at the end of 1992, Japanese banks had a market share of 11.7 percent.[33] The

---

[32]ibid. p. 298.

[33]By contrast, the U.S. banks had a share of 3.7%. See Houlder (1993) for details.

recent slump in the property market has altered the risk complexion of lending to this sector and, as a consequence, influenced the Japanese banks' exposure to this sector.

Though no information is available about the maturity composition of Japanese banks' lending, huge lending to the financial services sector and to wholesale distribution suggests their greater involvement in the shorter end of the market.

8.1.4 Activities of Japanese Securities Companies in London

It was only in the early 1970s that Japan's leading securities houses (the Big Four) first wished to participate in the London market. Prior to that, they had preferred to do business in Amsterdam or Luxembourg rather than London.[34] As mentioned in Section 5.3.1, foreign investors' demand for Japanese securities was the major part of their business in this earlier phase. Later, the new Foreign Exchange Law (1980) of Japan, which liberalized in principle all cross-border transactions, led to a spurt in Japanese demand for foreign securities. The affiliates of Japanese securities companies in London were well placed to carry out Japan-related business. A third phase of expansion in London ensued around 1985 when the Japanese securities companies became active as underwriters for the Eurobond issues of their Japanese clients. Today, for the Japanese securities companies, their subsidiaries in London are among the most important in terms of number of personnel committed, volume of trading conducted and revenue generated.[35] Of the many overseas outposts of Japanese securities companies, their London subsidiaries have been continually enlarging their service offerings.

Keeping pace with the boom in the Euromarkets, a series of financial and securities market reforms were instituted in London, including the establishment of the London International Financial Futures Exchange (LIFFE) in September 1982, the implementation of the 'Big-Bang' reforms in October 1986,[36] and the enactment of the Financial Services Act in November 1986. These reforms led to serious reorganization in the securities industry. In response to these changes, the London subsidiaries of Japanese securities companies embarked upon a series of services expansions and diversification

---

[34]Kitamura (1991) p. 109.

[35]Nikko Research Center (1988) p. 183.

[36]The Big Bang abolished the separation of jobber and broker services and fixed commission system (for securities trading) and started the operation of the SEAQ system.

initiatives. They participate in the "SEAQ International" system as market makers. The stock market crash of October 1987 brought about a slump in the international markets in London and, in a succession of moves, British and American securities firms announced curtailment of operations and cuts in personnel. However, the Japanese securities companies continued to expand during this phase. Table 8.5 provides a list of product areas in which Japanese securities companies claimed a capability even before the Big Bang. Later, the Big Four expanded further in several directions. They were reportedly expanding their London equity operations as the 1990s began and have increased the number of U.K. stocks in which they make market. Nomura is now also active in U.K. gilts. By establishing their banking subsidiaries, the Big Four added new areas of operations after 1987 to become integrated investment banking institutions.

Table 8.5: The Product Range of Japanese Securities Cos. in London

Product	Nomura	Daiwa	Nikko	Yamaichi
UK equities market making	x			
International equities market making	x		x	
Gilts primary dealing				
Futures options and swaps	x	x	x	x
Eurobond market making	x	x	x	x
Eurobond underwriting	x	x	x	x
Euro-commercial paper	x		x	
Sterling commercial paper				
US treasuries market making		x		
Equity issues	x	x	x	x
Retail stockbroking		x	x	x
Retail banking				
Wholesale banking				x
Foreign exchange	x		x	
Mergers and acquisitions	x	x		x
Commodities				
Bullion				
Consumer finance				
Unit trusts				
Fund management	x	x	x	x
Private client investment	x			x
Mortgages (sterling)				
Venture capital	x	x		x
Insurance				
Number of Products offered (As of October 1986)	12	9	9	10

Source: The Economist; quoted in Scott-Quinn (1990b)

Table 6.6 has depicted the competitive position of Japanese securities companies in the Eurobond league table for the period 1983-94. In Chapter 6, it has further been proved that the dramatic rise of Japanese securities companies in the league table was attributed primarily to the equity-warrant related bonds issued by Japanese companies in the Euromarkets. The privatization programs in the U.K. such as British Telecom and British Petroleum were interesting developments for the Japanese securities companies in London because 10 percent or so of the total equity issues were automatically scheduled for a Japanese tranche.[37] This provided the Japanese securities companies with an easy entry into the international equity market.

London is the main source of revenue for Japanese securities companies in their overseas operations. Thus, of the total net profit earned by the Big Four in Europe, London has been contributing between one half and two-thirds (see Table 5.6). However, it is only major Japanese securities companies that have enjoyed the wide range of securities business and better results. The newly established subsidiaries of smaller securities companies usually start their business by trading Japanese stocks and shares and have difficulty entering into profitable business.[38]

8.1.5 Impact of the Japanese Financial Presence on London

What implications does the dominant Japanese financial presence have for London? The question can be answered from the point of view of various parties. For the users of financial services, the presence of a large number of suppliers is a real boon. More competition definitely implies lower price and a variety of choices. Not only international clients but domestic clients, too, must also have gained from the aggressive market strategy of the Japanese financial institutions in London. For the employment market, foreign financial institutions provide additional employment opportunities. Japanese banks in the U.K. are the second largest group of foreign banks after the U.S. as employers.[39] They employ more than 5000 local staff. For the Exchequer, the presence of foreign institutions has meant additional sources of revenue. It is estimated that more than half of Britain's invisible receipts come from banking and insurance. To take

---

[37]Prindl (1989) p. 31.

[38]Kitamura (1991) p. 110.

[39]London Chamber of Commerce and Industry (1991) p. 41.

an example, Britain was seen to have earned over £9 billion in income from financial services in 1987; the Japanese participants may provide over a third of this.[40] For the domestic financial institutions, foreign financial institutions pose a real challenge. The fact that foreigners concentrate on international financial markets cannot be an argument when one notices that foreign multinational financial institutions have cornered a larger slice of the market than local multinational financial institutions. Furthermore, the intrusion of foreigners in the domestic markets often raises concern. In this regard, the insignificant share of the Japanese banks' sterling lending to U.K. residents has raised no alarm so far. However, any increase in this share might generate criticism.

For London, it has been a matter of sheer prestige to continue to play the role of the leading financial center in Europe. In the wake of Europe after 1992, where Paris and Frankfurt are aspiring for greater roles, a large populace of foreign financial institutions in the City of London reinforces its position. In the City, where the ideology of self-regulation has been prevalent, foreign financial institutions have not posed any problems for the authorities. Though Japanese financial institution have often been charged with over-presence in the City of London, this was more aimed at gaining greater accessibility for British financial institutions in the Japanese financial markets than for any wrong-doing on their part. Thus, the Japanese financial institutions justify their presence in London by an equal contribution to the national good.

8.2 Case Study II: Japanese Financial Institutions in Germany

The strength of Germany as a leading industrial nation[41] derives from its success as an export-oriented economy.[42] Its industrial strength has been reinforced by the prestige of the monetary sector where monetary stability has made the Deutsche mark the second most important international currency for transactions, interventions, capital movements and reserves.[43] The monetary policy of the Deutsche Bundesbank has earned it the status

---

[40]Prindl (1987) p. 31.

[41]It ranks third, behind the United States and Japan, in the world in terms of GNP.

[42]Exports account for about 30 percent of Germany's GNP.

[43]Götz and Müller (1990) p. 5. The German currency accounted for 19 percent of world reserves in foreign exchange at end-1989 and some 30 percent in the ECU basket of the European Monetary System.

of a model central bank in the world.[44] Germany's financial sector also exhibits numerous liberal features. Unlike the financial institutions in the U.S. and Japan, German financial institutions function as universal banks and combine commercial and investment banking under the same roof. Germany was the earliest among the continental European countries to deregulate interest rates,[45] make the currency fully convertible and abolish all controls on the capital controls. Except for the need to liberalize its money markets and introduce stock exchange reforms, deregulation has not been a pressing and debatable topic in Germany.

The city of Frankfurt is Germany's main financial center. Practically, all leading German banks have headquarters in Frankfurt. It accounts for more than 60 percent of all equity market turnover and more than 70 percent of all bond market turnover in Germany[46]. With the seat of the Deutsche Bundesbank, the Deutsche Börse AG, German Futures Exchange (Deutsche Termin Börse), and the European Monetary Institute in the city, Frankfurt competes with Paris as the second most important financial center in Europe after London.

The attractiveness of Germany for foreign financial institutions was limited until 1985. This was largely because of the institutional regulations that circumscribed the freedom of foreign institutions. In 1971, there were just 59 offices (29 branches and 30 subsidiaries) of foreign banks in Germany and, between 1971-85, the total increased to 105 (63 branches and 42 subsidiaries).[47] After 1985, when foreign financial institutions were allowed to participate in new market segments, financial institutions from many countries rushed towards Frankfurt. At present (as of September 1992), foreign financial institutions from 57 countries have 360 offices (including 108 subsidiaries, 56 branches and about 200 representative offices) in Germany.[48] Measured in terms of the total

---

[44]The Bundesbank's monetary decisions lead and influence the interest rate levels and exchange rate of other European countries.

[45]The deposit rates were *de facto* completed deregulated by 1973.

[46]Götz and Müller (1990) p. 5.

[47]Deutsche Bundesbank.

[48]The total number includes the offices of non-banking foreign financial institutions also. [Die Bank (1992) p.554].According to the Bundesbank, only foreign banks have a total of 143 offices (56 branches and 87 subsidiaries) in Germany as of the end of January 1993.

number of offices, Japanese, U.S. and French banks are the main national groups present in Germany. The majority of foreign banks (41 branches, 63 subsidiaries and 149 representative offices)[49] are based in Frankfurt. Hamburg, because of its traditional role in foreign trade (with 9 subsidiaries and 15 branches), and Düsseldorf, because of its position in the industrial geography of Germany (4 subsidiaries and 6 branches), are the other prominent cities where foreign banks have opened offices.

The foreign banks in Germany exhibit a high concentration ratio; thus, of the 141 foreign institutions covered by the Association of Foreign Bankers Association in its report for the year 1991, the top 10 account for over 35 percent of the total business volume of all foreign banks.[50] However, since 1985, the share of foreign banks in the business volume of the entire German banking system has been below 5 percent;[51] it recently declined from 4.2 percent in 1985 to 3.84 percent at the end of 1991.[52] However, within the group of commercial banks, foreign banks have a relatively high market share at 14.7 percent as of the end of 1991.[53]

8.2.1 Indicators of the Bilateral Economic Relationship between Japan and Germany

Among the Member States of the EU, Germany is Japan's largest trading partner and accounts for roughly one-third of the total value of trade between Japan and the EU. (see Table 8.6 for details.) As in London, Japanese trading firms were the first to arrive in Germany followed by Japanese manufacturing companies. Although the Japanese trading companies were initially the ones to start direct investment activity around the mid-1950s, the Japanese manufacturing companies had overtaken them in number by

---

[49]As of the end of October, 1991 (information obtained from Landeszentralbank, Hessen).

[50]The top 20 foreign banks do more than 50 percent of the total business carried out by foreign banks in Germany. [Calculations from the annual reports of the Verband der Auslandsbanken in Deutschland].

[51]Since the Deutsche Bundesbank started publishing statistics about the German subsidiaries of foreign banks from 1987 onwards with data going back to 1985, the market share figures until 1984 cover only foreign bank branches.

[52]Deutsche Bundesbank (1992b).

[53]ibid.

Table 8.6: Selected Indicators of the Economic Relationship between Japan and Germany

	1980	1993
Japanese exports to Germany (US $ in million)	5,756	17,782
Germany's share in Japanese exports to EU	34.6	32.5
Japanese imports from Germany (US $ in million)	2,501	8,571
Germany's share in Japanese imports from EU	31.9	33.2
Outward FDI to Germany(cumulative total in US $ million)	498	7,334
Germany's share in Japanese FDI to Europe	11.1	8.8
Inward FDI from Germany (cumulative total in $ million)	NA	546[2]
Germany's share in European FDI to Japan		18.1
Number of Japanese manufacturing units in Germany	20*	111**
Number of German-affiliated companies in Japan	NA	63°

[2]for the period 1950-88
*as of January 1983; ** as of January 1992
°as of March 1990

Source: MOF, Bank of Japan, JETRO etc.

1973.[54] The industrial city of Düsseldorf was the center of their activity throughout the 1960s and 1970s.

In terms of value, Germany received a larger share of Japan's manufacturing FDI to Europe in the 1970s and early 1980s. Thus, in 1980, Germany's share (11.1%) in the total Japanese FDI to Europe was second only to that of the U.K. After 1985, Germany's share has declined to about 9 percent primarily as a result of Japan's huge financial FDI elsewhere in Europe. Seem from the point of view of the number of manufacturing units, Germany hosts over 101 manufacturing affiliates of Japanese companies and ranks third in Europe, after the U.K. and France. Despite the fact that Japanese FDI to Germany has increased ten fold in absolute terms, Japanese exports to Germany have not declined. This implies that FDI to Germany was not guided by the motive of export substitution. Recently, however, increasing labor costs have discouraged Japanese multinationals from coming to Germany. Yet another indicator of the bilateral relationship between Japan and Germany is that Germany's FDI to Japan is the largest of all the EU countries and represents more than 18 percent of the total FDI from Europe to Japan.

---

[54]See Kumar (1991) p. 215.

8.2.2 The Japanese Financial Presence in Germany: A Brief History[55]

Japanese financial institutions, though latecomers on the German financial scene, have become the largest group in terms of the number of offices. Since Germany is not a major international banking center,[56] foreign financial institutions are attracted to it for reasons other than international financial business. As explained below, the arrival of Japanese banks into Germany in the 1960s and 1970s presents a classical case of the "banks following the client" hypothesis.

The first Japanese bank to arrive in Germany was the Bank of Tokyo which reopened its branch in Hamburg in 1954 after the War. The second bank to do so was the Fuji Bank which opened its branch in Düsseldorf in 1963. Following Fuji Bank's example, all the city banks, except Taiyo Kobe Bank and Tokai Bank[57], opened branches in Düsseldorf between 1963-75. Apart from this, the Bank of Tokyo and Industrial Bank of Japan (IBJ) opened their Frankfurt subsidiaries during this period.[58] Thus, at the end of 1977, Japanese banks had 12 branches, 2 subsidiaries and 10 representative offices in Germany. Other than Japanese banks, the Big Four Japanese securities companies also had subsidiaries in Frankfurt.[59] It is noteworthy that, between 1977 and 1984, no new branches or subsidiaries were opened by Japanese banks in Germany.

In 1985, a second wave of the arrival of Japanese financial institutions in Germany started. It was more a response to the deregulation of the German capital markets that allowed foreign financial institutions to underwrite Euro-DM bonds, provided they were residents in Germany. The Japanese banks, which were left out of this new business opportunity because of the reciprocity reasons, were allowed entry into this market

---

[55]Because of the prevalence of the universal banking system in Germany, foreign commercial banks and securities firms are not classified separately. Hence the discussion of Japanese banks and securities companies has been undertaken simultaneously in this case study.

[56]When analyzed by center, Germany accounted for about 5 percent of the total international banking business at the end of 1990. See Bank of England Quarterly Bulletin (1991b) p.237.

[57]Taiyo Kobe Bank opened its branch in Hamburg and Tokai in Frankfurt.

[58]The Deutsche Bank has a minority stake (16.67%) in IBJ's subsidiary, making it the first strategic alliance between financial institutions of the two countries.

[59]Nomura and Daiwa in 1973, Yamaichi in 1974 and Nikko in 1977.

segment only after October 1987. Thereafter, practically all major city banks sought entry into the financial center of Frankfurt as subsidiaries. Sumitomo, Fuji, and Mitsubishi opened their subsidiaries in October 1988[60] and a host of others followed between 1989-91. As of June 1994, Japanese banks have 15 branches, 19 subsidiaries and 20 representative offices in Germany.[61] In addition to that, Japanese securities companies have 6 subsidiaries and 10 representative offices.[62] The importance of Frankfurt for Japanese financial institutions is revealed by the fact that all subsidiaries located there undertake securities business. Other than Düsseldorf and Hamburg, some banks have sub-branches in Munich and 7 banks have opened representative offices in Berlin to explore business potential in the former East Germany and the rest of eastern Europe.[63]

8.2.3 Activities of Japanese Financial Institutions in Germany

The city of Düsseldorf was the first to attract Japanese banks. Being the industrial and trading center of Germany, over half the Japanese enterprises (both trading and manufacturing) in Germany were attracted towards Düsseldorf in the 1960s and 1970. The Japanese City banks followed to serve these clients. Up to 1985, Japanese enterprises constituted the core business target for these banks. Because of Germany being a major trading partner for Japan, trade-related financing continues to be a very important business area. Industrial financing of manufacturing affiliates of Japanese companies in Germany has been another important area. After 1986, securities related business and off-balance sheet business attracted maximum attention of Japanese institutions in Frankfurt. Table 8.7 provides data about the balance sheet structure of Japanese financial institutions in Germany and makes a simultaneous comparison with the U.S. banks.

Thus, interbank business constitutes the core interest area for the Japanese on both sides of their balance sheet. In the absence of a retail network for deposit collection, their dire need for DM refinancing is amply illustrated by half of their liabilities coming

---

[60]MTCB Bank Deutschland was another strategic alliance created between Mitsubishi Trust and Westdeutsche Landesbank in October 1988.

[61]Information obtained from MOF.

[62]Information obtained from Landeszentralbank, Hessen.

[63]It would be of interest to mention briefly that, as of April 1992, German banks have 11 branches and 7 representative offices in Japan (Information obtained from the MOF).

Table 8.7: Balance Sheet Structure of Japanese and US Banks in Germany

(% of Balance sheet total)

	Japanese banks		US banks	
	1986*	**1991***	**1986**	**1991**
(A) Assets				
Interbank (under 4 yrs.)	40.66	39.24	22.34	21.06
Interbank (4 yrs. and longer)	8.74	4.38	1.67	0.33
Securities	13.35	16.82	20.75	22.36
Non-bank clients (under 4yrs.)	26.41	25.56	23.48	26.20
Non-bank clients (4 yrs. and longer)	8.28	6.76	18.20	17.82
Investments	0.25	0.15	0.70	0.83
Leasing assets		0.24		1.27
(B) Liabilities				
Interbank (under 4 yrs.)	50.37	42.66	28.94	35.07
Interbank (4 yrs. and longer)	32.07	31.38	30.68	18.65
Non-bank clients (under 4 yrs.)	4.50	4.18	14.70	18.05
Non-bank clients (4 yrs. and longer)	0.91	3.26	8.55	7.63
Bonds issued	0.00	0.00	0.35	1.54
Own acceptances and promisory notes	0.15	0.68	0.45	0.03
Share capital	6.18	9.93	3.63	2.98
Capital reserves	0.18	0.42	1.56	1.86
(C) Off-balance sheet items				
Endorsements	6.25	5.26	6.62	1.92
Guarantees	5.80	5.82	7.85	6.34
Balance Sheet total (DM in Million)	25504	32685	46517	59775
Reporting institutions	**[11]**	**[32]**	**[28]**	**[28]**

*For some institutions, fiscal year end in March of following year

Source: Verband der Auslandsbanken in Deutschland, Annual Reports

from the short-term interbank market. This contrasts with the U.S. banks, which raise around 15 percent of their funds from non-bank clients and hence have lower interbank liabilities. The Japanese and the U.S. banks are equally active in supplying short-term credit to non-bank clients but the U.S. banks are more involved in medium and long-term credit to non-banks. The securities holding of Japanese banks in Germany is lower, and that of U.S. banks is higher, than the average (15%) of all foreign banks in Germany. Whereas the U.S. banks have reduced their involvement in off-balance sheet business, the Japanese banks continue to be active in this market segment. For Japanese banks as a whole, Japanese enterprises still constitute the largest client group. In a survey of foreign banks in Germany, the ratio between Japanese and German clients for

Japanese banks was 80:20 for two banks, 60:40 for one and 50:50 for one.[64] These banks also confirmed "following domestic client" as their main motive for coming to Germany.[65]

Virtually no published information is available about other types of business conducted by Japanese financial institutions. For example, nothing is known about the securities business (underwriting and brokerage) done by Japanese securities companies. One study found out that Japanese banks had a share of 0.8 percent in all the Euro-DM bonds issued in 1987 and ranked fourth after the U.S., Swiss, and British banks.[66] In 1988, their share increased to 2.1 percent and they were ranked third.[67] The improvement in the share of Japanese banks must be seen in the light of the fact that they obtained permission to lead Euro-DM bonds in October 1987 only. The share of Japanese institutions in securities business must have increased significantly because the Japanese institutional investors have raised their holdings of DM government bonds dramatically in recent years.[68] Thus, in 1990, Nomura alone had a 3.1 percent share in the Euro-DM bonds market.[69] The fact that interest rates in Germany after unification were higher than in the U.S. also led to a diversion of Japanese money that otherwise went into U.S. markets throughout the 1980s. This naturally meant more securities- related business for Japanese financial institutions. Various deregulation in the German capital market, such as entry of foreign financial institutions in the syndicate for trading government bonds (1986),[70] diversification of bond products (1986), revitalization measures for the stock exchange (1987), permission to issue domestic securities in foreign currencies (1990), the opening of the German Futures Exchange (1990), permission to issue DM Commer-

---

[64]See Hofmann (1989) p. 42-43 and 58-59.

[65]ibid.

[66]ibid. p. 76.

[67]ibid.

[68]Roughly 6 percent of their foreign holding around March 1989 was in DM and Japanese buyers account for 20 percent of the DM paper placed outside Germany. See Lee (1989b) p. 102.

[69]Euromoney.

[70]At present (as of August 1992), there are 55 German subsidiaries of foreign financial institutions in the government bond consortium which comprises 113 banks.

cial Papers (January 1991) and abolition of the quota limit of foreign banks in government bond consortium (October 1991),[71] are likely to add to the attractiveness of the German capital market for Japanese investors and financial institutions alike.

Foreign banks and securities companies have pursued a variety of strategies in entering the German equity market. Whereas British clearing banks have acquired existing private merchant banks, U.S. securities firms and banks have tended to build up their own operations, based on their strength in equity derivatives. Japanese banks and securities companies appear to have focused on serving Japanese investors.

The Performance of Japanese Financial Institutions in Germany. In 1987, the Bundesbank started publishing data on the profitability of foreign banks. However, the figures are aggregate and do not help in gauging the performance of individual national groups. The Association of Foreign Banks in Germany regularly publishes summary figures about various groups in its annual reports. According to this report, the main source of income for Japanese banks is interest earning, accounting for about 80 percent of total earnings in 1991. Similarly, interest paid is the largest item on the expenditure side.[72] Commission and fee income constituted only 4 percent of their total earnings in the year 1991.[73] Thus, in comparison with the U.S. banks, the investment banking activities of Japanese financial institutions do not contribute significantly to overall profitability. Table 8.8 provides data on comparative performance for Japanese and U.S. banks in Germany. In comparison with the U.S. banks, the low interest surplus (0.86% of business volume) earned by Japanese banks hints at the aggressive price policy adopted by them. Even in fee income business (mostly investment banking), Japanese banks earn considerably less than American banks. However, with lower administrative costs, Japanese banks appear more cost efficient than their American counterparts. The annual profits after tax have been very marginal in Germany for all types of foreign banks, largely because of heavy taxation, particularly the capital taxes.

---

[71]Until October 1991, foreign banks had a fixed quota of 20 percent in the consortium.

[72]Verband der Auslandsbanken in Deutschland (1993) p. 57.

[73]The US banks in Germany obtained about 50 percent of their earning from interest income and 7 percent from commissions and fee income in 1991. See Verband der Auslandsbanken in Deutschland (1993) p. 57.

Table 8.8: Profitability of Japanese and US banks in Germany

(% of business volume)

	Japanese banks		US banks	
	1986*	1991*	1986	1991
Interest surplus	0.87	1.26	2.30	2.46
Commission or Fee surplus	0.40	0.22	0.81	0.76
Administrative expenses	0.58	1.04	2.07	2.38
Operating profits	0.69	0.45	1.04	0.84
Annual profit before taxes	0.70	0.48	0.80	0.79
Annual profits after taxes	0.24	0.10	0.38	0.56
Annual Profit (in DM million)	**68.73**	**38.12**	**203.93**	**362.79**

*for some institutions, fiscal year ends in March of following year

Source: Verband der Auslandsbanken in Deutschland, Annual Reports

8.2.4 Impact of the Japanese Financial Presence on German Financial Markets

Japanese financial institutions in Germany are still behind American banks when it comes to providing various kinds of innovative banking services, such as foreign exchange business, M&A business, cash management systems, swap related business, etc. In the recent past, Japanese banks in Frankfurt have started establishing contact with small and medium-sized firms in southern Germany for new business. With reference to a survey conducted by Greenwich Associates, in which 350 of the top 500 hundred German firms were surveyed, 6 percent of those questioned had Japanese banks as their main bank, 25 percent of them maintained regular contact with some Japanese bank, and with another 30 percent, Japanese banks had tried to establish contact.[74]

A detailed study of competitive strengths of foreign banks in Germany has been carried out by Hofmann (1989). According to this study:

> "Foreign banks compete mainly with the commercial banks...Their business strategy shows that they compete more for lending business than for deposit taking...it can be stated that foreign banks compete mostly on the shorter end of the banking business. They occupy important positions in the fee-income business and since the 'Restliberalisierung,' they make their presence felt in lead managing the Euro-DM bonds. Further, foreign

[74]Quoted in Hofmann (1989) p. 42.

banks (particularly Japanese) use pricing policy as an instrument for market share. "[75]

Since the Japanese financial presence in Frankfurt is of recent origin, it is too early to trace its impact on German markets. How far they succeed will depend upon their efforts in gaining a respectable share of the potential markets of the former East Germany and rest of eastern Europe. However, because of the strong position of the big banks in Germany[76], the close relationship between the big banks and industry[77] and the heavy reliance of German industry on bank financing, foreign banks in Germany perceive the banking market as difficult to penetrate.[78] Practically all foreign banks complain about the problem posed by the condition of dotation (endowment) capital which is also subject to tax. This has been viewed as a serious handicap in their growth.[79]

8.3   Summary and Conclusions

The two case studies of the Japanese financial presence in Europe testify the country-specific approaches adopted by Japanese financial institutions. In the United Kingdom, though international financial markets have been the main attraction for Japanese institutions, strong bilateral economic relations between Japan and the United Kingdom have increased the amount of involvement of Japanese banks and securities companies in the domestic financial markets, too. On the other hand, in Germany, Japanese banks' arrival represented the classic case of banks following their clients. The presence of Japanese trading companies and later huge Japanese FDI provided Japanese banks with their initial business opportunities. Later, the liberalization of the domestic capital market attracted the attention of Japanese banks and securities companies towards the domestic capital markets. However, Japanese banks or securities companies do not show any involvement in the retail deposit markets of the United Kingdom or Germany.

---

[75]ibid. pp. 105-110.

[76]The three big banks account for more than 37% of the business volume in the banking industry.

[77]Many German banks are important shareholders (either for their own account or for their clients) in Germany industries.

[78]Frankfurter Allgemeine Zeitung (1990).

[79]Tsuji (1990) p. 13.

Concluding Observations

The focus of this research work is on the Japanese financial presence in Europe. An important reason for the choice of the topic was the dramatic increase in the network of offices opened by Japanese financial institutions and the growth in their market share of international financial markets after 1985. It was alleged that Japanese banks and securities companies are positioning themselves for a dominant role in international financial markets. The research work was intended to test the validity of this statement and provide evidence for and against it.

The main findings of the study and supporting arguments are summarized below.

The Japanese financial institutions that are active internationally are also the most dominant in their domestic financial markets. This shows the importance of home market in overseas expansion. A secured domestic position, therefore, should be seen as a prerequisite for international expansion.

Japanese financial institutions in Europe show a kind of herding behavior, both in their presence and business strategy. This is reflected in the concentration of their network of offices in a few European countries and in their similar investment portfolio. The joining of several Japanese banks in a loan syndicate or participation of several securities companies in an underwriting syndicate are examples of this behavior. The theoretical value of this finding is that herding behavior makes business riskier and risk-diversification more difficult.

Deregulation of cross-border financial transactions and large capital flows from Japan hastened the overseas expansion of Japanese financial institutions. Whereas the huge portfolio investment in foreign securities provided Japanese securities companies with additional business opportunities, the need for foreign currency funds at home to finance these portfolio investments induced Japanese banks to commit short-term foreign currency liabilities abroad. With this kind of maturity transformation occurring at the macro-level, it appeared as if Japan were performing the role of an international financial intermediary.

The expansion process in Europe was influenced by a variety of factors, some of which went beyond the economic reasoning of following the clients and network advantages. In the case of Japanese banks, their arrival into Europe was initially influenced by the Japanese FDI to Europe. The subsequent expansion has been guided by a multitude of factors. The (1) desire to participate in international financial markets; (2) need to serve as funding conduits for their home offices; (3) necessity of a foothold in the integrated European financial markets; and (4) wish to benefit from the liberal financial regulations in certain countries were motives which justified their expansion in the 1980s. Because of their monolithic size and top ranking in league tables of financial institutions, the compulsion to develop themselves into global institutions also played a role in this process.

Since the internationalization of securities business, in general, is contingent upon cross-border integration of the securities markets and the volume of cross-border trade in securities, the expansion of securities firms in foreign markets has been slower than that of banks. This is true of both the U.S. and the Japanese financial institutions. In the Japanese case, the dominance of portfolio investment in Japan's capital outflows gave a boost to the internationalization of non-bank financial intermediaries, particularly Japanese securities companies. Here again, the differences in the domestic setting of the Japanese banks and securities companies have been an important variable influencing their overseas strategy.

The sources of the Japanese financial institutions' international competitiveness are to be found in the low-cost capital, strong ties with domestic clients, and in the conventional measures of competitiveness, such as size, productivity and cost-efficiency. The cost of capital advantage available to banks and securities companies has been eroded by various developments in the domestic and international arena. The contention of strong ties with domestic clients may be an argument for following them overseas. However, it does not justify continued profitable expansion.

The results of a multiple regression analysis provide empirical proof for the fact that increasing Japanese FDI to Europe, low cost of capital at home and deregulation in the financial sector reinforced the growth of Japanese banks in the European Union. Apparently the appreciating home currency and its low international use did not yield Japanese banks any competitive advantage.

To sum up all the above findings, the surge of the Japanese financial institutions in foreign markets in the 1980s has been a replica of their domestic strength earned through a conducive domestic environment. The changed domestic environment after the downturn of the Japanese stock market and perpetuating economic recession supports this point. Japanese financial institutions curtailed their foreign activity between 1991 and 1994 to cope with the deteriorating domestic asset quality and rescue the "core" segments of their business.

A major conclusion of this research work is that the international position of Japanese financial institutions during the 1980s was assessed more with reference to their swelling market share in international financial markets than in terms of their international competitiveness. In this regard, the strength of Japanese financial institutions has been grossly over-estimated. Their dramatic expansion after mid-1980s does not necessarily imply improvements in their international competitiveness. Hence, for the internationally active financial institutions from other industrialized countries, the competitive challenge posed by Japanese banks and securities companies needs to be re-assessed in the light of the evidence provided in this study.

Future Directions for Research. The present study is based primarily on a macro-analysis of the Japanese banks' and securities companies' presence in Europe; all types of banks and securities companies were studied collectively. There is a need for more research into the internationalization of different types of financial institutions according to their functional specialization and size. Through such an analysis, one could evaluate the impact of the unique domestic position of each type of institution on their overseas strategy and performance. Further, case studies of individual institutions may help in improving our perception of the internationalization process.

The empirical testing of the determinants of Japanese banking presence in the EU was a modest attempt to clarify their internationalization process. The findings of the regression model in this study could be extended to individual European countries to check their generalizability. Inclusion of country-specific determinants may help in making the model more effective and improve upon its predictive power. No attempts have so far been made to test empirically the determinants of securities firms' internationalization. This is an area where more research is needed.

An investigation of foreign financial presence in a country necessitates an assessment of its impact on the host financial markets. Any such analysis warrants a prudent choice of indicators for measuring the impact of foreign financial presence on monetary policy, competition, prices and stability of the host financial system. Though brief reference has been made in the case studies (see Chapter 8) to the consequences of the Japanese financial presence for the financial markets of the United Kingdom and Germany, the analysis is limited and requires a full-length independent study.

Bibliography

Aderhold, R. et al. (1991). "Competitiveness in the Global Swap Market", in: *Federal Reserve Bank of New York (1991)*. pp. 42-64.

Aggarwal, R. (1992). "The Globalization of the Japanese Financial Service Firms: Role of Domestic Economic and Regulatory Policies", in: Aharoni, Y. (ed.). *Coalitions and Competitions: The Global Expansion of Service Firms*. London: Routledge.

Aggarwal, R. and J. Durnford (1989). "Market Assessment of International Banking Activity: A Study of U.S. Bank Holding Companies". *Quarterly Review of Economics and Business*. Vol. 29. No. 1, pp. 58-67.

AIESEC (1981). *International Banking Activities in the Eighties*. Frankfurt am Main: Fritz Knapp Verlag.

Alexander, J. and C. Jones (1992). "Global Banking: Global Gamble". *The Banker*. February, pp. 8-17.

Aliber, R. Z. (1976). "Towards a Theory of International Banking". *Federal Reserve Bank of San Francisco Economic Review*. Spring.

Aliber, R. Z. (1984). "International Banking: A Survey". *Journal of Money, Credit, and Banking*. Vol. 16, pp. 661-678.

Aliber, R. Z. (1987). "Financial Liberalization in Japan". *Geston 2000*. Vol. 3, No. 4, pp. 77-100.

Aliber, R. Z. (1989). "Protection and the Structure of the Banking Industry in an International Context", in: Giersch, H. (ed.). *Services in World Economic Growth*. Tübingen: J. C. B. Mohr. pp. 198-218.

Ando, A. and A. Auerbach (1988). "The Cost of Capital in the U.S. and Japan: a Comparison". *Journal of the Japanese and International Economies*. Vol. 2, No.2, pp. 134-158.

Ando, A. and A. Auerbach (1990). "The Cost of Capital in the U.S. and Japan: Recent Evidence and Further Results". *Journal of the Japanese and International Economies*. Vol. 3, No.4, pp. 323-350.

Aoki, M. (1988). *Information, Incentives and Bargaining in the Japanese Economy*. Cambridge: Cambridge University Press.

Arora, D. (1991). *Investment Banking in Japan*. Frankfurt am Main: Peter Lang.

Arthur Andersen & Co. (1986). *The Decade of Change: Banking in Europe - the Next Ten Years*. London: Lafferty Publications.

Arthur Anderson & Co. (1989). *European Capital Markets: A strategic Forecast*. London: The Economist Publication.

Bachman, J. W. (1976). "Euromarket Still Tiered". *The Money Manager.* September, p. 10.

Baker, G. (1994). "Regional Rivals Hot on its Heels". *Financial Times.* October 19, p.15.

Baker, G. (1995a). "Trapped in Stagnant Waters". *Financial Times.* February 22, p.19.

Baker, G. (1995b). "Benefits of Building a Bloc". Financial Times. May 17,   p. 11.

Balder, J. M. et al. (1991). "Competitiveness in the Eurocredit Market", in: *Federal Reserve Bank of New York (1991).* pp. 26-41.

Bank for International Settlements. *Annual Reports.* Various years.

Bank for International Settlements (1983). "The International Interbank Market - A Descriptive Study". *BIS Economic Papers No. 8.* Basle. July.

Bank for International Settlements (1986). *Recent Innovations in International Banking.* Basle. April.

Bank for International Settlements (1988). *International Convergence of Capital Measurement and Capital Standards.* Basle. July.

Bank for International Settlements (1989). "The Nationality Structure of the International Banking Market: 1983-88". *International Banking and Financial Market Developments.* Basle. August, pp. 15-22.

Bank for International Settlements (1990). *Survey of Foreign Exchange Market Activity.* Basle. February.

Bank of England (1991a). *Annual Report under the Banking Act 1987 for 1990/91.* London. February.

Bank of England (1991b). "Developments in International Banking and Capital markets". *Bank of England Quarterly Bulletin.* May, pp. 234-243.

Bank of England (1992). *Annual Report under the Banking Act 1987 for 1991/92.* London. February.

Bank of England (1993). "Cross-border Alliances in Banking and Financial Services in the Single Market". *Bank of England Quarterly Bulletin.* Vol. 33, No. 3, August, pp. 372-378.

Bank of England (1994). *Annual Report under the Banking Act 1987 for 1993/94.* London. February.

Bank of Japan. *Balance of Payments Monthly.* Various issues.

Bank of Japan. *Comparative Economic and Financial Statistics: Japan and Other Major Countries.* Various years.

Bank of Japan. *Economic Statistics Annual.* Various years.

Bank of Japan. *Economic Statistics Monthly.* Various issues.

Bank of Japan (1984). "Stepped-up Capital Movements In and Out of Japan and their Effect on the Japanese Financial Market". *Special Paper No. 112.* Tokyo. March.

Bank of Japan (1991a). "Credit Risk Management of Financial Institutions Related to Lending". *Special Paper No. 205*. Tokyo. September.

Bank of Japan (1991b). "Recent Developments in Lending Rates: Changing Behavior of Banks under Interest Rate Liberalization". *Special Paper No. 206*. Tokyo. September.

Bank of Japan (1991c). "Tōkei no chūshin ni mita kokusai kinyū-shijō no dōkō" (Trends in International Financial Markets: Based on BIS Statistics). *Nihon Ginko Geppo*. March, pp. 17-36.

Bank of Japan (1992a). "Analysis of Recent Changes in the Relationship between Banks and Corporations Based on Financial Data of Corporations". *Special Paper No. 217*. Tokyo. July.

Bank of Japan (1992b). "Developments in Cross-border Securities Investment in 1991". *Special Paper No. 215*. Tokyo. June.

Bank of Japan (1993a). "Functions of Stock Markets: Implications for Corporate Financial activities". *Special Paper No. 225*. Tokyo. February.

Bank of Japan (1993b). "Summary of Results of the Tokyo Foreign Exchange Market Survey (conducted in April 1992)". *Bank of Japan Quarterly Bulletin*. Vol. 1, No. 1. February, pp. 37-45.

Bank of Tokyo (1990). "A Japanese View on Structural Developments of European Banking". *Tokyo Financial Review*. December, Vol. 15, No. 12. pp. 1-5.

Bank of Tokyo (1991). "Internationalization of the Yen". *Tokyo Financial Review*. December. Vol. 16, No. 12.

Banker, The (1995). "Japan's Hidden Agenda". February, p. 6.

Banker Research Unit (1981). *Japanese Banking and Capital Markets*. London: The Financial Times Business Publishing Ltd.

Bellanger, S. (1987). "The Japanese Invasion". *The Bankers Magazine*. Vol. 170, No. 4. July-August, pp. 50-54.

Benston, G. J. et al. (1982). "Scale Economies in Banking: A Restructuring and Reassessment". *Journal of Money, Credit, and Banking*. Vol. 14, No. 4, pp. 435-456.

Berglöf, E. (1990). "Corporate Control and Financial Deregulation". *Wirtschaftspolitische Blätter*. Vol. 37, No. 2/3, pp. 145-154.

Bernheim, B. and J. Shoven (1987). "Taxation and the Cost of Capital: An International Comparison". in Walker, C. and M. Bloomfield (eds.). *Consumption Tax: A Better Alternative?* Cambridge, MA: Ballinger.

Bildersee, J. S. et al. (1990). "The International Price-Earning Ratio Phenomenon: A Partial Explanation". *Japan and the World Economy*. Vol. 2, pp. 263-282.

Blanden, M. (1991). "Small Bang in Belgium". *The Banker*. March.

Blattner, N. (1992). "Competitiveness in Banking: Selected Recent Contributions and Research Priorities". in: Blattner, N. et al. (eds.). *Competitiveness in Banking*. Heidelberg: Physica-Verlag.

Blitz, J. (1993). "All Change in Foreign Exchanges". *Financial Times*. April 2, p. 15.

Bond Underwriters Association of Japan (1992). *Bond Review*. No. 427. March.

Bond Underwriters Association of Japan (1993). *Bond Market in Japan*.

Borio, C. E. V. (1990a). "Leverage and Financing of Non-financial Companies: An International Perspective". *BIS Economic Papers No. 27*. Basle. May.

Borio, C. E. V. (1990b). "Banks' Involvement in Highly leveraged Transactions". *BIS Economic Papers No. 28*. Basle. October.

Brandy, Simon (1988). "The Sun Rises again in the West". *Euromoney*. December.

Bresser, K.-L. (1981). "Market Position and Market Behavior of Foreign Banks in Europe", in: *AIESEC (1981)*. pp. 33-42.

Brimmer, A. and F. Dahl (1975). "Growth of American International Banking: Implications for Public Policy". *Journal of Finance*. Vol. 30. May, pp. 341-363.

Bröker, G. (1989). *Competition in Banking*. Paris: OECD.

Bryant, R.C. (1987). *International Financial Intermediation*. Washington DC: The Brookings Institutions.

Buckley, P. J. et al. (1992). "Foreign Market Servicing Strategies of UK Retail Financial Service Firms in Continental Europe", in: Young, S. and J. Hamill (eds.). *Europe and the Multinationals: Issues and Responses for the 1990s*. Aldershot: Edward Elgar. pp. 159-182.

Burton, F. N. and F. H. Saelens (1983). "Trends in the Growth of Japanese International Banking in Western Europe". *Intereconomics*. July/August, pp. 172-176.

Burton, F. N. and F. H. Saelens (1986). "The European Investment of Japanese Financial Institutions". *Columbia Journal of World Business*. Vol. 21, No. 4, pp. 27-33.

Büschgen, H. E. and K. Richolt (eds.) (1989). *Handbuch des internationalen Bankgeschäfts*. Wiesbaden: Gabler.

Callier, P. (1986). "Professional Trading, Exchange Rate Risk and the Growth of International Banking: A Note". *Banca Nazionale del Lavoro Quarterly Review*. December, pp. 423-428.

Cargill, T. F. (1985). "A US Perspective on Japanese Financial Liberalization". *Bank of Japan Monetary and Economic Studies*. May, pp. 115-161.

Cargill, T. F. (1988). *The Transition of Finance in Japan and the United States: A Comparative Perspective*. Stanford: Hoover Institution Press.

Casson, M. (1989). The Economic Theory of Multinational Banking: An International Approach. Discussion Paper No. 133. University of Reading, Department of Economics.

Casson, M. (1990). "Evolution of Multinational Banks: A Theoretical Perspective", in: *Jones (1990)*. pp. 14-29.

Caves, R. E. (1977). "Discussion" in: Federal Reserve Bank of Boston (ed.). *Key Issues in International Banking*. October.

Cecchini, P. et al. (1988). *The European Challenge: 1992 - The Benefits of a Single Market*. London: Wildwood House.

Chase Manhattan Bank (1980). "*U.S. and Japanese Semiconductor Industries: A Financial Comparison*". June.

Cho, K. R. (1985). *Multinational Bank: Their Identities and Determinants*. Ann Arbor: UMI Research Press.

Clark, J. A. (1988). "Economies of Scale and Scope at Depository Financial Institutions". *Federal Reserve Bank of Kansas City Economic Review*. Sept-October.

Cohen, R. B. (1989). The Foreign Challenge to U.S. Commercial Banks", in: Noyelle, T. (ed.). *New York's Financial Markets: The Challenge of globalization*. London: Westview Press. pp. 31-50.

Connors, D. (1994). "Global Banking: Top Twenty Take to Travel". *The Banker*. February, pp. 49-52.

Connors, D. (1995). "Global Banking: Far and Wide". *The Banker*. February, pp. 68-71.

Cooper, S. K. et al. (1989). "U.S. Activities of Pacific-rim and European banks: Evidence for a Global Integrated Market for Bank Credit?" *The Review of Research in Banking and Finance*. Vol. 5, No. 2, pp. 1-25.

Corrigan, E. G. (1989). "Trends in International Banking in the United States and Japan". *Federal Reserve Bank of New York Quarterly Review*. Autumn, pp. 1-6.

Corrigan, T. (1993). "Tokyo Reforms Feed through to London". *Financial Times*. April 5, p. 17.

Coulbeck, N. (1984). *The Multinational Banking Industry*. London: Croom Helm.

Damanpour, F. (1986). "A Survey of Market Structure and Activities of Foreign Banking in the United States". *Columbia Journal of World Business*. Vol. 21, No. 4, pp. 35-46.

Damanpour, F. (1990). *The Evolution of Foreign Banking Institutions in the United States*. New York: Quorum Books.

Danton, G. (1992). "Major International Banks' Performance: 1980-91". *Bank of England Quarterly Bulletin*. August, pp. 288-297.

Darby, M. R. (1986). "The internationalization of American Banking and Finance: Structure, Risk and World Interest rates". *Journal of International Money and Finance. Vol. 5, pp. 403-428.*

Dean, J. and H. G. Grubel (1979). "Regulatory Issues and the Theory of Multinational Banking", in: Edwards, F. (ed.). *Issues in Financial Regulation*. New York: Columbia University Press.

Dermine, J. (1990). *European Banking After 1992*. Oxford: Basil Blackwell.

Despres, E., C. P. Kindleberger, and W. S. Salant (1966). "The Dollar and World Liquidity: A Minority View". *The Economist*. Vol. 218. February. Reprinted in: Kindleberger, C. P. (ed.) (1981). *International Money*. London: George Allen and Unwin. pp. 42-52.

Deutsche Bundesbank (1987). Die Auslandsbanken - eine neue Untergruppe der Bankenstatistik, in: *Monthly Bulletin of German Bundesbank*. January, pp. 32-37.

Deutsche Bundesbank (1992a). *Balance of Payments statistics*. Statistical Supplements to the Monthly Reports of the Deutsche Bundesbank. Series 3. September.

Deutsche Bundesbank (1992b). *Banking Statistics by Category of Banks*. Statistical Supplements to the Monthly Reports of the Deutsche Bundesbank. Series 1. March.

Die Bank (1992). "Die Auslandsbanken in der Bundesrepublik". September, pp. 554-560.

Dietrich, J. K. (1990). "Consequences of 1992 for Competition in Financial Services: Banking". Paper presented to the Conference on Financial Regulation and Monetary Arrangements after 1992. Gothenburg School of Economics, Sweden. May, pp. 21-23.

Dohner, R. S. and H. S. Terrell (1988). "The Determinants of the Growth of Multinational Banking Organizations: 1972-86". *International Finance Discussion Papers No. 326*. Board of Governors of the Federal Reserve System. June.

Dufey, G. (1990). "The Role of Japanese Financial Institutions Abroad", in: *Goodhart and Sutija (1990)*. pp. 132-166.

Dufey, G. and I. H. Giddy (1978). *The International Money Market*. London: Prentice Hall.

Dunning, J. H. (1981). *International Production and the Multinational enterprise*. London: Allen and Unwin.

Durand, M. and C. Giorno (1987). "Indicators of International Competitiveness". *OECD Economic Studies*. No. 9, Autumn.

Düser, J. T. (1990). *International Strategies of Japanese Banks: The European Perspective*. London: Macmillan.

Economist, The (1986). "Japanese Investment Bankers Head for the Big Wide World". April 19.

Economist, The (1989). "Japanese Banks Abroad: A Subtler Approach". July 8, p. 80.

Economist, The (1990a). "Japanese Finance: A Survey". December 8, pp. 1-22.

Economist, The (1990b). "Survey of International Capital Markets". July 21, pp. 16-18.

Economist, The (1990c). "Japanese Change their Style Abroad". July 28, pp. 81-82.

Edwards, F. R. and H. T. Patrick (1992). *Regulating International Financial Markets: Issues and Policies*. Boston/Dordrecht/London: Kluwer Academic Publishers.

Emerson, M. et al. (1990). *Economics of 1992: the EC Commission's Assessment of the Economic Effects of Completing the Internal Market*. Oxford: Oxford University Press.

Enderwick, P. (1990). "The International Competitiveness of Japanese Service Industries: a Cause for Concern?". *California Management Review*. Vol. 32, Summer, pp. 22-37.

Engels, W. (1989). "Finanzmacht Japan". *Wirtschaftswoche*. No. 25. June 16.

Etzioni, A. (1968). *The Active Society: A Theory of Societal and Political Processes*. New York: The Free Press.

Euromoney, *Annual Financing Report*. March issue. Various years.

Euromoney (1990a). *"New Boys on the Street: Mergers and Amalgamation"*. February, pp. 45-52.

Euromoney (1990b). "The 1990 International Brokers Poll". May, p. 75.

Euromoney (1991a). "Equity Research Country Tables". May, p. 6.

Euromoney (1991b). "International Equities". *Special Supplement to Euromoney*. March, p. 24.

Euromoney (1992). "International Equities: Healthy Appetites All Round". *Special Supplement to Euromoney*. March, pp. 28-30.

Euromoney (1994). "Investors' Plans Unveiled". February, p. 50.

Export Import Bank of Japan (1991). *Kaigai-tōshi kenkyū-jōhō* (Survey of Japan's Foreign Direct Investment). Tokyo.

Fassbender, H. and R. Leichtfuss (1990). "Banking im neuen Europa: Eine Zwischenbilanz". *Die Bank*. May, pp. 244-255.

Federal Reserve Bank of New York (1991). *International Competitiveness of U.S. Financial Firms: Products, Markets and Conventional Performance Measures: A Staff Study*. New York. May.

Federal Reserve Bank of New York (1992). *International Competitiveness of U.S. Financial Firms: The Dynamics of Financial Industry Change: A Staff Study*. New York. May.

Federation of Bankers Association of Japan [Zenginkyo] (1994a). *Japanese Banks '94*. Tokyo: International Affairs Department.

Federation of Bankers Association of Japan [Zenginkyo] (1994b). *The Banking System in Japan*. Tokyo.

Federation of Bankers Association of Japan [Zenginkyo] (1994c). *Zenginkyo Financial Review*. No. 19, Tokyo: International Affairs Department.

Feldman, R. A. (1986). *Japanese Financial Markets: Deficits, Dilemmas and Deregulations*. Cambridge, Mass.: MIT Press.

Feldman, R. A. et al. (1991). "Role of Foreign Securities Companies in Japan", in: *Foundation for Advanced Information and Research (1991)*. pp. 426-438.

Feldstein, M. (1983). "Domestic Saving and International Capital Movements in the Long Run and the Short Run". *European Economic Review*. Vol. 21, pp. 129-151.

Fels, G. and G. Sutija (eds.) (1990). *Protectionism and International Banking* New York: St. Martin's Press.

Fieleke, N. S. (1977). "The Growth of United States Banking Abroad: An Analytical Survey". Federal Reserve Bank of Boston (1977). *Key Issues in International Banking*. October, pp. 9-40.

Financial System Research Council (1991). *On a New Japanese Financial System: Report*. Translated by Federation of Bankers Associations of Japan. Tokyo. June.

Flaherty, M. and H. Itami (1982). "Financial Systems and Capital Acquisitions". Stanford University.

Foundation for Advanced Information and Research [FAIR] (1991). *Japan's Financial Markets*. Fair Fact Series II. Tokyo: FAIR, Japan.

Frank, D. (1990). "Japanese Eurobond Strength Deceptive". *Global Finance*. February, p. 24.

Frankel, A. B. and P. B. Morgan (1992). "Deregulation and Competition in Japanese Banking". *Federal Reserve Bulletin*. August, pp. 579-593.

Frankel, J. A. (1991). "Japanese Finance in the 1980s: A Survey", in: Krugman, P. (ed.). *Trade with Japan: Has the Door Opened Wider?*. Chicago/London: The University of Chicago Press.

Frankfurter Allgemeine Zeitung (1990). "Eine Stütze des Finanzplatzes Frankfurt". November 27.

Freedman, C. (1977). "Micro Theory of International Financial Intermediation". *American Economic Review*. Vol. 66, No. 1, pp. 172-179.

French, K. and J. Poterba (1989). "Are Japanese Stock Prices too High?" National Bureau of Economic Research Working Paper No. 3290. March.

Friend, I. and I. Tokutsu (1987). "The Cost of Capital to Corporations in Japan and the USA". *Journal of Banking and Finance*. Vol. 11, No. 2.

Friesen, C. M. (1986). *International Bank Supervision*. London: Euromoney Publications.

Froot, K. A. (1991). "Japanese Foreign Direct Investment". National Bureau of Economic Research Working Paper No. 3737. June.

Fuji Bank (1990). "The Yen Taking on a More International Role". *Fuji Economic Review*. July-August.

Fujita, M. and K. Ishigaki (1986). "The Internationalization of Japanese Banking", in: Taylor, M. and N. Thrift (eds.). *Multinationals and the Restructuring of the World Economy - The Geography of Multinationals*. Vol. 2. London: Croom Helm.

Fukao, M. (1990). "Liberalization of Japan's Foreign Exchange Controls and Structural Changes in the Balance of Payments". *Bank of Japan Monetary and Economic Studies*. September, Vol. 8, No. 2, pp. 1-65.

Fukao, M. (1991). "Exchange Rate Movements and Capital-Asset Ratio of Banks: On the Concept of Structural Positions". *Bank of Japan Monetary and Economic Studies*. Vol. 9, No. 2, pp. 91-101.

Fukao, M. and K. Okina (1989). "Internationalization of Financial Markets and Balance of Payments Imbalances: A Japanese Perspective". *Carnegie-Rochester Conference Series on Public Policy*. Vol. 30, Spring, pp. 167-220.

Funabashi, M. (1991). "Participation of Foreign Financial Institutions", in: *Foundation for Advanced Information and Research (1991)*. pp. 418-425.

Fürer, G. (1990). *Risk Management im internationalen Bankgeschäft*. Bankwirtschaftliche Forschungen. Band 129. Institut für Bankwirtschaft an der Hochschule St. Gallen. Stuttgart: Verlag Paul Haupt.

Gamble, A. (1991). "EMU and European Capital Markets: Towards a Unified Financial Market". *Common Market Law Review*. Vol. 28, pp. 319-333.

Gapper, J. and N. Cohen (1994). "They've really got a hold on EU: US investment banks are increasingly dominant in European financial markets. *Financial Times*. April 20, 1994, p.13

Gardner, E. P. M. and P. Molyneux (1990). *Changes in Western European Banking*. London: Unwin Hymann.

Gardner, M. J. and D. L. Mills (1988). *Managing Financial Institutions*. Chicago: The Dryden Press.

Germidis, D. and Ch.-A. Michalet (1984). *International Banks and Financial Markets in Developing Countries*. Paris: OECD.

Giddy, I. H. (1983)".The Theory and Industrial Organization of International Banking", in: Hawkins, R., R. Levich and G. Wihlborg (eds.). *The Internationalization of Financial Markets and National Economic Policy*. (Research in International Business and Finance - A Research Annual). Vol. 3. London: Greenwich. pp. 195-243.

Glüder, D. (1988). *Die Entstehung multinationaler Banken: Ein Beitrag zur ökonomischen Analyse von Institutionen*. Wiesbaden: Gabler.

Goldberg, L. G. and A. Saunders (1980). "The Causes of U.S. Bank Expansion Overseas: The Case of Great Britain". *Journal of Money, Credit, and Banking*. Vol. 12, No. 4, pp. 630-643.

Goldberg, L. G. and A. Saunders (1981a). "The Determinants of Foreign Banking Activity in the United States". *Journal of Banking and Finance*. Vol. 5, No. 1, pp. 17-32.

Goldberg, L. G. and A. Saunders (1981b). "The Growth of Organizational Forms of Foreign Banks in the U.S.". *Journal of Money, Credit, and Banking*. Vol. 13, No. 3, pp. 365-374.

Goldberg, L. G. and D. Johnson (1990). "The Determinants of US Banking Activity Abroad". *Journal of International Money and Finance*. Vol. 9, No. 2, pp. 123-137.

Goldberg, L. G. and G. A. Hanweck (1991). "The Growth of the World's 300 Largest Banking Organizations by Country". *Journal of Banking and Finance*. Vol. 15, pp. 207-223.

Goodhart, C. A. E. and G. Sutija (eds.) (1990). *Japanese Financial Growth*. Washington Square, N.Y.: New York University Press.

Götz, R. J. and J. Müller (1990). *Frankfurt: A Banking and Financial Services Center*. Frankfurt am Main: Institut für Kapitalmarktforschung.

Graf von Pückler, A. (1989). "Auslandsbanken in Italien". *Die Bank*. March, pp. 174-176.

Gramlich, D. (1990). *Operatives Auslandsgeschäft deutscher Kreditinstitute*. Wiesbaden: Gabler.

Gray, J. M. and P. H. Gray (1981). "The Multinational Bank: A Financial MNC?" *Journal of Banking and Finance*. Vol. 5, pp. 33-63.

Grilli, V. (1989). "Financial Markets and 1992". *Brookings Papers on Economic Activity*. No. 2, pp. 301-324.

Grosse, R. and L. G. Goldberg (1991). "Foreign Bank Activity in the United States: An Analysis by Country of Origin". *Journal of Banking and Finance*. Vol. 15, pp. 1093-1112.

Group of Thirty (1982). *Risks in International Banking*. New York.

Grubel, H. G. (1977). "A Theory of Multinational Banking". *Banca Nazionale del Lavoro Quarterly Review*. December, pp. 349-363.

Gurley, J. and E. Shaw (1960). *Money in a Theory of Finance*. Washington DC: Brookings Institution.

Guttantag, J. and R. Herring (1985). "Disaster Myopia in International Banking", in: *Essays in International Finance*. No. 164. Princeton: Princeton University. September.

Haberman, G. (1987). "Capital Requirements of Commercial and Investment Banks: Contrasts in Regulation". *Federal Reserve Bank of New York Quarterly Review*. Autumn, pp. 1-10.

Hagura, N. (1978). "Japanese International Banking: Why Competition will Get Stiffer". *Euromoney*. March, pp. iii-vii.

Hakim, J. (1986). *The International Investment Banking Revolution: Strategies for Global Securities Trading*. London: Economist Publication.

Hale, D. (1990). *"How Should the U.S. Respond to the Japanese Challenge in Financial Services"*. Hearing before the Task Force on International Competitiveness of the U.S. Financial Institutions of the Committee on Banking, Finance and Urban Affairs, House of Representatives, August, pp. 24-51.

Hall, M. J. B. (1992). "Implementation of the BIS Rules on Capital Adequacy Assessment: A Comparative Study of the Approaches Adopted in the UK, the USA and Japan". *BNL Quarterly Review*. No. 180, pp. 35-57.

Hanley, T. H. et al. (1986). *The Japanese Banks: Positioning for Competitive Advantage*. New York: Salomon Brothers Inc. November.

Hanley, T. H. et al. (1987). *European Bank Equity Conference: The Competitive Position of U.S. Multinational Banks in a Global Marketplace*. New York: Salomon Brothers Inc. November.

Hanley, T. H. et al. (1988a). *The Japanese Banks - At a Crossroads*. New York: Salomon Brothers Inc. July.

Hanley, T. H. et al. (1988b). *Domestic and International Bank Stock Investing: A Global Approach*. New York: Salomon Brothers Inc. March.

Hanley, T. H. et al. (1989). *The Japanese Banks: Emerging into Global Markets*. New York: Salomon Brothers Inc. September.

Hanley, T. H. et al. (1990). *A Review of Bank Performance: 1990 Edition*. New York: Salomon Brothers Inc. April.

Hanzawa, M. (1991). "The Tokyo Offshore Market", in: *Foundation for Advanced Information and Research (1991)*. pp. 283-302.

Harada, Y. and K. Inogawa (1992). "Saikin no kokusai-shūshi no ugoki ni tsuite" (Recent Changes in the Balance of Payments). *Fainansu*. April, pp. 72-79.

Hart, H. T. and J. Piersma (1990). "Direct Representation in International Financial Markets: The Case of Foreign Banks in Amsterdam". *Tijdschrift voor Econ. en Soc. Geografie*. Vol. 81, No. 2, pp. 82-92.

Haslem, J. A. et al. (1986). "A Statistical Analysis of International Banking Measures and Relative Profitability". *Management International Review*. Vol. 26, No. 2, pp. 5-13.

Hatsopoulos, G. (1983). *"High Cost of Capital: Handicap of American business"*. A study sponsored by the American Business Conference and Thermo Electrical Corporation. April.

Hatsopoulos, G. and S. Brooks (1986). "The Gaps in the Cost of Capital: Causes, Effects, and Remedies". in: Landau, R. and D. Jorgson (eds.). *Technology and Economic Policy*. Cambridge, MA: Ballinger.

Hawawini, G. and M. Schill (1993). "The Japanese Presence in the European Financial Sector: Historical Perspective and Future Prospects". Revised version of a paper presented at the conference on Japanese Direct Investment in a Unifying Europe:

Impacts on Japan and the European Community, INSEAD Euro-Asia Centre, Fountainbleau, France, June 26-27, 1992

Healey, D. T. (1991). *Japanese Capital Exports and Asian Economic Development.* Paris: OECD.

Heinkel, R. L. and M. D. Levi (1992). "The Structure of International Banking". *Journal of International Money and Finance.* Vol. 11, pp. 251-272.

Heitger, B. and J. Stehn (1989). "Japanische Direktinvestitionen in der EG - ein trojanisches Pferd für 1993?". *Die Weltwirtschaft. No. 1, pp. 124-136.*

Helleiner, E. (1990). "Money and Influence: Japanese Power in the international Monetary and Financial System", in: Newland, K. (ed.). *The International Relations of Japan.* London: Macmillan.

Hellwig, M. (1992). "Comment on Blattner's: Competitiveness in Banking: Selected Recent Contributions and Research Priorities". in: Blattner, N. et al. (eds.). *Competitiveness in Banking.* Heidelberg: Physica-Verlag.

Herring, R. I. (1985). "The Interbank Market", in: Savona, P. and Sutija, G. (eds.). *Eurodollars and International Banking.* Basingstoke: Macmillan.

Hirota, H. (1990). "The Attitude of Japanese Banks Towards a Single European Market in 1992". *Revue de la Banque/Bank- en Financiewezen.* Vol. 54, No. 1, pp. 17-21.

Hirtle, B. (1991). "Factors Affecting the Competitiveness of Internationally Active Financial Institutions". *Federal Reserve Bank of New York Quarterly Review.* Spring, pp. 38-51.

Hitachi Research Institute (1991). *Banking Strategies for the 21st Century.* Tokyo.

Hodder, J. E. and A. E. Tschoegl (1985). "Some Aspects of Japanese Corporate Finance". *Journal of Financial and Quantitative Analysis.* Vol. 20, No. 2, pp. 173-191.

Hofmann, S. (1989). *Die Beurteilung der Inlandskonkurrenz der Foreign Banks in der Bundesrepublik Deutschland.* Erlangen-Nürnberg: Veröffentlichungen des Lehrstuhls für Allgemeine Bank- und Versicherungs- Betriebswirtschaftslehre an der Friedrich-Alexander-Universität.

Holden, D. (1983). "Japanese Bank Strategy in the United States". *Oriental Economist.* October, pp. 22-25.

Holloway, N. (1989). "The Jaded Giants: Overseas Profits Elude Japan's Financial Institutions". *Far Eastern Economic Review.* June 1, pp. 54-56.

Holmes, P. et al. (1991). "Competitiveness in the Global Market for Foreign Exchange", in: *Federal Reserve Bank of New York (1991).* pp. 65-88.

Horiuchi, A. (1989). "Informational Properties of the Japanese Financial System". *Japan and the World Economy.* Vol. 1, No. 3, pp. 255-278.

Houlder, V. (1993). "Weighted Down with Debtors". *Financial Times.* March 5, p. 10.

Houpt, J. (1988). *International Trends for U.S. Banks and Banking Markets.* Staff Study No. 156. Board of Governors of the Federal Reserve System. May.

Howell, M. and A. Cozzini (1992). *International Equity Flows: Reemerging Markets. London: Baring Brothers.* November.

Hu, Yao-Su (1992). "Global or Stateless Corporations are National Firms with International Operations". *California Management Review.* Winter, pp. 107-126.

Hultman, C. W. (1990). *The Environment of International Banking.* Englewood Cliffs, N.J.: Prentice Hall.

Hultman, C. W. and L. R. McGee (1989). "Factors Affecting the Foreign Banking Presence in the U.S.". *Journal of Banking and Finance.* Vol. 13, pp. 386-396.

Hultman, C. W. and J. Ramsey (1975). "Cyclical Behavior of Foreign Direct Investment in the United States". *Rivista di Internationale e Commerciali.* November, pp. 1098-1102.

IBCA Ltd. (1991). *Japanese Banks' Statistical Compendium.* London: IBCA.

Independent, The (1990). "End of Japanese Surplus in Sight". February 2.

Inoue, Y. (1989). "Globalization of Business Finance". *Japanese Economic Studies.* Vol. 17, No. 4, Summer, pp. 41-91.

Inoue, Y. (1992). "An Aspect of the Changing Japanese Business Management Practice: Shift in the Asset Base of the Economy through Increasing Financial Activities during the 1980s" (in Japanese). Bulletin of the Institute of Business Administration, Senshu University. No. 98. January.

Institute for Financial Affairs (1991). "Bank Restructuring through Mergers Predicted for 1991". *Kinzai Financial Briefings.* March 14, No. 5.

International Monetary Fund. *International Financial Statistics.* Washington. Various issues.

International Monetary Fund (1989). "Capital Account Developments in Japan and the Federal Republic of Germany: Institutional Differences and Structural Changes. Supplementary Note 5, in: *World Economic Outlook.* pp. 84-89.

Ishikawa, K. (1990). *Japan and the Challenge of Europe 1992.* London: Royal Institute of International Affairs.

Iwami, T. (1989). "The Internationalization of Japanese Banking: The Factors Affecting its Rapid Growth". *Journal of International Economic Studies.* No. 3, pp. 85-110.

Jacobs, K. P. (1975). "The Development of International and Multinational Banking in Europe". *Columbia Journal of World Business.* Winter, pp. 33-39.

Jacoby, A. (1987). "Risk Spreading and Expansion of Banks through Overseas Offices". *Bank of Israel Banking Review.* No. 1, pp. 12-19.

Jain, A. K. (1986). "International Lending Patterns of U.S. Commercial Banks". *Journal of International Business Studies.* Vol. 17, pp. 73-88.

Jain, A. K. (1988). "Uncertainty and Oligopolistic Reaction: An Examination of Leadership Behavior in International Banking". *The Review of Research in Banking and Finance*. Fall, pp. 17-44.

Jain, A. K. and S. Gupta (1987). "Some Evidence on 'Herding' Behavior of U.S. Banks". *Journal of Money, Credit and Banking*. Vol. 19, No. 1, pp. 78-89.

Japan Center for International Finance [JCIF] (1990). "A Survey of the Opinions and Strategies of Foreign Financial Institutions with Regard to the Tokyo Money and Capital Market". *JCIF Policy Study Series*, No. 15 and 15-II. August.

Japan Center for International Finance [JCIF] (1991). "*The Expansion of Japanese Banks: Is it a Lasting Trend?*" Tokyo.

Japan External Trade Organization [JETRO] (1991). *Directory of Japanese Affiliated Companies in the EC*. Tokyo.

Japan External Trade Organization [JETRO] (1992). *Eighth Survey of Japanese Manufacturers in Europe*. Tokyo.

Japan Securities Dealers Association (1992). *Shōkengyo hō* (Bulletin of Securities Business). No. 491. March.

Japan Securities Research Institute (1992a). *Securities Market in Japan: 1992*. Tokyo.

Japan Securities Research Institute (1992b). *Capital Markets and Financial Services in Japan: Regulations and Practice*. Tokyo.

Johnston, R. B. (1983). *The Economics of the Euromarket: History, Theory and Policy*. London: Macmillan.

Jones, G. (1990). "Competitive Advantages in British Multinational Banking since 1890", in : *Jones (1990)*. pp. 30-61.

Jones, G. (ed.) (1990). *Banks as Multinationals*. London: Routledge.

Jones, R. and M. Barrett (1988). "The Best of Times - The Worst of Times". *Euromoney, Annual Financing Report*. March.

Juttner, D. J. (1989). *International Finance and Global Financial Markets*. Sydney: Longman Cheshire.

Kajüter, P. (1994). "Internationale Strategische Allianzen im europäischen Finanzsektor". *Die Bank*. April, pp. 196-201

Kaven, J. P. (1991). "Chancen und Strategien der Auslandsbanken in Deutschland". *Kreditwesen*. February, pp. 7-9.

Kawai, M. (1988). "Japan's Demand for Long-Term External Assets in the 1980s". Working Paper in Economics No. 214. Institute of Social Sciences, University of Tokyo. July.

Kay, S. J. (1989). "Mutual Recognition: Integration of the Financial Sector in the European Community". *Federal Reserve Bulletin*. September, pp. 591-609.

Kester, W. and T. Luehrman (1992). "The myth of Japan's Low-Cost Capital". *Harvard Business Review*. May-June, pp. 130-138.

Khoury, S. J. (1980). *Dynamics of International Banking*. New York: Praeger Publishers.

Khoury, S. J. (1990). *The Deregulations of the World Financial Markets: Myths, Realities and Impact*. New York: Quorum Books.

Kindleberger, C. P. (1965). "Balance of Payments Deficits and the International Market for Liquidity", in: *Essays in International Finance*. No. 46. Princeton: Princeton University. May.

Kinyū Zaisei Jijō (in Japanese). Various issues.

Kinzer, D. (1992). "Outlook for Japanese Bank Rating". *Moody's Special Comment*. April.

Kitamura, T. (1991). "Investment in Financial Services", in: *Sumitomo-Life Research Institute (1991)*. pp. 86-117.

Kogut, B. (1988). "Country Patterns in International Competitions: Appropriability and Oligopolisitic Agreement", in Hood, N. and J. Vahlne (eds.). *Strategies in Global Competition*. London: Croom Helm.

Kohn, S. J. (1990). "The Benefits and Pitfalls of Joint Ventures". *The Bankers Magazine*. May/June, pp. 12-18.

Konzul, J. P. (1970). "American Banks in Europe", in: Kindleberger, C.P. (ed.). *The International Corporation*. Cambridge, Mass.: MIT Press.

Koy-Samusch, G. (1992). "Strategie und Profitabilität japanischer Banken in Europa". in: Deutsche Industrie- und Handelskammer in Japan (ed.) *Japanische Investitionen in Europa*. Tokyo, pp. 54-65.

Kreps, D. (1990). "*A Japanese Juggernaut into Financial Services: Is It Real?*" Hearing before the Task Force on International Competitiveness of the U.S. Financial Institutions of the Committee on Banking, Finance and Urban Affairs, House of Representatives, August, pp. 74-93.

Krüger, R. (1989). "Die Bedeutung des internationalen Bankgeschäfts für die Rentabilität einer Geschäftsbank", in: *Büschgen and Richolt (1989)*.

Krugman, P. (ed.) (1991). *Trade with Japan: Has the Door Opened Wider?*. Chicago/London: The University of Chicago Press.

Kudoh, K. (1989). "International Capital Movements, Domestic Assets and the Current Account". *Journal of the Japanese and International Economics*. Vol. 3, pp. 189-208.

Kumar, B. N. (1991). "Japanese Direct Investment in West Germany: Trends, Strategies and Management Practices", in: Moris, J. (ed.) *Japan and the Global Economy: Issues and Trend in the 1990s*. London/New York: Routledge.

Kurosawa, Y. (1989). "Issues in International Finance: The Over-presence of Japanese Banks". *Capital Market Research Institute (CaMRI) Review*. December, No. 10, pp. 2-16.

Kusukawa, T. (1991). "International Banking". Speech delivered at the Financial Times conference held on February 13-14, 1991 in London. *Fuji Economic Review.* July-August, pp. 1-7.

Lamb, A. (1986). "International Banking in London". *Bank of England Quarterly Bulletin.* Vol. 26, No. 3, pp. 367-378.

Lamfalussy, A. (1971). "European Capital Markets and Financial Intermediation by the United States", in: Kindleberger, C.P. and A. Shonfield (ed.). *North American and Western European Economic Policies. London: Macmillan. pp. 209-222.*

Landeszentralbank, Hessen (1990). "Auslandsbanken in Frankfurt". *Frankfurter Finanzmarkt-Bericht.* No. 2/90, November.

Lary, H. B. (1963). *Problems of the U.S. as World Trader and Banker.* New York: National Bureau of Economic Research.

Lee, P. (1989a). "Bonds A-Plenty - Not Much Profit". *Euromoney.* Annual Financing Report. March, pp. 3-32.

Lee, P. (1989b). "Foreign Banks are Still Arriving in Frankfurt as Others Quit". *Euromoney.* March, pp. 95-105.

Lee, P. (1991). "ECU Bonds: Hue and Cry". *Euromoney.* July, pp. 39-46.

Lewis, J. (1989). "Room at the Top, But Not for Sitting Tenants: Annual Foreign Exchange Review. *Euromoney.* May, pp. 79-88.

Lewis, M. K. (1987). "International and Multinational Banking". *British Review of Economic Studies.* Vol. 9, No. 20, pp. 27-55.

Lewis, M. K. and K. T. Davis (1987). *Domestic and International Banking.* New York/London/Sydney: Philip Allan.

Litan, R. (1990). "Commentary: U.S. Banking in an Increasingly Integrated and Competitive World Economy". *Journal of Financial Services Research.* Vol. 4, pp. 341-344.

Llewellyn, D. T. (1979). "International Financial Intermediation", in: Frowen, S.F. (ed.). *A Framework for International Banking.* Würzburg: Physica-Verlag.

Loopesko, B. E. (1992). "The Importance of the Cost of Capital to the Competitiveness of U.S. banks". in: *Federal Reserve Bank of New York (1992).* pp. 209-221.

Makus, K. D. (1986). Auslandsfilialen westdeutscher Geschäftsbanken in betriebswirtschaftlicher Sicht. Dissertation: Göttingen University.

Marr, M. W. et al. (1989). "The Competitive Effects of U.S. and Japanese Commercial Bank Participation in Eurobond Underwriting". *Financial Management.* Winter, pp. 47-54.

Mason, M. (1994). "Europe and the Japanese Banking Challenge". *Journal of Public Policy.* Vol. 13, No. 3, pp. 255-278

Mattione, R. P. (1991). *A Dangerous Dependence? Equity-linked Bond Issues, Corporate Profitability, and Financing in Japan*. Mimeo, Morgan Guaranty Trust Company of New York. Tokyo. September.

Mattione, R. P. (1992a). *A Capital Cost Disadvantage for Japan*. Tokyo: JP Morgan. April.

Mattione, R. P. (1992b). *Can Japan's Banks Meet the BIS Rules?* Tokyo: JP Morgan. April.

McCauley, R. N. and S. A. Zimmer (1989). "Explaining International Differences in the Cost of Capital". *Federal Reserve Bank of New York Quarterly Review*. Summer, pp. ?

McCauley, R. N. and S. A. Zimmer (1991). "The Cost of Capital for Securities Firms in the United States and Japan". *Federal Reserve Bank of New York Quarterly Review*. Autumn, Vol. 16, No. 3, pp. 14-27.

McKenzie, C. (1992). "Recent Developments in Japan's Financial Markets", in: *McKenzie and Stutchbury (1992)*. pp. 27-44.

McKenzie, C. and M. Stutchbury (eds.) (1992). *Japanese Financial Markets and the Role of the Yen*. Sydney: Allen and Unwin.

McMillen, M. E. (1981). "Market Position and Market Behavior of Foreign Banks in Europe", in: *AIESEC (1981)*. 43-51.

Meerschwam, D. M. (1991). *Breaking Financial Boundaries: Global Capital, National Deregulations and Financial Services Firms*. Boston: Harvard Business School Press.

Métais, J. (1979). "Le processus de multinationalisation des grandes banques commerciales". *Revue écomonomique*. No. 3, May, p. 487.

Métais, J. (1990). "International Strategies of French Banks", in: de Boissieu, C. (ed.). *Banking in France*. London: Routledge.

Middleton, P. (1990). "Moving Across Europe - The Response of European Financial Institutions to 1992". *Revue de la Banque/Bank- en Financiewezen*. January, Vol. 54, No. 1, pp. 23-26.

Ministry of Finance, Japan. *Ōkurashō-kokusai- kinyūkyoku-nenpō* (Annual Report of the International Finance Bureau). Various years.

Minsitry of Finance, Japan. *Ōkurashō-ginkōkyoku-nenpō* (Annual Report of the Banking Bureau). Various years.

Ministry of Finance, Japan (1991). *Ōkurashō-shōkenkyoku-nenpō* (Annual Report of the Securities Bureau).

Ministry of International Trade and Industry [MITI] (1989). *Kaigai-tōshi tokei sōran* (Statistics on Overseas Investments). Report No. 3. May.

Ministry of International Trade and Industry [MITI] (1991). *Kaigai-tōshi tokei sōran* (Statistics on Overseas Investments). Report No. 4. November.

Ministry of International Trade and Industry [MITI] (1992). "The 21st Survey of Japanese Business Activities Abroad". *News from MITI*. February.

Mitsubishi Bank. *Annual Reports*. Various years.

Mitsui Bank (1989). "Main Bank, Primary Securities Brokerages, and their Business with Corporations. *Tokyo Report*. No. 5. November.

Molyneux, P., D.M. Llyod-Williams and J. Thornton (1994). "Competitive Conditions in European Banking". *Journal of Banking and Finance*. Vol. 18, pp. 445-459.

Moody's Inc. (1989). "Bank Risk: US Compared with Europe and Japan". *Market Update*. October, p. 17.

Moody's Inc. (1991). "Outlook for Japanese Bank Rating". *Moody's Special Comment*. March.

Moody's Inc. (1992). "The Future of the Japanese Banking Industry". *Moody's Special Comment*. June.

Moody's Investors Service (1992). *Moody's Credit Opinions: Financial Institutions*. New York. July.

Mori, N. and Y. Tsutsui (1989). "Bank Market Structure and Performance: Evidence from Japan". *The Economic Studies Quarterly*. Vol. 40, No. 4, pp. 296-316.

Mullineux, A. W. (1987). *International Banking and Financial Systems: A Comparison*. London: Graham and Trotman.

Mullineux, A. W. (ed.) (1992). *European Banking*. Oxford: Blackwell.

Münch, D. (1990). "Schlechte Zeiten für Auslandsbanken". *Bankkaufmann*. November, pp. 39-44.

Nakaishi, A. (1991). "The Foreign Exchange Market", in: *Foundation for Advanced Information and Research (1991)*. pp.245-259.

Nakamoto, M. (1991). "The New Relationship: Survey of Japan in the UK". *Financial Times*. 20 September.

Nakao, S. (1989). "Euro-dollar Borrowing of Japan Through London Financial Market". *Osaka City University Economic Review*. Vol. 24, No. 1, pp. 25-46.

Nakao, S. (1992). "What has Made Asian Financial Markets Active in 1980s". *Osaka City University Economic Review*. Vol. 27, No. 1, pp. 33-50.

Nakao, S. (1993). "The Stock Market in Japan and the Globalization of Japanese Money". *Osaka City University Economic Review*. Vol. 28, No. 1, January.

Naruse, T. (1990). "Japanese Presence in London". *Tokyo Financial Review*. June, Vol. 15, No. 6, pp. 1-5.

Niehans, J. (1983). Financial Innovation, Multinational Banking and Monetary Policy. *Journal of Banking and Finance*. December, Vol. 7, No. 4, pp. 537-552.

Nigh, D. et al. (1986). "The Role of Location Related Factors in U.S. Banking Involvement Abroad". *Journal of International Business Studies*. Fall, pp. 59-72.

Nikami, K. (1991). "Management of Japan's Securities Companies". *Japanese Economic Studies*. Spring, pp. 43-73.

Nikkei Newsletter on Bond and Money (1990). Shōken-renketsu kessan: Shūeki kōzō ni henka (Securities-related Settlement of Accounts: Changes in the Profitability Structure). June.

Nikko Research Center (1988). *The New Tide of the Japanese Securities Market*. Tokyo.

Noel Alexander Associates (1991a). *New Foreign Bank Offices in London: 1990*. February.

Noel Alexander Associates (1991b). *New Foreign Securities Houses in London: 1990*. February.

Noguchi, A. et al. (1991). "Changes and New Developments in Life Insurance Companies", in: *Foundation for Advanced Information and Research (1991)*. pp. 404-409.

Nomura Research Institute (1986). *The World Economy and Financial Markets in 1995 - Japan's Role and Challenges*. Tokyo.

Nomura Research Institute (1988). *Investment Opportunities in Europe: 1992 and Beyond*. London.

Nomura Securities Co. (1990a). *Nomura Fact Book*. March.

Nomura Securities Co. (1990b). Annual Reports. Various years.

OECD. *Financial Statistics Monthly*. Various issues.

OECD (1992a). "International and Foreign Bond Markets". *Financial Market Trends*. No. 51. February, pp. 46-64.

OECD (1992b). *Banks under Stress*. Paris: OECD.

Official Journal of the European Communities (1990). "Amended Proposal for a Council Directive on Investment Services in the Securities Field". No. C 42. February.

Official Journal of the European Community (1992). "Amended Proposal for a Council Directive on Capital Adequacy of Investment Firms and Credit Institutions". No. C 50. January.

Okumura, H. (1989). "Features of the Japanese Stock Market". *Rivista internationale di Scienze economische Commerciali*. Vol. 36, No. 12, pp. 1063-1073.

Oriental Economist (1976). "Japanese Banks Move for Internationalization". November, pp. 6-10.

Osugi, K. (1990). "Japan's Experience of Financial Deregulations since 1984 in an International Perspective". *BIS Economic Papers No. 26*. Basle. January.

Ozawa, T. (1989). *Recycling Japan's Surpluses for Developing Countries*. Paris: OECD.

Ozawa, T. (1991). "Japan in a New Phase of Multinationalism and Industrial Upgrading: Functional Integration of Trade, Growth and FDI". *Journal of World Trade*. Vol. 25, No. 1, pp. 43-60.

Ozawa, T. and S. Hine (1993). "A strategic shift from International to Multinational Banking: A "Macro-Developmental" Paradigm of Japanese banks *qua* Multinationals". *BNL Quarterly Review*, No. 186, September, pp. 251-274

Parkes, C. and D. Waller (1992). "Politics Comes to the Finanzplatz". *Financial Times*. January 24.

Patel, J. (1992). "Top Exchanges Ranked by Foreign Equity Turnover". *Euromoney*. June, p. 48.

Pecchioli, R. M. (1983). *The Internationalization of Banking: The Policy Issues*. Paris: OECD.

Plender, J. (1987). "London's Big Bang in International Context". *International Affairs*. Vol. 63, No. 1, pp. 39-48.

Porter, M. (1990). "The Competitive Advantage of Nations", *Harvard Business Review*. March-April, pp. 73-93.

Poterba, J. M. (1991). "Comparing the Cost of Capital in the United States and Japan: A Survey of Methods". *Federal Reserve Bank of New York Quarterly Review*. Vol. 15, No. 4, Winter, pp. 20-32.

Poulsen, A. (1986). "Japanese Bank Regulation and the Activities of U.S. Offices of Japanese Banks". *Journal of Money, Credit, and Banking*. Vol. 18, No. 3, pp. 366-373.

Price Waterhouse (1988). *Research on the Cost of Non-Europe in Financial Services*. Vol. 9. Luxembourg: EC.

Prindl, A. (1987). "Japan's Role in Britain's Invisible Trading". *Banking World*. May, p. 31.

Prindl, A. (1989). "Change and Continuity in Japanese Finance". *Banking World*. March, pp. 21-24 and April, pp. 30-33.

Rhoades, S. A. (1983). "Concentration of World Banking and the Role of the US Banks among the 100 Largest, 1956-80". *Journal of Banking and Finance*. Vol. 7, pp. 427-437.

Robinson, J. S. (1972). *Multinational Banking*. Leiden: A.W. Sijthoff.

Rose, H. (1994a). "London as an International Financial Centre: A Narrative History". *The City Research Project*, Subject Report XIII. London Business School. July.

Rose, H. (1994b). "International Banking Developments and London's Position as an International Financial Centre". *The City Research Project*, Subject Report XII. London Business School. July.

Rose, P. S. (1991). *Japanese Banking and Investment in the United States*. New York: Quorum Books.

Rowley, A. (1989). "Mean Streets: Big Four's Invasion Stumbles in New York". *Far Eastern Economic Review*. June 1, pp. 56-67.

Ryan, C. (1990). "Trade Liberalization and Financial Services". *The World Economy*. Vol. 13, No. 3, pp. 349-366.

Sagari, S. (1986). The Financial Services Industry: An International Perspective. Dissertation: New York University.

Sakakibara, E. (1984). "The Japanese Financial System in Transition", in: Agmon, T., R. G. Hawkins and R. M. Levich (eds.). *The Future of the International Monetary System*. Lexington, Mass.: D.C. Heath. pp. 157-185.

Sakakibara, E. et al. (1982). The Japanese Financial System in Comparative Perspective. Presented to the Joint Economic Committee, U.S. Congress. March.

Sakakibara, E. and R. A. Feldman (1983). "The Japanese Financial System in Comparative Perspective". *Journal of Comparative Economies*. Vol. 7, No. 1, pp. 1-24.

Sakuma, H. (1991). "The Public Bond Market", in: *Foundation for Advanced Information and Research (1991)*. pp. 126-143.

Salant, W. S. (1972). "Financial Intermediation as an Explanation of Enduring 'Deficits' in the Balance of Payments", in: Machlup, F., Salant, W. S. and L. Tarshis (ed.). *International Mobility and Movement of Capital*. New York: National Bureau of Economic Research. pp. 607-659.

Sargen, N. P. (1991). "U.S.-Japanese Competition in Financial Services: Japanese Domination is not the Issue". *Journal of Asian Economics*. Vol. 2, No. 2, pp. 317-324.

Saunders, A. (1986). "The Interbank Market, Contagion Effects and International Financial Crisis". Working Paper No. 385. Salomon Brothers Center for the Study of Financial Institutions. New York University. June.

Sawayama, H. (1991). "Japan's Short-term Financial Markets". *Japanese Economic Studies*. Spring, pp. 3-17.

Sazanami, Y. (1991). "Determinants of Japanese Foreign Direct Investment -Locational Attractiveness of European Countries to Japanese Multinationals". Keio Economic Society Discussion Paper Series No. 9102. Tokyo: Keio University.

Schaede, U. (1990). *Der neue japanische Kapitalmarkt: Finanzfutures in Japan*. Wiesbaden: Gabler.

Schissel, H. (1989)".They have Got a Little Niche". *Euromoney,* Special Supplement on France. July, pp. 8-12.

Schmid, P. (1990). *Strategisches Bankmarketing zur Betreuung multinationaler Unternehmungen: Grundlagen und Anwendungen bei Schweizer Grossbanken*. Bern: Haupt Verlag.

Scholtens, L. J. R. (1992). "On the Determinants of International Banking". Research Memorandum No. 9205. University of Amsterdam. February.

Schütte, H. (ed.) (1994). *The Global Competitiveness of the Asian Firm*. New York: St. Martin Press.

Scott-Quinn, B. (1990a). "US Investment Banks as Multinationals", in: *Jones (1990)*. pp. 268-293.

Scott-Quinn, B. (1990b). *Investment Banking: Theory and Practice*. London: Euromoney Publications.

Senda, J. (1991). "Changes in the Japanese Financial System", in: *Foundation for Advanced Information and Research (1991)*. pp. 3-13.

Senda, J. (1992). "Impacts of the EC Single Market 1992 on Japanese Banks and Securities Firms". in: Matsugi, T. and A. Oberhauser (eds.). *Economic Cooperation in the 1990s*. Berlin: Dunkers & Humbolt.

Shale, T. (1992). "Forex Fiasco Forces Radical Rethinking". *Euromoney*. March, pp. 49-52.

Sheard, P. (1989). "The Main Bank System and Corporate Monitoring and Control in Japan". *Journal of Economic Behavior and Organization*. Vol. 11, pp. 399-422.

Sheard, P. (1992a). "Japanese Corporate Finance and Behavior: Recent Developments and the Impact of Deregulation", in: *McKenzie and Stutchbury (1992)*. pp. 55-72.

Sheard, P. (1992b). "Stable Shareholdings, Corporate Governance, and the Japanese Firm". Discussion Paper No. 281, Australian National University and Bank of Japan, September.

Shigehara, K. (1991). "External Dimension of Europe 1992: Its Effects on the Relationship between Europe, the United States and Japan". *Bank of Japan Monetary and Economic Studies*. Vol. 9, No. 1, pp. 87-102.

Shigyo, K. (1991). "Fuji Bank's International Business: Influencing Factors and Strategic Response". Unpublished manuscript. February.

Shimamura, T. (1989). "Japanese Financial System: Creation and Changes". *Japanese Economic Studies*. Vol. 17, No. 3, pp. 43-88.

Shinkai, Y. (1988). "The Internationalization of Finance in Japan", in: Inoguchi, T. and I. Okimoto (eds.). *The Political Economy of Japan: Vol. 2, The Changing International Context*. Stanford: Stanford University Press. pp. 249-271.

Spindler, J. A. et al. (1991). "The Performance of Internationally Active Banks and Securities Firms Based on Conventional Measures of Competitiveness", in: *Federal Reserve Bank of New York (1991)*. pp. 173-192.

Steil, B. (1993), *Competition, Integration and Regulations in EC Capital Markets*. London: Royal Institute of International Affairs.

Steil, B. (1995), *Illusions of Liberalisation: Securities regulation in Japan and the EC*. London: Royal Institute of International Affairs.

Sumitomo Life Research Institute (1991). *Japanese Direct Investment in the EC*. Aldershot: Avebury, The Academic Publishing Group.

Suto, M. (1992). "The Securities Industry in Japan: An Overview of Market Structure, Corporate Strategies and Current Issues", in: *Japan Securities Research Institute (1992b)*. pp. 81-100.

Suzuki, K. and H. Ishiyama (1991). "Changes in Corporate Fund Raising and Fund Management", in: *Foundation for Advanced Information and Research (1991)*. pp. 45-63.

Suzuki, Yoshio (ed.) (1987). *The Japanese Financial System*. Oxford: Clarendon Press.

Suzuki, Yoshio (1989). *Japan's Economic Performance and International Role*. Tokyo: University of Tokyo Press.

Suzuki, Yukio (1993). "The Relationship between Banks and Businesses: Where will the Main Bank System Go from Here?". *CaMRI Review*. January, No. 29, pp. 31-37.

Swoboda, A. K. (1982). "International Banking: Current Issues in Perspective". *Journal of Banking and Finance*. Vol. 6, pp. 323-348.

Tachibanaki, T. and K. Mitusi (1991). "Economies of Scope and Shareholding of Banks in Japan". *Journal of the Japanese and International Economies*. Vol. 5, pp. 261-281.

Taiyo Kobe Bank (1989). "Long-Term Capital Account and the Exchange Rate in Japan" (in Japanese). *Monthly Review*.

Takagaki, T. (1986). "Japanese Banking in Europe". *International Banking Review: Europe*. SPG Bankers' Edition. pp. 45-47.

Takagi, S. (1989). "The Japanese Equity Market". *Journal of Banking and Finance*. Vol. 13, pp. 537-570.

Takagi, S. (ed.)(1993) *Japanese Capital Markets: New Developments in Regulations and Institutions*. Cambridge, Mass.: Blackwell.

Takeda, M. and P. Turner (1992). "The Liberalization of Japan's Financial Markets: Some Major Themes". *BIS Economic Papers No. 34*. Basle November.

Takeda, S. (1992). "Ginkō Shōken no naigai-shinshutsu-jōkyō to gyosei kadai" (Situation of Inroads by Japanese and Foreign Banks and Securities Firms). Kinyu Zaisei Jijo. June 8.

Tatewaki, K. (1990). *Banking and Finance in Japan: An Introduction to the Tokyo Market*. London: Routledge.

Tavlas, G. S. and Y. Ozeki (1992). *The Internationalization of Currencies: An appraisal of the Japanese Yen*. Washington DC: IMF.

Tazaki, S. (1983). "Blooming Foreign Departments of Securities Firms". *Oriental Economist*. January, pp. 16-23.

Teranishi, J. (1986). "The "Catch-up" Process, Financial System and Japan's Rise as a Capital Exporter". *Hitotsubashi Journal of Economics*. Vol. 27, pp. 133-146.

Teranishi, J. (1990). "Financial System and the Industrialization of Japan: 1900-1970". *Banco Nationale del Lavoro Quarterly Review*. No. 174, pp. 309-341.

Teranishi, J. (1991). Finance and Economic Development in Postwar Japan. Unpublished manuscript. January.

Terrell, H. (1979). "U.S. Banks in Japan and Japanese Banks in the United States: An Empirical Comparison". *Economic Review of Federal Reserve Bank of San Francisco.* Summer, pp. 18-30.

Terrell, H. et al. (1989). "The U.S. and U.K. Activities of Japanese Banks: 1980-88". *International Finance Discussion Papers No. 361.* Board of Governors of the Federal Reserve System. September.

Thomsen, S. and P. Nichlaides (1991). *The Evolution of Japanese Direct Investment in Europe.* New York/London: Harvester Wheatsheaf.

Thomson, R. (1992). "Most of the Japan's Leading Brokers End Year in Red". *Financial Times.* May 16-17, p. 12.

Thomson, R. and E. Terazono (1992). "Shadow of Guilt Falls across Derivatives". *Financial Times.* January 22, p. 14.

Thornton, J. (1991). "Concentration in World Banking, the Cost of Capital and the Rise of Japanese Banks". *British Review of Economic Issues.* Vol. 13, No. 30, pp. 57-77.

Tickell, A. (1994). "Banking on Britain? The Changing Role and Geography of Japanese Banks in Britain". *Journal of the Regional Studies Association.* Vol. 28, No. 3, pp. 291-304.

Tobin, J. (1984). "On the Efficiency of the Financial System". *Lloyds Bank Review.* No. 153, pp. 1-15.

Tokunaga, S. (1992). "Moneyless Direct Investment and Development of Asian Financial Markets: Financial Linkages between Local and Offshore centers", in: Tokunaga, S. (ed.). *Japan's Foreign Investment and Asian Economic Interdependence: Production, Trade and Financial Systems.* Tokyo: University of Tokyo Press.

Tokyo Stock Exchange (1990). *Annual Securities Statistics* for 1989. Tokyo. April.

Tokyo Stock Exchange (1992a). *Annual Securities Statistics* for 1991. Tokyo. April.

Tokyo Stock Exchange (1992b). *Fact Book.* Tokyo: International Affairs Department.

Tschoegl, A. E. (1987). "International Retail Banking as a Strategy: An Assessment". *Journal of International Business Studies.* Summer, pp. 67-88.

Tsuji, N. (1990). "Finanzplatz Deutschland aus japanischer Sicht". Lecture delivered at Institut für Kapitalmarktforschung, J. W. Goethe University, Frankfurt am Main. November 11.

Tsutsui, Y. (1990). "Japan's Banking industry: Collusion under Regulation". *Japanese Economic Studies.* Spring, pp. 53-92.

Turner, P. (1991). "Capital Flows in the 1980s: A Survey of Major Trends". *BIS Economic Papers No. 30.* Basle. April.

Tynan, N. (1993). "Global Banking: The Elusive Goal". *The Banker.* February, pp. 27-31.

Ueda, K. (1989). "Japanese Capital Outflows: 1970-86". University of Tokyo. Faculty of Economics. Discussion Paper No. 89-F-11. October.

Ueda, K. (1990). "Are Japanese Stock Prices Too High?". *Journal of the Japanese and International Economies*. Vol. 4, pp. 351-370.

Ungefehr, F. (1990). "Offshore-Zentren (XIV): Japan Offshore Market". *Die Bank*. November, pp. 635-637.

United Nations Center for Transnational Corporations [UNCTC] (1981). *Transnational Banks: Operations, Strategies and their Effects in Developing Countries*. New York.

United Nations Center for Transnational Corporations [UNCTC] (1989). "Transnational Banks and International Capital Markets", in: *Foreign Direct Investment and Transnational Corporations in Services*. New York.

Ursacki, T. and I. Vertinsky (1992). "Choice of Entry Timing and Scale by Foreign Banks in Japan and Korea". *Journal of Banking and Finance*. Vol. 16, pp. 405-421.

U.S. Department of Commerce (1983). *A Historical Comparison of the Cost of Financial Capital*. April.

Usuki, M. (1991). "The Future of Corporate Finance", in: *Foundation for Advanced Information and Research (1991)*. pp. 31-44.

Verband der Auslandsbanen in Deutschland. *Die Auslandsbanken in der Bundesrepublik Deutschland*. Annual Reports. Various issues.

Viner, A. (1987). *Inside Japan's Financial Markets*. London: The Economist Publishing Ltd.

Wallich, H. and M. I. Wallich (1976). "Banking and Finance", in: Patrick, H. and H. Rosovsky (eds.). *Asia's New Giant*. Washington: Brookings.

Walter, H. (1983). *Standortpolitik multinationaler Banken*. Frankfurt am Main: Verlag Harri Deutsch.

Walter, I. (1989). "Competitive Performance and Strategic Positioning in International Financial Services", in: Sato, R. and J. Nelson (eds.). *Beyond Trade Friction: Japan-U.S. Economic Relations*. Cambridge: Cambridge University Press.

Walter, I. (1990). "European Financial Integration and its Implications for the United States". INSEAD, Research and Development of Pedagogical Material. Working Paper No. 90/22/FIN.

Walter, I. and R. C. Smith (1990). *Investment Banking in Europe: Restructuring for the 1990s*. Oxford: Basil Blackwell.

Walton, R. J. and D. Trimble (1987). "Japanese Banks in London". *Bank of England Quarterly Bulletin*. November. pp. 518-524.

Ward, V. M. (1985). Power and Interdependence Revisited: The State and Commercial Banks in International Financial Markets. Unpublished doctoral dissertation. University of Maryland.

Warner, F. (1991). *Anglo-Japanese Financial Relations: A Golden Tide.* Oxford: Basil Blackwell.

Watanabe, K. and Muraoka, H. (1991)".Money Markets", in: *Foundation for Advanced Information and Research (1991).* pp. 67-83.

Weston, R. (1980). *Domestic and Multinational Banking.* London: Croom Helm.

Widmer, A. W. (1989). "Das Emissionsgeschäft japanischer Schuldner in der Schweiz. *Die Bank.* August, pp. 439-446.

Wohlmannsteller, G. (1991). *Finanzplatz Tokio.* Frankfurt am Main: Fritz Knapp Verlag.

Yamasaki, T. (1990). "Japan's Foreign Securities Investment". *Tokyo Financial Review.* Vol. 15, No. 4. April, pp. 1-6.

Yamazawa, I. (1990). "EC '92 and the Outsider's View: The Japanese Economy". Paper presented at the WWZ conference on 'The EC After 92: Perspective for the Outsider' in Basle, Switzerland on August 22-24, 1990.

Yannopoulos, G. N. (1983). "The Growth of Transnational Banking", in: Casson, M. (ed.). *The Growth of International Business.* London: Allen and Unwin.

Yoshizawa, K. (1991). "Japanese Banks' Strategies in the 1990s" *Tokyo Financial Review.* Vol. 16, No. 4. April.

Yukihara, T. (1991). "Sortimentspolitik japanischer Wertpapiergesellschaften im In- und Ausland", in: Süchting, J. and E. van Hooven (eds.). *Handbuch des Bankmarketing.* Wiesbaden: Gabler. pp. 461-484.

Zechner, J. R. (1983). "The Effects of the Current Turbulent Times on American Multinational Banking". *Journal of Banking and Finance.* Vol. 7, pp. 625-637.

Zimmer, S. A. and R. N. McCauley (1992). "Bank Cost of Capital and International Competition". in: *Federal Reserve Bank of New York (1992).* pp. 166-208.

Zimmerman, G. C. (1989). "The Growing Presence of Japanese Banks in California". *Federal Reserve Bank of San Francisco.* Summer, pp. 3-17.

Zysman, J. (1983). *Governments, Markets and Growth: Financial Systems and the Politics of Industrial Change.* Ithaca, NY: Cornell University Press.

Author Index